A HISTORY OF EARLY
CHRISTIAN LITERATURE

EDGAR J. GOODSPEED

A HISTORY OF EARLY CHRISTIAN LITERATURE

REVISED AND
ENLARGED BY
ROBERT M. GRANT

PHOENIX BOOKS

THE UNIVERSITY OF CHICAGO PRESS

This book is also available in a clothbound edition from

THE UNIVERSITY OF CHICAGO PRESS

THE UNIVERSITY OF CHICAGO PRESS, CHICAGO 60637
GEORGE ALLEN AND UNWIN, LTD., LONDON, W.C. 1
The University of Toronto Press, Toronto 5, Canada

EDITOR'S PREFACE

Edgar J. Goodspeed was one of the most distinguished scholars ever to write and teach at the University of Chicago. A man of almost universal interests and sympathies, he was prominent in New Testament and patristic studies during most of his ninety years. He combined meticulous accuracy with creative insight. Although he is best known for *An American Translation* of the New Testament, his English version of the Apostolic Fathers is superb, and his translation of the Apocrypha does not come far behind. His theories about the New Testament books have won widespread agreement, although—like all such theories—they have not proved universally acceptable. Beyond technical scholarship, he wrote a lively detective story entitled *The Curse in the Colophon*, as well as a fascinating and revealing autobiography, *As I Remember*.

One of his most important works is *A History of Early Christian Literature*. This book, begun in 1929 but completed only in 1941, is a masterly and—unlike many other such histories—eminently readable study of patristic writings to the early fourth century. Since it has been out of print for some time, the University of Chicago Press decided to make it available in a revised form. Hence this new edition.

I have tried to retain as much of the Goodspeed flavor as possible, recalling that a reviewer praised the "clarity, brevity, and accuracy" of the book. At the same time, I have incorporated descriptions of new discoveries in early Christian literature and have modified the arrangement to some extent to provide, I hope, even more clarity. Because I am not as sure how the New Testament canon developed as Goodspeed was, I have changed some of the sequences of books, with the result that the narrative is not as continuous as it was.

This edition, however, is by no means a completely new book. It is a revision of Goodspeed's work, and although I cannot claim that he would have agreed completely with all the changes, I do suggest that he would not have found its approach very different from his own. Toward the end I have added a chapter, "Eusebius and Early Christian Literature," which seems to me to round out the story.

ROBERT M. GRANT

DIVINITY SCHOOL
UNIVERSITY OF CHICAGO

GOODSPEED'S PREFACE

To many the New Testament appears as an island of religious literature in an ancient sea. That it is the beginning of a new continent of literature escapes them. Yet the New Testament was the source of a whole range of literary movements that in a few generations gave Christianity a literature that in sheer bulk and vigor dominated the ancient scene.

The New Testament was really the bursting forth of a great spring of religious expression that flowed on copiously far and wide for five hundred years. This literature sprang not only out of Christian life and experience but also directly out of the New Testament. Its first literary models and patterns were found in the sermons, letters, revelations, gospels, and acts of the New Testament. There was something about the Christian experience that drove men to record it in books, to express it, defend it, and explain it. This is an aspect of early Christianity too often forgotten.

Much of this literature has perished, although the discoveries and studies of the last sixty years have recovered some long-lost pieces of striking interest. But not a few of these lost writings can be pictured and in part recovered from mentions of them and quotations from them in later writers, particularly from Eusebius.

That remarkable young man came to Caesarea in Palestine about A.D. 280 to study with Pamphilus in the library the latter had assembled there along with the library of Origen. Eusebius not only catalogued these books, he read them; and to good purpose, for when in A.D. 303 he published the first edition of his *Church History*, it covered much of the history of Christian literature as well as of Christian life. That is why he is so constantly referred to in these pages. Eusebius was so devoted to Pamphilus, his friend and teacher, that he adopted him as his father and ever after called himself the son of Pamphilus. It was in his *Life of Pamphilus*, now lost, that he included the catalogue of his library. Ah, Eusebius! Immortal cataloguer, who read and summarized the books he catalogued!

Half a century or more later, Jerome flourished. He wrote in Latin, and he still influences the religious and learned worlds through his version of the Bible, the Latin Vulgate. He wrote a short dictionary of Christian biography which he called *On Illustrious Men* (*De viris illustribus*). He sometimes leaned heavily on Eusebius for his information, but his book has some independent value, too, and will be frequently referred to in this and every book on early Christian literature.

And then there is Photius, most extraordinary of them all; that Byzantine officer who, while master of the horse, suddenly emerged as the logical man for patriarch of Constantinople. He was not even in holy orders and had to go through a series of rapid clerical ordinations and promotions to achieve in a single week the transformation from soldier to prelate. This was a thing Roman ecclesiasticism could not tolerate, and it gave lasting offense to the Church of Rome.

And yet what we know as the *Library* of Photius, his *Bibliotheca*, is one of our chief helps in the recovery of early Christian literature. For it seems that, when he and his brother Tarasius were stationed at different places in the empire, Photius sent Tarasius summaries of a whole library of ancient works as he read them. They formed, in fact, a kind of medieval book club. And these book reviews by Photius, made, it would seem, for his faraway brother's enlightenment, still play a notable part in the study of these same books, too many of which have disappeared altogether since Photius wrote them, about A.D. 890.

With these and other lesser aids from the fourth century onward, we can do much to fill the gaps in our early Christian library. And certainly the development of Christian thought and life can never be understood from the New Testament alone. Early Christian literature is an indispensable aid for its understanding. The rise of the rites, creeds, doctrines, clergy, and liturgy is reflected here, in that heroic age when Christianity moved through persecution and conflict to become the religion of the empire.

The field of study assigned to me during almost forty years of service at Chicago was Biblical and Patristic Greek, and most of the positions taken in these pages were worked out with groups of graduate students of early Christian literature there, in the course of those years. But new discoveries in recent years have surprisingly supplemented our patristic resources and encouraged us to anticipate still greater reinforcements in the years to come. It is with this in mind that I have added a chapter on the works of early Christian literature that are still conspicuously missing and to be looked for.

I am once more indebted to my brother, Charles T. B. Goodspeed, of the profession of Tertullian and Minucius Felix, who has generously assisted me with the proofs of this book.

This book has been written primarily for continuous reading; but to facilitate casual consultation also, dates have been purposely repeated with each mention of the names of ancient writers with whom the casual reader can hardly be expected to be familiar.

EDGAR J. GOODSPEED

BEL-AIR, LOS ANGELES

CONTENTS

CONTENTS

1

EARLY CHRISTIAN LITERATURE

Primitive Christianity Not Literary

Christianity began as a proclamation and a response. Its founder wrote nothing. He called upon men to follow him, to take part in the inauguration of the reign of God. His earliest followers continued this course. They were further committed to it by their expectation of his return in triumph to judge the world. They had no thought of producing a literature; indeed, during the first fifteen years or so after his death there are no traces of their having produced any written documents.

This delay in creating literary materials is hard to explain in the light of the literature produced by other Jewish groups, notably the community at Qumran by the Dead Sea but also by those other groups out of which various apocalyptic predictions emerged. It was doubtless due not only to the expectation of Jesus' imminent return but also to the early Christian belief that the Old Testament, if properly understood, clearly pointed toward Christianity and did not need to be supplemented. Furthermore, in early times the teaching of Jesus, committed to memory, was being transmitted by word of mouth with such a degree of exactness that no written record seemed necessary; and this teaching was primarily regarded as providing the true interpretation of the Old Testament books.

Among the rabbis and their disciples, traditions were handed down orally, and in some instances these were not committed to writing until the late second century. The most important example of this process of transmission is to be found in the treatise that now forms part of the Mishnah, the *Pirke Aboth* or "Chapters of the Fathers."

The Oral Gospel

Such oral tradition was evidently known to Paul, who quoted it as something handed down to him (I Cor. 11:23, the account of the

1

Last Supper; I Cor. 15:3, traditions about the Resurrection). He clearly knew commandments of the Lord (I Cor. 7:10) which he could differentiate from his own counsel (I Cor. 7:12, 25), as well as traditions about the Lord's coming from heaven (I Thess. 4:15). Luke refers to such tradition in Acts 20:35. "Remembering the words of the Lord Jesus, how he said, 'It is more blessed to give than to receive.'" Similar formulas occur in the letter of Clement of Rome to the Corinthians (13:1; 46:7)—perhaps based on Acts; Polycarp of Smyrna, about twenty years later, quotes Jesus with the words—probably derived from *I Clement*—"remembering what the Lord said" (Phil. 2:3). Not only does the manner of quotation in all these instances suggest memorized material but the items quoted cannot be found in these forms in any written gospel. It is reasonable to suppose that they were derived from oral tradition.

But have we actual mention of such a work—if anything so nebulous can be called a "work"—on the part of any early Christian writer? Sometimes it is thought that what Papias (*ca.* A.D. 120) says of Matthew compiling the *logia* in "a Hebrew dialect," and each one translating them as best he could, is an attempt to describe just such a work. But *logia* does not mean "sayings," and what Matthew compiled probably consisted of Old Testament oracles interpreted in relation to Jesus. The process of oral transmission is probably mentioned in Luke's opening sentence: "Just as the original eye-witnesses who became teachers of the message have handed it down to us" (1:2). And whether or not the Gnostic *Gospel of Thomas* is actually based on oral tradition (see chap. iv), it contains a collection, or a series of collections, ultimately derived from word-of-mouth transmission, and it clearly purports to be a record of this kind of material.

Although this elusive oral tradition must have had a great influence on Christian preaching—echoes of it have been found in many of the epistles—and on the gospels that were later written, we cannot recover it in any detail. It certainly contained some characteristic pieces of Jesus' teaching, with accounts of his last days in Jerusalem and his later appearances to the disciples. We might expect relics of it to survive in the gospels, but New Testament study is not yet in a position—if it ever will be—to pronounce exactly which portions of the gospel materials come directly from Jesus, which from the disciples. The difficulty, of course, lies in the fact that all the materials were transmitted through the disciples.

It is true that the written gospels, when they appeared, sprang up under the shadow of the oral tradition and were largely derived from it. The evangelists intended to arrange and to record the tradition as it had come to them, as well as to indicate what it had come to mean in their time. From the point of view of the story of Christian literature, the work of the evangelists is significant because it does come later and shows that a period of oral tradition preceded that of written documents. A full generation seems to have passed before Christians produced written gospels, and then they arose in Greek, not in Hebrew or Aramaic, and in circles not often close to Jewish Palestine.

Letters and Gospels

With the letters of Paul and the earliest gospels a new and extraordinary force began to find written expression, a force destined powerfully to affect the life of mankind as a whole. From small and obscure beginnings, mere personal letters, for the most part, long left unpublished, this literary phase of Christianity gradually gathered strength, until it became a great tide not only potent in itself but influencing other literatures as well.

Its beginnings were in the Greek world, as far as we know, and for a century Greek seems to have been its sole vehicle; then it spread and appeared in Latin and Syriac and, in the third century, in Coptic, although at first the Christian literature of these languages consisted of translations made from Greek. Many of the earliest Christians were bilingual; but they wrote in Greek.

Organization of the Literature

This voluminous literature breaks conveniently for us at the Council of Nicaea in 325, for the actions there taken so colored the subsequent literature that it can hardly be mistaken; every page of it bears their stamp. An even more practical terminus is afforded by the *Church History* of Eusebius, published in A.D. 326, for that book is in no small degree a history of early Christian literature as well as of the march of events, and Eusebius gives us information on not a few books that he had examined but are now lost. It is safe to say that no book is more in the hands of the student of early Christian literature than the *Church History* of Eusebius, long available in English in the annotated edition of

A. C. McGiffert,[1] and more recently in the translations of Lawlor and Oulton (1927–28) and of Lake and Oulton (1926, 1932).[2]

Again, a convenient break in the literature of these first three Christian centuries can be noted with Irenaeus of Lyons, who about A.D. 185 wrote his principal work, the *Refutation of Gnosticism* (also known as *Against Heresies*). He begins a new period in Christian literature because with him the self-consciously orthodox Christianity of the Catholic Church is clearly set forth in contradistinction from the sects.

What has come down to us from Christian writers before Irenaeus can be grouped in four volumes of unequal but moderate size: the New Testament, the Apostolic Fathers, the early Greek apologists, and the uncanonical gospels, acts, and apocalypses (along with a few Gnostic works of various kinds). But these four groups of books are not to be thought of as absolutely separate or successive. The Apostolic Fathers overlap some of the New Testament books in date, and some of the apologies are earlier than some of the Apostolic Fathers. Uncanonical gospels, acts, and apocalypses are scattered over the years from A.D. 100 on, so that some of them are close to the later books of the New Testament. In purpose, too, the various groups of writings often coincide. The purpose of *I Clement* is not totally different from that of I Peter. Both Ignatius and the author of the Johannine gospel and epistles are opposed to Docetism and to Judaizing. There are apologetic materials in the New Testament as well as in the writings of the later apologists. This situation is not surprising when we bear in mind the continuity of the Christian church.

To a considerable extent this earliest Christian literature before Irenaeus reproduced literary types already developed and standardized in books that we find in the New Testament—letters, apocalypses, gospels, and acts. Most of them were anonymous or pseudonymous; they provided the popular background against which

---

[1] Arthur C. McGiffert, *Eusebius* ("Select Library of Nicene and Post-Nicene Fathers of the Christian Church: Second Series," Vol. I [New York, 1890]).

[2] H. J. Lawlor and J. E. L. Oulton, *Eusebius: The Ecclesiastical History and Martyrs of Palestine* (2 vols.; London, 1927–28); Kirsopp Lake and J. E. L. Oulton, *Eusebius: The Ecclesiastical History, with an English Translation* ("Loeb Library" [2 vols.; London and New York, 1926, 1932]).

arose the products of more self-conscious Christian leaders who wrote under their own names.

Order of Treatment

The order in which these writings can best be arranged and approached presents a difficult problem, which has been variously dealt with but not solved. The earlier literature can be grouped according to type as letters, revelations, gospels, and acts, with the individual works arranged chronologically within the several groups. But when the more conscious literary movement begins, with the apologists and the writers against the sects, the scene is constantly changing from West to East and back again, and soon in the West we have Latin writers at work simultaneously with Greek, gradually taking over the Western literary field from them. The arrangement by types of literature—apologies, antiheretical works, commentaries, and so forth—is helpful, but with such a treatment those diligent writers who worked in three or four different types would have to be taken up over and over again. So it seems preferable to present the work of each of these many-sided individuals as a unit in relation to his times and problems; this is obviously the best way to describe the writings of men like Irenaeus, Clement, Tertullian, Hippolytus, and Origen.

Literary Expansion

The literary disposition that began to pervade Greek Christianity in the earlier years of the second century swelled to a flood in the last third of that century and reached proportions that amaze the modern reader. The volume, variety, and vigor of this literature must be realized if we are to understand what manner of faith it was that was beginning to turn the Greco-Roman world upside down, for not the least of the elements of its strength was the intellectual attack it was making upon paganism.

We have been too much inclined to pass by all this literature and go directly to the New Testament, as though it existed apart from the contemporary and later Christian literature. And it is true that it was in the books of the New Testament and in the earliest collections of them—of the letters of Paul and of the Four Gospels —that the letter and gospel types were first set powerfully before the early church; and the Revelation and the Acts offered patterns for the apocalypses and acts that were to come. But the development of Christian thought did not stop with the writing of the

New Testament, and although none of these later writers achieved the insight of Paul, the first of its authors, they have something of value to contribute to our understanding of historical Christianity, the development of Christian doctrine, and the extraordinary movement, so largely literary, that in a century and a half after its formation made the New Testament the religious authority of that ancient world.

It was the conviction of the early church that the acceptance of the gospel released new powers in the human spirit, and never was this truer than in these first centuries when in the defense and advocacy of Christianity men like Irenaeus, Tertullian, and Origen stood forth to fight the literary battle for the new faith. It was an age of writers, publishers, books, and readers to a degree that may well surprise the modern reader and give him a new idea of the intelligence and reading interest of Christian circles in the second and third centuries.

A few Christian books not included in the New Testament may well be older than some of those that found a place in it, and they throw light upon the situations in which canonical books were written. In origin the books are interrelated, for all come from, and find their places in, the ongoing life of the church. But the story of the New Testament books has often been told and need not be repeated here. The reader is referred instead to introductions to the New Testament that emphasize the literary and historical circumstances of the New Testament books.[3] In the present study, it will be enough to assume the existence of these circumstances without undertaking to repeat what has already been said in print about New Testament origins.

---

[3] See, e.g., R. M. Grant, *A Historical Introduction to the New Testament* (London, New York, 1963).

LETTERS

Paul's Letters

The earliest form of Christian writing was naturally the letter, the personal communication from man to man or man to group of men, such as first-century Greeks and Romans, and Jews as well, constantly wrote. In the hands of Paul this simplest form of composition had developed into a powerful instrument of religious instruction, and by A.D. 90 the collection and publication of his letters had standardized it as a Christian literary type. This is the background of all the other early Christian letters, particularly of what we know as the *Letter of Clement*.

Clement of Rome

Toward the end of the first century, perhaps about A.D. 95, something like a revolt broke out among the Christians at Corinth against the officers of the church, the presbyters or elders as they were called. This disturbance became so notorious that news of it reached Rome and distressed the church there. The Roman church accordingly sent a long letter to the Corinthians, urging them to harmonize their differences and to show their church officers the respect due them. The letter does not name its writer. It is written simply in the name of "the church of God that sojourns in Rome to the church of God that sojourns in Corinth," but it was recognized very early as the work of Clement, the head of the Roman church from about A.D. 88 to 97. Ancient writers, from Dionysius of Corinth (*ca.* A.D. 170) down, agree in ascribing the letter to Clement; Eusebius himself does so in his *Church History* (iii. 16; iv. 23. 11). Dionysius wrote to Soter, bishop of Rome between 166 and 174, that it was the custom of the Corinthian church to read Clement's letter from time to time in its meetings. So religiously useful did the letter prove that it passed into some early New Testaments, such as the Codex Alexandrinus of the fifth century, and into a Syriac manuscript of the New Testament in the Harclean version written in the twelfth century, in which the *Letter of Clement*[1] immediately followed the general, or Catholic letters, to which it was evidently believed to belong.

The position of presbyter or elder first comes into prominence in the Acts, written about A.D. 90 or soon after. The Corinthians had from the beginning made much of spiritual endowments (I Cor. 12–14), and it is easy to see how the new regard for church officers might have encountered difficulty in gaining support in that church. Clement, however, speaks as though the office was of long standing and the Corinthian disloyalty to it an innovation. He rebukes them sharply for their attitude and dwells upon the bad effects discord always produces. He urges them to follow the example of the great figures of Scripture; he is remarkably familiar with the Greek version of the Jewish Bible and quotes it copiously. He reminds them of the humility of Christ and points to the harmony of the natural world. He tells the story of the phoenix, described by Herodotus (ii. 73) and Pliny the Elder (*Natural History* x. 2), among others. After a long admonition to lead a godly life, Clement returns to the Corinthian situation (chap. 44), points out that the officers of the church derive their leadership in succession from the apostles, and urges upon them love, forgiveness, humility, and reconciliation. After a prayer (59:3–61:3) he closes with a summary of the letter.

It may seem strange that the Roman church should take upon itself the direction of the church at Corinth, but a number of events in Christian history had prepared the way for such a step. The Roman church saw that the churches of Asia needed to be reminded to love their enemies and to respect the emperor, and thus transmitted I Peter to convey this corrective. As the Revelation had claimed the authority of a Christian prophet writing in the name of Jesus himself, the Roman church wrote in the name of the chief of the apostles. This it could do, the ancients thought, since it was the custodian of his tomb and so of his memory and his teaching.

In writing to the Corinthians, however, it needed no such aids for its message and wrote simply as the church of God that sojourned in Rome. The apology with which it begins is explained

---

[1] Followed by the so-called *II Clement*.

by the probable persecution of the church. "Because of the sudden and successive misfortunes and disasters that have overtaken us," Clement begins, "we think that we have been too slow to pay attention to the matters under dispute among you, beloved."

The influence of Hebrews on the *Letter of Clement* is very marked. It is here that we first find Hebrews reflected in Christian literature, for Clement is largely interspersed with thoughts and expressions from it.

The acquaintance of Clement with the collected letters of Paul is also clear; he is the first Christian writer to quote one of Paul's letters expressly: "Take up the letter of the blessed Paul, the apostle; what did he first write you, at the beginning of the gospel preaching?" chapter 47 begins, and then continues with an unmistakable reference to I Cor. 1:10–12. Not only I Corinthians but Romans and Ephesians are clearly reflected in Clement.

This knowledge of the collected letters of Paul on the part of Clement suggests that we should push the earliest possible date of Clement's letter down ten or fifteen years later than A.D. 75, suggested by Lake as the *terminus a quo*, although it is not certain exactly when the Pauline letters were collected. More important is Clement's reference to the envoys of the Roman church as having "lived among us . . . from youth to old age" (64). Since the Roman church was probably not established until about A.D. 40, this remark may well point to the date of the letter as A.D. 85 —or later.

The resemblances of the *Letter of Clement* to I Peter are generally, and rightly, taken to show Clement's use of that letter. Their similarities may conceivably be the result of the parallels in the situations involved, for both are Roman letters to the Christians of the East, *I Clement* to those of Greece and I Peter to those of Asia Minor. But Peter's reference to himself as a "fellow elder" (5:1) has nothing to do with Clement's insistence upon the authority of elders at Corinth. The fact that in both letters those who oversee the churches are called elders, and the churches called "sheepfolds," points toward the continuity of doctrine and discipline at Rome, not primarily to literary relationships.

Clement cannot be said to show acquaintance with any written gospel; his quotations of Jesus' words in chapters 13 and 46 are highly stylized and seem more naturally explained as being de-

rived from catechetical teaching. In both chapters they are introduced with the words "remembering" or "remember the words of
the Lord Jesus"—the way of introducing a quotation from oral
tradition, as in Acts 20:35 (see p. 2).

Lightfoot in his great commentary on the epistles of Clement,
which Harnack called the finest commentary we have on any
Church Father, says that Clement's characteristics are compre-
hensiveness, order, and moderation. The *Letter* is certainly a fine
example of first-century Christian teaching, and it almost won a
place in the New Testament. It was accepted as scripture by
Clement of Alexandria, writing between A.D. 190 and 210. The
so-called *II Clement* became attached to it, and the two stand
after the Revelation in the Alexandrian manuscript of the Greek
Bible. They are mentioned as part of the New Testament in the
Apostolic Canons, a Syrian work of about A.D. 400, and stand between the Catholic letters and those of Paul in the Harclean Syriac
New Testament manuscript already noted. Abu'l Barakat (1363),
in his account of Christian Arabic literature, speaks of the two
letters of Clement as belonging to the New Testament. But on
the Greek side, the *Stichometry of Nicephorus*, a list of books of
scripture giving the size of each in lines of Homeric length (*ca.*
A.D. 850), lists them among the rejected books, its "apocrypha."
But, in or out the New Testament, *I Clement* is a noble monu-
ment of Christian attitudes in Rome toward the end of the first
century.

Modern Discoveries

Yet for all its ancient renown—it was one of the best-known books
of early Christian literature—until 1875 *I Clement* was known to
the modern world only through a single defective Greek manuscript—the fifth-century Codex Alexandrinus, from which a leaf
was lost just before the end of the letter. As no other versions
were known to exist, no one knew how much or how little was
really gone until, in 1873, Bryennius discovered in Constantinople
a complete Greek text of it in a manuscript dated A.D. 1056. This
text he published in 1875. One Syriac, one Latin, and two Coptic
manuscripts of it have since been found, one of these last a papyrus
leaf-book of the fourth century.

Clement himself was spoken of in the *Shepherd* of Hermas,
about A.D. 100 (*Vision* ii. 4. 3); and his letter is mentioned or

quoted by Dionysius of Corinth, about 170 (*Church History* iv.
23. 11); by Hegesippus in his *Memoirs*, now lost, about 180
(*Church History* iv. 22. 1); by Irenaeus, 181–89 (*Against Heresies*
iii. 3. 3); by Clement of Alexandria several times; by Origen (*On
First Principles* ii. 3. 6, etc.); and by Eusebius (*Church History*
iv. 22. 1, etc.). Although its almost complete disappearance in
medieval Greek manuscripts shows its decline in prestige, its translation into Latin, Syriac, and Coptic shows its wide currency in
the early period, and the fact that *II Clement* does not accompany
it in the Latin and Coptic versions shows at how early a date these
translations must have been made.

The Apostolic Fathers and the Didache

It was the Codex Alexandrinus that first made the *Letter of
Clement* known in Europe, and when Cyril Lucar, patriarch of
Constantinople, sent that manuscript to the king of England in
1628, one of the first acts of the royal librarian Patrick Young
was to edit and publish the *Letters of Clement* in 1633. The subsequent publication of the *Letter of Barnabas*, the *Letter of Polycarp*, and the Ignatian letters made it posible for Cotelier in 1672
to publish the *Works of the Holy Fathers Who Flourished in
Apostolic Times* (*temporibus Apostolicis*); when Ittig in 1699
carried on that task, he called his collection a library of Apostolic
Fathers (*Bibliotheca Patrum Apostolicorum*). In the principal
collections of Apostolic Fathers to this day (Severus of Antioch;
Lightfoot; Gebhardt, Harnack, and Zahn; Lake), Clement has
usually had the place of honor, at first probably because he was
identified with the Clement mentioned in Phil. 4:3, but more
recently because his letter is so clearly the earliest writing outside
of the New Testament that we possess.

The Apostolic Fathers in the nineteenth century consisted of
I–II Clement, the letters of Ignatius and Polycarp, together with
the *Martyrdom* of the latter, the *Letter of Barnabas*, the *Shepherd*
of Hermas, and—because of a seventeenth-century error—the *Letter to Diognetus*, actually an apologetic work. With these writings
was sometimes associated what remains of the writings of Papias,
a contemporary of Polycarp.

In 1883, however, the situation was changed when Bryennius
published, from the Constantinople manuscript of A.D. 1056 (now
at Jerusalem), the text of the *Teaching of the Lord through the*

Twelve Apostles for the Gentiles. This little manual of church discipline, usually called the *Didache* ("teaching"), immediately evoked a great deal of controversy, which is not yet at an end. The first six chapters of the manual contain moral instruction, largely Jewish in nature and partly based on the teaching of Jesus, which was to be recited before baptism. Chapters 7–10 consist of instructions about baptism, prayer, and what seems to be the eucharist. Chapters 11–15 deal with the reception of various kinds of ministers—apostles, prophets, and teachers—who are about to be supplanted by the appointment of bishops and deacons. The last chapter is an apocalypse apparently based on Matthew 24. Naturally the question of the date of this book was raised, and it has been located all the way from A.D. 70 to A.D. 180. A *terminus ante quem* is provided by a quotation from it as scripture in Clement of Alexandria (*Miscellanies* i. 100), between 190 and 200.

The book was later known to Eusebius, Athanasius, and a few others and was incorporated in the third-century *Didascalia* and the fourth-century *Apostolic Constitutions*. In recent times two small Greek fragments of the fourth century (*Oxyrhynchus Papyri* xv.1782; *Didache* 1:3^b–4^a, 2:7^b–3:2^a) and one Coptic fragment of the fifth century (British Museum, Or. MS, 9271, 10:3^b–12:2^a) have been discovered. To the prayers over wine and bread the Coptic fragment adds a prayer over chrism. In addition, Ethiopic and Georgian versions have been found. The situation became even more complicated when O. von Gebhardt, in 1884, printed a copy of a twelfth-century manuscript with a Latin version of *Didache* 1:1–2.6^a, and J. Schlecht, in 1899, published a Latin document (eleventh-century manuscript) entitled *De doctrina apostolorum* (*On the Teaching of the Apostles*) closely parallel to *Didache* 1–6 and *Barnabas* 18–20.

All sorts of theories have been set forth to explain the interrelations of the Greek *Didache* with the parallel texts. Goodspeed argued that both Latin versions represented the original Greek edition composed early in the second century, perhaps at Antioch; this was used when *Barnabas* 18–20 was added to the first seventeen chapters and also, about A.D. 150, when the existing *Didache* was compiled. A more likely view is that *De doctrina apostolorum*, which lacks the clearly Christian section in the *Didache*, 1:3–2:1, represents the Jewish original "two ways" on which the first part of the *Didache* is based, and that in turn *Barnabas* 18–20 is based on the *Didache*.

The ideas of the *Didache* do not vary greatly from those expressed in the Gospel of Matthew, and it appears that, at least in the latter half of the *Didache*, that gospel was used. Some of the coincidences in the first part may have resulted from the use of common oral traditions. J.-P. Audet, who published a very thorough study of the little work in 1958, has argued that the first half (through 11:2) comes from about A.D. 70, while the rest was added not long afterwards. Perhaps as a whole the book should be dated about the last third of the first century, possibly around A.D. 90. Its Jewish-Christian tone indicates its place of origin as the East, perhaps Syria or Alexandria.

Later on, Eusebius puts "the so-called Teachings of the Apostles" among the books that are disputed and rejected (*Church History* iii. 25. 4). Athanasius in his *Festal Letter* of A.D. 367 omits it from the New Testament but says that it and the *Shepherd* of Hermas may be read by new converts and persons preparing for baptism. The *Didache* is listed among the "apocrypha" or rejected books in the *List of Sixty Canonical Books* and in the *Stichometry of Nicephorus*. It was no longer especially useful, since it had been assimilated and modernized in later manuals of discipline, and it survived only as occasional reading among the monks of Egypt.

Ignatius of Antioch

Early in the second century a Christian prisoner guarded by ten Roman soldiers was being taken through western Asia Minor to Rome, where he was to be executed. He was the bishop of Antioch, in Syria, and his name was Ignatius. News of his coming had preceded him, and when at Laodicea his guards took the north fork of the road that led through Philadelphia to Smyrna, Christian messengers hurried along the south fork, through Tralles and Magnesia to Ephesus, to tell the brethren that he had gone the other way and that they must go to Smyrna if they hoped to see him. A number of them did so, and when, very soon after, his guards took him on to Troas, one of these brethren went with him to that port. A little later his party touched at Philippi, on their way westward. That is the last we see of Ignatius. But at Smyrna and Troas he managed to write seven letters that, though of no great length, are of extraordinary interest.

Although he was the bishop of Antioch, it is only when Ignatius enters the circle of the churches of Asia that he writes anything significant enough to be preserved. We know of no writings of his from the years at Antioch, and of none after he left Troas for Rome; and it may be that his one sudden burst of literary activity at Smyrna and Troas was stimulated by the Christian leaders of Asia—Polycarp of Smyrna and Onesimus of Ephesus—or by the circumstances under which he wrote.

We can hardly suppose that his brutal guards—"ten leopards," he called them—did anything to facilitate his letter-writing in the way of providing him with writing materials or forwarding his letters. But an Ephesian deacon named Burrhus, who came to Smyrna with his bishop Onesimus and three others from Ephesus to see and cheer him, seems to have assisted him as far as Troas and helped with his letter-writing there. In fact, he was probably his amanuensis. Ignatius says that the Ephesians and Smyrnaeans had been instrumental in getting him this assistance.

While he was at Smyrna, Ignatius recognized this expression of Christian sympathy by writing a letter to each of these churches. He also addressed one to the Christians of Rome, preparing them for his coming and urging that nothing be done to prevent his martyrdom, to which he had now fully made up his mind. This attitude of Ignatius can be understood if we remember the terrible prospect of a cruel death to which he must have been striving to adjust himself through these weeks of travel.

His guards took him on from Ephesus to Troas, and there he wrote three more letters: one to the church at Smyrna, where he had been so kindly treated; one to the church of Philadelphia, with which he had had a hurried contact on his way to Smyrna; and one to Polycarp, the bishop of Smyrna, who had evidently done all that could be done for him during his stay in that city. The persecution at Antioch was now over, and Ignatius wished the Asian churches to write letters of encouragement to his old flock, especially as he could not rally them himself. He was being hurried on to Neapolis, and even with the aid of Burrhus could not write to all the churches through which he would pass on his way to Rome. He asked Polycarp to do this for him, so that his triumphal progress might continue all the way to the city of his martyrdom.

We catch one more glimpse of him at Philippi, where he met the church. Then he disappears from our ken, for the later book on the *Martyrdom of Ignatius* has little historical worth. We can only suppose that he was thrown to the lions in the Coliseum;

Eusebius places the date about A.D. 107–8. The exact date is uncertain.

Second-century Christianity was clouded over by a wide variety of schismatic movements: Docetism, Judaizing, Marcionism, Gnosticism, and Montanism. The first two are reflected and opposed in the letters of Ignatius and the letters and Gospel of John. Ignatius is the first Christian writer to describe the Docetic position—that Christ's suffering was not real but only a "semblance" (*dokein*), so that he only seemed to suffer. Against these views, Ignatius insisted in his letters to the Trallians and the Smyrnaeans that Christ's sufferings were real, and he bitterly retorted that the holders of such views were themselves but "semblance." He criticized the Judaizers in writing to the Magnesians and the Philadelphians; these Judaizers had an exaggerated idea of the self-sufficiency of the Old Testament and seemed to be occupied with Jewish rites.

Against the obvious danger of division within and among the churches, Ignatius urges unity upon believers, and he finds the surest guaranty of this in a uniform church organization, under the leadership of bishop, elders (presbyters), and deacons. "Do nothing without the bishop" is his remedy (*Philadelphians* 7). Christians must be in harmony with their bishop and, since the bishop has the mind of Christ, in harmony with Christ and the Father. Ignatius is strongly ecclesiastical in his views; he certainly believes that outside the church there is no salvation and that to be within the church requires obedience to the bishop and presbyters. He is the first true advocate of the threefold ministry, although it was not for another fifty years or so that this kind of organization became universal.

The style of Ignatius owes much to the Greco-Roman rhetoric of his time, with its fondness for paradox and vivid imagery. His is a good example of what was called the Asian style, as opposed to the more restrained Attic. The stylistic influence of the Hellenistic-Jewish treatise on martyrdom that we know as IV Maccabees seems particularly apparent.[2]

It may be that the Christian leaders of Asia, Polycarp of Smyrna and Onesimus of Ephesus, urged upon Ignatius the duty of attacking the false doctrines current among their churches. His

---

2 See H. Riesenfeld in *Texte und Untersuchungen* 79 (Berlin, 1961), pp. 312–22.

immediate position, as a Christian confessor, a man already condemned to death for his faith and on the way to execution,
naturally gave his words great weight. But it seems unnecessary
to ascribe much influence to Ignatius' fellow bishops. As bishop
of Antioch, or indeed of Syria (*Rom.* 2:2), he was quite capable
of assessing the situation for himself, as we learn from his account
of his dealings with the Philadelphians.

Ignatius speaks in his letters of the aid the brethren of Ephesus
and Smyrna had given him in writing and sending his letters, and,
of course, without such local aid a prisoner like him could not
have either written or sent them. The Ephesians and Smyrnaeans
had sent Burrhus of Ephesus (*Eph.* 2:1) with Ignatius to Troas
to write or carry his letters (*Philad.* 11:2; *Smyrn.* 12:1). Ignatius
directs Polycarp to write to the churches in the cities he is likely
to pass through on the rest of his journey to Rome. And a few
weeks later we find Polycarp sending a collection of his letters
to the church at Philippi. The free interchange of letters among
the churches of Asia, Macedonia, and Syria that is implied or
reflected in the letters of Ignatius and Polycarp shows in what
close touch these churches, and probably the other leading
churches of Italy and Greece, already were. Paul's letters to the
churches had led the way in this, and the letter collection that
begins the Revelation, together with Hebrews, I Peter, and *I
Clement,* had continued it. These churches of East and West were
in frequent communication by letter and these letters sometimes
rose to the stature of permanent contributions to the growing
treasures of what was to be Christian literature.

Polycarp of Smyrna

The letter of Polycarp to the Philippians is an immediate sequel
to the letters of Ignatius. Ignatius had been taken by his guards
from Troas to Neapolis and thence, it appears, to Philippi, where
the Philippian Christian leaders had visited him (Pol. *Phil.* 9:1).
After his departure they had written to Polycarp, asking him to
send their letter with his to Antioch, for Ignatius had requested
them to write to the Christians of his diocese. They had also
asked Polycarp to send them whatever letters of Ignatius he could,
and this he did writing them on his own account a kind of
covering letter. He urged them to be harmonious, steadfast, and
faithful but said nothing about the threefold ministry of which

Ignatius made so much; in writing he simply grouped himself with his presbyters: "Polycarp and the elders with him."[3] He evidently wrote his letter within a few weeks of Ignatius' departure for Rome, for he had no news of his fate and asked the Philippians if they had any.

Not only in polity but in doctrine and in his use of Christian literature does Polycarp stand apart from Ignatius. Ignatius is the first writer to show acquaintance with Matthew, and he knows the Pauline letters, but Polycarp also knows the Pauline letters, including the Pastorals, the Acts, Hebrews, and I Peter, and uses Christian literature much more frequently than Ignatius does. His style, however, lacks the rugged vigor and the very unconventional metaphors that make Ignatius interesting and sometimes perplexing.

A striking difficulty arises when we try to reconcile two passages in Polycarp's letter. In the first (chap. 9), he clearly regards Ignatius as dead, a martyr with other martyrs; in the second (chap. 13), he asks for further information about him, evidently writing soon after Ignatius' departure for Rome. Chiefly because of this discrepancy, P. N. Harrison has argued that the letter really consists of two letters, one (chaps. 13–14) written in the year when Ignatius was martyred, the other (chaps. 1–12) written at a time of crisis in the Philippian church, perhaps just before Marcion left Asia Minor for Rome, about A.D. 135.[4] It is possible, however, that Polycarp treats Ignatius' zeal for martyrdom as certain to achieve its goal, and that the one letter was written early rather than late. It is by no means certain that Polycarp has Marcion in view at this time.

Forms of the Ignatian Letters

This brings up the matter of the forms in which the Ignatian letters have come down to us. Eusebius speaks of seven letters (*Church History* iii. 36): *Ephesians, Magnesians, Trallians,* and *Romans,* written from Smyrna, and *Philadelphians, Smyrnaeans,* and *Polycarp,* written from Troas. In the manuscripts of Ignatius, however, the letters begin with *Smyrnaeans* and *Polycarp,* continuing with *Ephesians, Magnesians, Philadelphias, Trallians;* these

---

[3] Presumably he writes as bishop; he mentions both presbyters and deacons.
[4] *Polycarp's Two Epistles to the Philippians* (Cambridge, 1936).

are followed by a string of spurious letters that cannot be dated earlier than the latter part of the fourth century, among which *Romans* appears following a late and unhistorical account of the *Martyrdom of Ignatius*, to which it has evidently given rise. The order in which the genuine letters thus appear—*Smyrnaeans, Polycarp, Ephesians, Magnesians, Philadelphians, Trallians, Romans*—recalls Polycarp's words to the Philippians regarding what he was sending them: "We send you, as you asked, the letters of Ignatius which were sent to us by him [that would be *Smyrnaeans* and *Polycarp*] and such others as we had in our possession [that is, those to other churches of which Burrhus would have retained copies]." This is perhaps the original order in which Polycarp circulated the collection, much as the Pauline letter collection had been put in circulation perhaps twenty-five years earlier. That Polycarp has that collection in the back of his mind is shown when he says to the Philippians, "Neither am I nor is any other like me able to follow the wisdom of the blessed and glorious Paul, who . . . when he was absent wrote letters to you" (3:2). The collection he is now sending them cannot compare with that of the Pauline letters; yet he also speaks of the endurance the Philippians had seen with their own eyes "not only in the blessed Ignatius and Zosimus and Rufus . . . but in Paul himself and in the other apostles" (9:1), thus suggesting that Ignatius, like Paul, is a martyr and so deserves a hearing.

Both Ignatius and Polycarp were well aware of the great value the collected letters of Paul had possessed for the churches; they speak of it (*Eph.* 12:2; Pol. *Phil.* 11:3) very much as though they had had that collection of the martyred Paul in mind in creating this new collection by the soon-to-be-martyred Ignatius. Ignatius' remark to the Ephesians that Paul "in every letter makes mention of [*mnemoneuei*] you" may point to Ephesus as the place where Paul's letters had been collected and published.

It is not necessary to suppose that Polycarp painfully sent around among the Asian churches and gathered up the letters of Ignatius. He tells the Philippians that he is sending them "the letters of Ignatius which were sent to us by him, and such others as we had in our possession." How does Polycarp happen to have any others besides Ignatius' letters to himself and to his church at Smyrna? He has already made a collection, it appears, before the Philippians ask him for it; indeed, Ignatius has told them to ask, for he understands what Polycarp has in mind. Apparently

Burrhus, the deacon of Ephesus, who had accompanied Ignatius from Smyrna to Troas had kept copies of the letters he wrote for him for the use of his principals, Polycarp and Onesimus, and that Ignatius was aware of this and was agreeable to it. It is reasonable, then, to suppose that the letter to the Romans was among the letters Polycarp had in his possession and that he sent copies of it to the Philippians.

Two other forms of the Ignatian letters illustrate their popularity in ancient times. For they were not only generally accompanied by from six to ten spurious letters ascribed to Ignatius and written in his name, probably late in the fourth century, but each letter was interpolated and expanded, as Greek and Latin texts show. On the other hand, three of them—*Polycarp*, *Ephesians*, and *Romans*—are found in Syriac much abbreviated. The letters of Ignatius were, therefore, known in the early church in at least four different forms:

1. The seven genuine letters, known to Eusebius in A.D. 326.
2. These seven letters, accompanied by ten spurious ones.[5]
3. The seven letters individually expanded and interpolated and accompanied by several spurious letters.
4. In Syriac three letters—*Polycarp*, *Ephesians*, *Romans*—compressed, on no particular principle, to a little more than half their original length.

Polycarp's *Letter to the Philippians* was not usually copied with the Ignatian letters; indeed, no complete Greek text of it is known, and although a group of Greek manuscripts preserves almost nine chapters of it, and Eusebius in his *Church History* (iii. 36. 14, 15) supplies the thirteenth, for the other four chapters we are dependent upon the Latin version.

Nearly sixty years later, in A.D. 167, Polycarp suffered martyrdom in Smyrna, at the age of eighty-six. An account of this, sub-

---

[5] In the Latin text which contains the seven genuine letters in the translation made or directed by Robert Grosseteste, bishop of Lincoln (*ca.* 1250), the contents are: *Smyrnaeans, Polycarp, Ephesians, Magnesians, Philadelphians, Trallians, Mary of Cassobola to Ignatius, Ignatius to Mary of Cassobola, Tarsians, Antiochenes, Hero,* the *Martyrdom* (numbered the twelfth letter), and *Romans* (numbered the thirteenth). Then follows the correspondence of Ignatius with John the Evangelist and with St. Mary (four letters). The longer Greek form has a *Letter to the Philippians* also but usually contains only thirteen letters. We also possess most of *Smyrnaeans* in a fifth-century Greek papyrus (P. Berol. 10581), and there are Coptic fragments of several letters.

stantially historical, was embodied in a letter from the church of Smyrna to that of Philomelium, a town in Phrygia not far from Pisidian Antioch. It is the earliest example that has come down to us of that type of literature, the "martyrdom," which was to become so abundant. It will be more fully discussed in its chronological position in the development of Christian letter literature.

The Letter of Barnabas

The view Christians were to take of the Jewish scriptures was a serious problem for the early church for almost a century and a half. What were Christians to think of the Jewish Law? How were they to regard the utterances of the prophets? The Letter to the Romans and the Gospel of Matthew had grappled with these questions, and Marcion and Justin in the middle of the second century took opposite views on them. But about A.D. 130 a Christian teacher, probably in Alexandria, offered a compromise. The Jewish scriptures were true, not literally, as the Jews believed, but allegorically. When Genesis declared that Abraham circumcised 318 males of his household (14:14; 17:23), it meant to predict Jesus on the cross, for the Greek figures for 18 are iota eta (IH), the first two letters of Jesus' name, and the Greek figure for 300 is tau, or T, which could be taken as representing the cross. The allegorizing teacher who offered this interpretation was very proud of it. "No one has learned a truer lesson from me," he goes on, "but I know that you deserve it" (Barnabas 9:8, 9).

The food laws of Leviticus are also allegorized. They only mean that we are not to be like swine, wild beasts, or birds of prey. The six days of creation are the six thousand years the earth is to last before the Messiah's return, "for a day with him means a thousand years." So interpreted, the author finds the Jewish scriptures full of religious meaning and of predictions fulfilled in Christ.

One of these touches seems to date the book, for the writer speaks of the temple as having been destroyed and then rebuilt by those who had destroyed it, and he goes on, "It is happening. For because of the war it was destroyed by the enemy; now even the servants of the enemy will build it up again themselves" (16:14). This points to the heathen rebuilding of the temple of Jupiter on the temple site in Jerusalem, on the eve of the Bar-Cochba War of A.D. 132–35; this would date the Letter about A.D. 130–31, when Hadrian ordered the building of the new city. The literary environment of Barnabas is indicated by his use of Matthew, of Old Testament "testimonies," and of apocalyptic writings such as I Enoch, II Esdras, and II Baruch.

The *Letter of Barnabas* begins not in the usual fashion of Greek letters but in the informal epistolary style used in family letters, addressing its readers as "sons and daughters." Its tone changes suddenly at the end of chapter 17: "So much for this. Now let us pass to another lesson and teaching." (The words are *gnosis* and *didache*.) What follows is a bold statement of Christian ethics, the Way of Light against the Way of Darkness. It is cast in fifty-one curt commands of the "Thou shalt" and "Thou shalt not" order, twenty-three of them positive and twenty-eight negative (chap. 19). A brief description of the Way of the Black One follows, and a general exhortation concludes the book.

No one can miss the sharp cleavage at the end of chapter 17. The idle if ingenious fancies of the allegorical interpreter give way to the stern, blunt commandments of the Christian lawgiver, with only the crudest of transitions between. It is evident that two short Christian tracts have been put together. And this impression becomes a conviction when we find that each part has been found by itself in a Latin version. The Latin translation of *Barnabas* extends only through chapter 17, which is properly finished off with a doxology.

The Greek manuscripts of *Barnabas* have an interesting history. At first it was known in Greek only in a group of eight manuscripts, all copied directly or indirectly from an earlier manuscript from which several leaves had been lost, so that the text skipped from Polycarp *To the Philippians* 9:2 toward the end of one sentence to the *Letter of Barnabas* 5:7 in the middle of another. But in 1859, when Tischendorf found the Codex Sinaiticus at St. Catherine's on Mount Sinai, he saw at once that it contained the complete Greek text of *Barnabas*, and, fearing that the manuscript might be taken away from him the next morning, he sat up all night to copy that long-desired text. A few years later, in 1873, Bryennius made his famous discovery of the Constantinople manuscript, from which he published first the full Greek text of *I* and *II Clement* (1875), and then the long-lost *Didache* (1883). It also contained the full Greek text of *Barnabas*, and its readings Bryennius supplied for Hilgenfeld's edition of 1877.

The influence of the *Letter of Barnabas* was considerable, and it was long held in high regard. Clement of Alexandria, toward the end of the second century, accepted it as scripture and commented upon it in his lost *Outlines*. He spoke of Barnabas as an "apostle," but so, of course, did Acts (14:14). Origen, too, included it among his disputed books, which he himself accepted as scripture. The Sinaitic manuscript includes it in the New Testament, putting it after the Revelation and before Hermas. Jerome speaks of it as being read among the apocryphal writings (*On Illustrious Men* 6). The *Clermont List*, representing Egyptian usage about A.D. 300, has it at the end of the Catholic or general letters, between Jude and the Revelation of John. Eusebius classes it as disputed and rejected (*Church History* iii. 25. 4). The *List of the Sixty Canonical Books* mentions it among the rejected books, the apocrypha, and the *Stichometry of Nicephorus* (*ca.* A.D. 850) puts it with the disputed books—the Revelation of John, the *Revelation of Peter,* and the *Gospel of the Hebrews*—not among the rejected ones.

The Epistle of the Apostles

About the middle of the second century a Greek Christian of Asia, probably in the vicinity of Ephesus, wrote in the name of the apostles a letter to all the churches, gathering from the Four Gospels, the Acts, and other sources what he considered of most value and interest in the way of Christian history and tradition, ethics and expectation. He meant it as a kind of summary, for the whole world, from all the apostles, of Christian beliefs and hopes. Perhaps he felt that the growing number of Christian books must confuse simple minds, and he tried to condense all that material into one small book, about the length of I Corinthians. The idea of writing in the name of all the apostles was not new and had been taken up in the *Teaching of the Lord through the Twelve Apostles,* early in the second century, and again toward the end of it in the *Gospel of the Twelve Apostles.*

The only trace of the *Epistle of the Apostles* seems to occur in in the fifth-century Christian poet Commodian, who may reflect chapter 11 in the words "Vestigium umbra non facit" ("A phantom does not make a footprint"). But the book itself was entirely unknown until Carl Schmidt reported the discovery of a part of it in Coptic in 1895. A Latin fragment of it, a single leaf from the fifth century, came to light in 1908. Meanwhile in 1907 a work in Ethiopic called *The Testament of Our Lord in Galilee* had been reported and described, and was recognized by M. R.

James as including a version of the *Epistle of the Apostles;* it was published in 1913 and preserves the work in full. From these three sources, Coptic, Latin, and Ethiopic, Schmidt in 1919 published the text. But no part of it has yet been found in Greek, the original language of the book.

The writer of the *Epistle of the Apostles* names its authors as John, Thomas, Peter, Andrew, James, Philip, Bartholomew, Matthew, Nathanael, Judas the Zealot, and Cephas although John 1:42 explains that Cephas, so often mentioned in Paul, really means Peter. Nathanael is, of course, never mentioned in the gospel lists of apostles. The book begins with a warning against the "false apostles" Simon (meaning Simon Magus) and Cerinthus, the latter the earliest of the schismatic leaders (*ca.* A.D. 100). It records the creation by God the Father and his incarnation in God the Son. A summary of Jesus' miracles is given, followed by his crucifixion, burial, and resurrection. He rejoins the apostles, apparently in Galilee, and tells them of his experiences in the other world. He promises to release Peter from prison and instructs them to observe the Lord's Supper. They ask when he is to return, and he answers that it will be when a hundred and fifty years are past (so the Ethiopic; the Coptic has "When the hundred and twentieth part is fulfilled," evidently counting not from Jesus' birth but from his death). He teaches the apostles and answers their questions, promising them resurrection, and declaring that he will go with them as they preach. He predicts the conversion, work, and martyrdom of Paul and describes the signs of the end. He justifies the condemnation of the wicked but encourages the apostles to pray for sinners and commissions them as "fathers, servants, and masters." He explains the parable of the bridesmaids, giving each one the name of some virtue or faculty. The wise ones were Faith, Love, Grace, Peace, and Hope; the foolish were Knowledge, Understanding, Obedience, Patience, and Compassion. (This suggests the names given the twelve virgins in the *Shepherd* of Hermas, *Parable* 9:15.) After giving further moral instruction and the prediction of schismatic teaching, he is carried away on a cloud.

The writer's historical weakness is obvious; he can assemble only eleven apostles, although he counts both Cephas and Peter and includes Nathanael (of John 1:45–49). He describes Jesus as crucified by Pontius Pilate and Archelaus, although the latter disappeared from history in A.D. 6; Antipas, of course, is whom he meant.

He draws heavily upon the Four Gospels and the Acts and uses the Revelation of John, the *Revelation of Peter*, I Peter, and probably Ignatius (*Eph.* 7:2), the *Letter of Barnabas*, and the *Shepherd* of Hermas. He tells the famous story of Jesus and his alphabet teacher (chap. 4), which appears in the *Gospel of Thomas* and is quoted in Irenaeus (*Against Heresies* i. 20. 1), but we cannot be sure he derived the story from that gospel; he may have gotten it from tradition. He describes Jesus as quoting extensively from the Psalms (Pss. 3 [in full], 13, 49).

There are gropings toward a creed, as when the writer in chapter 3 proclaims his doctrine of God the Father and God the Son and in chapter 5 explains the five loaves as the symbol of our faith in "the Father, the Lord Almighty, and in Jesus Christ our Redeemer, in the Holy Spirit the Comforter, in the holy church, and in the forgiveness of sins." This was just at the time when the Roman church (A.D. 140–50) was first shaping its baptismal confession, which we know as the Apostles' Creed.

The fixing of the second coming "when a hundred and fifty years are past" points to a date between A.D. 140 and 150. Justin Martyr, in *Apology* xlvi. 1, speaks of Jesus as having been born one hundred and fifty years before he writes. Some touches sound as though Marcion were a contemporary of the writer; he flourished at just that time. On the whole, the *Epistle* was probably written between A.D. 140 and 160.

The Martyrdom of Justin

Early Christians were constantly liable to sporadic persecution, and one Christian leader after another met his death by martyrdom, as we have already seen in the case of Ignatius. After the middle of the second century we find a few accounts of the trials and sufferings of the martyrs, sometimes in the form of letters such as the one about Polycarp, to which we shall presently turn, sometimes in the form of court reporting, as in the account of the Roman Christian Justin, put to death between 163 and 167, when Q. Junius Rusticus was prefect of the city of Rome. The *Martyrdom of Justin* describes the interrogation of Justin and seven other Christians by the prefect. The prefect engages in a brief discussion with Justin, then inquires about the Christian allegiance of all the prisoners. When they insist that they are Christians, he threatens Justin and ridicules his ideas about heavenly reward. All the Christians refuse to offer sacrifice to the gods and are therefore beheaded; other Christians later obtain their bodies for burial, and perhaps for veneration.

The Martyrdom of Polycarp

Another account of martyrdom comes from about the same time. This is the *Martyrdom of Polycarp*, the famous bishop of Smyrna whose life spanned the years between Ignatius, early in the second century, and Irenaeus, toward its end. In 154 Polycarp had visited Rome to confer with the Roman bishop Anicetus about the day on which the institution of the Lord's Supper should be celebrated. Polycarp and the Christians of Asia observed it on the fourteenth of the month Nisan, no matter on what day of the week it fell; but the Roman church celebrated the death of Christ on Friday and his resurrection "on the Sunday following the first full moon after the vernal equinox." This was the "quartodeciman controversy" that was soon to divide Christianity. Polycarp and Anicetus could not agree about it, but they partook of the communion together and parted amicably. After his return to Smyrna, however, Polycarp was arrested and condemned to death; he suffered martyrdom by being bound to the stake, stabbed, and burned. This occurred in A.D. 166–67.

Polycarp was eighty-six years of age at the time of his martyrdom and had been bishop of Smyrna for at least fifty years. He was greatly respected and loved by Christians everywhere, and an account of his last days and death was very soon written in the form of a letter from the church at Smyrna to the one at Philomelium, two hundred miles to the east. It tells, for the most part with much restraint, of the arrest, examination, and execution of Polycarp. With it and the *Martyrdom of Justin* begins a new form of Christian literature that became immensely popular, the "acts of martyrdom"; the form was revived in more modern times with such effect in Foxe's *Book of Martyrs* (1563). Such narratives played an important part in early Christian history in keeping Christians steadfast in persecutions, as members of "the noble army of martyrs." The acts of martyrdom also played a very large part in such works as the *Golden Legend*, written in 1275 by Jacobus de Voragine, the archbishop of Genoa, translated into English and printed by Caxton in 1483, and in such great collections as the *Acta Sanctorum*, which contains sixty-nine volumes in both the Antwerp (1643–1910) and the Brussels (1845–1926) editions.

Further light is thrown upon the life of Polycarp by the accounts of Irenaeus, who when he was a boy in Asia had seen Polycarp and heard him; this he relates in a letter to his friend Florinus, which fortunately was preserved in Eusebius' *Church History* (v. 20. 4–8). Irenaeus tells us more about Polycarp in his work *Against Heresies* (iii. 3. 4), where he records Polycarp's appointment by the apostles as bishop in Asia, his journey to Rome to seen Anicetus, and his famous encounter with Marcion. Marcion asked him, "Do you know me?" "I know you for the firstborn of Satan," was Polycarp's sharp reply. Eusebius seems to have learned what he knew about Polycarp from Ignatius' *Letter to Polycarp*, Polycarp's *Letter to the Philippians*, the *Martyrdom of Polycarp*, and what Irenaeus had to say about him.

Eusebius copied most of the *Martyrdom of Polycarp* into the pages of his *Church History* (iv. 15). There are at least five Greek manuscripts of the *Martyrdom*. They end with a scribal note of unusual interest, for it states that the text was copied from the papers of Irenaeus by Gaius, who lived with him. Gaius' manuscript was copied by one Socrates, in Corinth, and his again by Pionius, possibly the martyr of that name who suffered in the Decian persecution (A.D. 250). This last scribe declares that Polycarp in a vision showed him where to find the outworn manuscript written by Socrates.

It is by no means certain that this scribal note—or, for that matter, any of the materials appended to the *Martyrdom* in chapters 21 and 22—belong to the original form of the work, which clearly ends with chapter 20. H. von Campenhausen has forcefully argued that the *Martyrdom* has suffered a good deal of interpolation, especially at the hands of an editor after Eusebius' time; this editor, impressed by the resemblance of Polycarp's sufferings to those of Jesus, has added details which bring out the parallel. Be this as it may—and acts of martyrdom have usually undergone a good deal of expansion—the *Martyrdom* contains a moving and generally convincing account of a tragic and heroic story, too often repeated in the second and third centuries, and it marks the beginning of the great literature of martyrology.

The Letter of the Gallican Churches

The position of Christians in the ancient world was extremely precarious; they might at any time be reported to the authorities, who would then have no choice but to proceed against them, as followers of an unauthorized religion. Any offense given to the rabble of a city by the Christians there might cause an outbreak of legal procedure against the church, and this is what occurred in the Gallican cities of Lyons and Vienne in A.D. 177 as the reign of Marcus Aurelius was drawing to its close. The pitiful and yet heroic story of those who suffered martyrdom in these places was soon afterward told in a letter from the "servants of God who sojourn in Vienne and Lyons, in Gaul, to the brethren throughout Asia and Phrygia." This letter ranks next to the *Martyrdom of Polycarp* and that of Justin as among the earliest acts of martyrdom. But the letter has disappeared, and for our knowledge of it we are dependent upon the copious extracts from it which Eusebius fortunately copied into the fifth book of his *Church History* (1–4).

The letter records the attack of the mob upon the brethren, the intervention of the city authorities against the Christians—the defense offered by one of them, Vettius Epagathus, the examination of the others, the defection of some and the steadfastness of others. Their slaves were examined and, in fear of torture, confessed that the Christians were guilty of the crimes usually charged against them—infanticide, cannibalism, and incest. Some of the brethren displayed conspicuous courage—Sanctus, a deacon of Vienne; Maturus; Attalus; and Blandina, a slave, whose mistress was also undergoing torture. Pothinus, the bishop of Lyons, a man over ninety, was so maltreated that he died in prison. The final sufferings of Maturus, Sanctus, Attalus, Blandina, Alexander, a physician, and a boy named Ponticus are narrated in some detail—how they were flogged, thrown to wild beasts, hung from stakes, and roasted on an iron chair.

The little letter, as far as can be judged from the portions Eusebius preserves, stands out as one of the classics of martyrological literature. Eusebius included it in his collection of acts of martyrdom, but that work has disappeared.

The Abgar Letters

The third century witnessed a marked rivalry among leading Christian centers regarding their apostolic founders: Rome took pride in the names of Peter and Paul; Ephesus rejoiced in the memory of John or Luke; and Alexandria, probably quite groundlessly, claimed the name of Mark. But the quaintest and boldest of such claims was that of the Syrian church of Edessa, which went straight back to Jesus himself. Syriac Christianity documented this great claim by two letters, believed to have been exchanged between Jesus and Abgar the Black, king of Edessa in A.D. 13–50. Abgar wrote to Jesus as follows:

Abgar, ruler of Edessa, to Jesus the excellent Savior, who has appeared in the country of Jerusalem, greeting. I have heard the reports of you and of your cures as performed by you without medicines or herbs. For it is said that you make the blind see and the lame walk, that you cleanse lepers and cast out foul spirits and demons, and that you heal those afflicted with lingering diseases, and raise the dead. After having heard all these things about you, I have concluded that one of two things must be true; either you are God, and having come down from heaven you do these things, or else you who do these things are the son of God. I have therefore written to you to ask you to take the trouble to come to me and heal the disease I have. For I have heard that the Jews are murmuring against you and are plotting to injure you. But I have a very small yet noble city, which is large enough for us both.

To this charming letter, Jesus is said to have replied:

Blessed are you who have believed in me without having seen me. For it is written of me, that those who have seen me will not believe in me, and those who have not seen me will believe and be saved. But in regard to what you have written me, that I should come to you, it is necessary for me to fulfil all things here for which I was sent, and after I have fulfilled them thus to be taken up again to him that sent me. But after I have been taken up I will send to you one of my disciples to heal your disease and give life to you and yours.

Syrian Christianity did not begin until about A.D. 172, with Tatian, and did not reach the stage of ecclesiastical consciousness implied in these letters until the middle of the third century, when they were probably written. Eusebius found them in the archives of Edessa and translated them from Syriac into Greek (*Church History* i. 13). They were early embellished with the story that Abgar's messenger painted a portrait of Jesus and took it back to Edessa. The fuller form of the correspondence, the *Teaching of Addai*, passed into Armenian and Greek. The original story became widely known in the West through Eusebius' account of it, especially in Rufinus' Latin version of Eusebius'. Jesus' letter has been found in a cave inscription at Edessa, and both letters in an inscription at Philippi. The Gelasian Decree stigmatized them as apocrypha.

Fragmentary Letters

Gnostic teachers also wrote "open letters" to their disciples, and Clement of Alexandria has preserved three fragments from letters of Valentinus in his *Miscellanies*. In addition, we possess a whole letter of the Valentinian Ptolemaeus to a certain Flora; in it he explains the nature of the true law of God.[6] Other letters have been discovered among the Gnostic writings found at Nag Hammadi in Egypt: these include two versions of a letter of Eugnostus, a letter of Peter and Philip, and a letter concerning the Father of the Universe and Adam, the First Man.

Beyond "open letters" such as these, there were naturally many private letters written by Christians—and, just as naturally, almost none of them survive. We should, however, mention what is probably the earliest extant letter of this kind, written by a young Christian named Besas to his mother Mary perhaps about the year 200.[7]

To my most honorable mother Mary, from Besas, many greetings in God. Above all, I pray to God the Father of truth and to the Paraclete Spirit that they may preserve you in soul and body and spirit: for the body, health; for the spirit, gladness; and for the soul, eternal life. And please do not hesitate, if you find anyone coming to me, to write me about your health so that when I hear I may rejoice. Do not neglect to send me the coat for the Paschal festival, and send my brother to me. I greet my father and my brothers. I pray that you may long be well.

Scholars have sometimes supposed that this letter reflects Gnostic thought, but it does not. The language is actually characteristic of the early Egyptian liturgy, the origins of which we can therefore place within the second century.[8]

---

6 For the letters of Valentinus and Ptolemaeus see R. M. Grant, *Gnosticism* (London, New York, 1961), 143-44, 184-90.

7 J. E. Powell, *The Rendel Harris Papyri* (Cambridge, 1936), No. 107.

8 For "Father of truth" see not only Gnostics but also *II Clement* 3:1, 20:5, and Origen *First Principles* ii. 6. 1; for "soul-body-spirit" see F. E. Brightman in *Journal of Theological Studies*, II (1900–1901), 273–74.

3

REVELATIONS

In later Judaism, a favorite type of religious instruction emerged in the apocalypse, which made use of symbols, sometimes grotesque, to interpret the present and forecast the future. The books of Daniel and Enoch were notable examples. Before the end of the first century, one early Christian writer made use of this style in the Revelation of John. This special kind of apocalyptic writing was revived among Christians in the second century when the Jewish collection of apocalypses known to us as II Esdras was given a Christian preface; then, after the middle of the third century, it was given a Christian conclusion and thus adopted into Christian literature.

But, in general, Jewish apocalyptic was not congenial with Greek Christianity, which instinctively found its own paths to apocalyptic expression of various kinds. Indeed, the first book of this more Greek kind followed almost immediately upon the publication of the Revelation of John and dealt not so much with the guilt and doom of empires as with the sense of sin and the need of repentance in the human heart. The Revelation of John was probably well known in Rome in the last years of the first century and no doubt had the general effect of leading Christian prophets to write down and publish their oracles; but its specific influence upon them was singularly slight.[1]

The continued influence of Hebrews upon the Roman church is reflected in the *Shepherd* of Hermas, perhaps begun in the last years of the first century, A.D. 95–100. Hermas was a Christian

---

[1] For instance, recent editors of the *Shepherd* of Hermas report finding only one line reminiscent of the Revelation—Vis. iv. 2. 1—whereas the Revelation, less than half the length of the *Shepherd*, is credited with at least seventy reminiscences of Daniel alone. On the other hand, there are a good many echoes of II Esdras (IV Ezra) in Hermas.

prophet in Rome, who understood Hebrews to teach that there could be no repentance for serious sins committed after baptism. The real meaning of Hebrews was that if anyone renounced his faith and became an apostate, he could never regain it and re-enter the church. Hermas records his interviews with the angel of repentance, who appeared to him in the guise of a shepherd and taught him that there might be one repentance for sin after baptism, but only one. It is from the prominence of the shepherd in the work that it takes its name.

Hermas was or had been a slave in Rome. His work, which probably grew gradually, begins with five Visions in which repentance is emphasized. In the third, the church appears to him as a woman and shows him a great tower being built, which also symbolizes the church. In the fourth, he is shown a hideous dragon, which foreshadows persecution. In the fifth, which is entitled an apocalypse and formed the introduction to the Commandments and Parables that make up the bulk of the book, the shepherd appears. The shepherd gives Hermas a new series of twelve commandments, diffuse in style and quite unlike the Ten Commandments of the Mosaic Law. In general, they explain how the repentant Christian should live. They are followed by ten parables, which deal with the operations of repentance and its theological bearings.

It is characteristic of the free spirit of the early Christian prophets that Hermas is not deterred by the Jewish Ten Commandments from offering twelve more, or by the parables of Jesus from hazarding ten of his own. Indeed, he shows much less influence of Paul and the early gospels, and even of the Greek Old Testament, than we might expect. The Revelation of John is full of reflections of the Old Testament, but this second Christian apocalypse shows very few indeed. It owes little or nothing to the old Jewish apocalyptic; it is not even pseudonymous; in fact, it possesses a naïve freshness and originality that along with its evident sincerity gave it its early influence, which reached not only to Egypt and Abyssinia but in later centuries, through the sect of the Manichees, as far east as Chinese Turkestan.

Hermas is described by the Muratorian writer (*ca.* A.D. 200) as the brother of Pius, the bishop of Rome, and as having written during his episcopate, A.D. 140–55. But parts of the *Shepherd* were probably written long before then, in fact, at the very end of the

first century, or very early in the second. Since the second vision
states that it should be the business of Clement to send copies of
the visions to other churches, these first visions may go back as
far as the last part of his leadership, or episcopate, which covered
the years 88–97. Hermas certainly expected the visions to be widely circulated among the churches, and his book did have a great
vogue in the second century. It found its way into more than one
early form of the New Testament and, translated into Latin, even
influenced Dante, whose guides Beatrice and Vergil evidently reflect Rhoda and the Shepherd.

Although Hermas has come down to us in Ethiopic and in two
Latin versions (one from the second century), no complete Greek
text of it has come to light. It stood at the end of the New Testament in the Sinaitic manuscript (fourth century), but the last
three-fourths of it are lost from that codex. The Athos manuscript
of it (fifteenth century), part of which is now at Leipzig, preserves about nine-tenths of the Greek but in an inaccurate and
badly written text. The Michigan papyrus (third century) contains almost a fourth of the Greek text but does not include the
part missing in the Athos manuscript. More than a dozen smaller
pieces, on parchment or papyrus, have come to light, some of them
covering parts missing from these more considerable manuscripts.
These numerous fragments from Egypt reflect its wide popularity
there, already evidenced by its acceptance as scripture by Clement
of Alexandria, Origen, and the scribe of the Sinaitic manuscript.
But Tertullian, at Carthage, though he at first accepted it, later
repudiated and condemned it. Irenaeus accepted it as scripture;
Eusebius classed it among the rejected writings, and Athanasius
excluded it from the New Testament but recommended it for
private reading by new converts.

The *Shepherd* manifestly gathers up the prophetic utterances
composed by Hermas over a series of years. The Michigan papyrus throws new light upon the literary development of his work,
for when complete this manuscript evidently began with what we
know as Vision 5 (which is called an "apocalypse" in the manuscripts) and contained the twelve commandments and the ten
parables.

At least three stages can be traced in the growth of Hermas'
work. He first published Visions 1–4, of which he was told to
give one copy to Clement for churches elsewhere, one to Grapte
for the widows and orphans, and one to the elders of the local

church, with whom he was to read the visions to the congregation. A few years later he completed the *Shepherd* proper, beginning with Vision 5 and including the twelve commandments and the ten parables. This is the form preserved in the third-century Michigan papyrus. Finally, the earlier work was prefixed to this, and in this longest form the *Shepherd* appeared in the later Greek manuscripts (Sinai, Athos) and in the various versions. There may have been even more stages in its publication (Parables 9 and 10 sound like later additions by Hermas), but this much is now certain. The whole makes a work much longer than any single book in the New Testament.

It has been suggested that in view of literary and theological differences among the various parts of the work, it should be assigned to three different authors. Hermas himself would have written Visions 1-4 at the beginning of the second century; later on, another author may have composed the very long Parable 9; and finally, the work would have been completed by a third writer, who created Vision 5 to introduce his own twelve commandments and the first eight parables, and then added Parable 10 as a kind of recapitulation.[2] Although the evidence favoring this view is impressive, it may just as well point not to three authors but to one not very competent author who wrote his book in three stages.

There is conjecture that Hermas got his idea of a shepherd as a revealer of truth from the *Poimandres*, or *Shepherd of Men*—written perhaps toward the end of the first Christian century—the most ancient of the Greek theosophical tracts ascribed to Hermes Trismegistus, meaning Thoth, the Egyptian god of wisdom. It is more likely, however, that if Hermas knew anything about that Hermetic teaching, it was through hearing it talked about. He was not a great reader, even of the books Christians prized most; but he would hear of shepherds, in the religious sense, just from going to church, where the Psalms ("The Lord is my shepherd") and the prophets would have familiarized him with the idea he utilized in his own work. The Epistle to the Hebrews, well known to the Roman church in his day, spoke of Christ as the great shepherd of the flock. And in I Peter Christ was described as "the shepherd and guardian of your souls." And while Hermas identifies his

---

2 S. Giet, *Hermas et les Pasteurs* (Paris, 1963); see also my review in *Gnomon* (1964), 357-59.

shepherd not with Christ but with the angel of repentance, Christian ministers were already spoken of as shepherds (Eph. 4:11). Moreover, Hermas is not greatly interested in theosophical speculations about the divine wisdom and intelligence. His concern is practical—with his own sins and weaknesses and with those of his wife and children and of his brethren in the Roman church.

The mention of Clement as still being active in the church may carry the first stage of the work back to A.D. 95 or 96, thus making the statement of the Muratorian writer that Hermas was the brother of Pius, bishop of Rome in A.D. 140–55, on every account difficult to accept. From his opening words, it is apparent that Hermas was exposed as an infant and picked up and reared for the slave market. It is hard to see how any brother of such a foundling could be identified, although it is not absolutely impossible.

With this work of Hermas the Roman church rounded out its literary contribution to first-century Christianity—the Gospel of Mark, I Peter, *I Clement,* and the *Shepherd*—a gospel, a church letter, a general letter to a whole province, and a revelation. No wonder Ignatius could write to the Roman church, "You have taught others" (*Rom.* 3:1). He probably had I Peter and *I Clement* in mind.

Direct divine revelation, or apocalyptic, was an idea familiar to the early church from the Hebrew prophets Ezekiel and Zechariah and from Jewish apocalypses like Daniel and Enoch. The Gospel of Mark, about A.D. 70, contained a striking apocalyptic passage (chap. 13) as did two letters of Paul, II Thessalonians (chap. 2) and I Corinthians (chap. 15).[3] But the Revelation of John, about A.D. 93, was the first Christian apocalypse and was much indebted to Daniel. The *Shepherd* of Hermas also took the form of a revelation, although it was influenced by Greek literature as well as Jewish.

Sometime between A.D. 125 and 150 a Greek Christian wrote an apocalypse in the name of Peter and introduced, for the first time, the pagan ideas of heaven and hell into Christian literature. The Orphic and Pythagorean religions had much to say about the punishments to be inflicted in the other world upon sinful men and women, and the Christian writer lays hold of these hideous pictures to warn men of the awful personal dangers of sin. Daniel

---

[3] See also the sixteenth chapter of the *Didache* which reflects the language and thought of Matthew 24.

and John had been concerned with the ultimate triumph of the Kingdom of God, but the *Revelation of Peter* is devoted to the precise punishments to be expected after death by individuals who commit certain sins. He does have something to say of the rewards of the faithful, but he is principally a preacher of hell-fire, a subject on which the teachers of Orphic and Pythagorean religion had had so much to say; indeed, we meet it as early as the *Odyssey* of Homer, when, in Book 11, Odysseus visits the underworld and sees the punishments endured by Sisyphus and Tantalus.

The *Revelation* runs somewhat as follows. Peter relates how, as they sat upon the Mount of Olives, he and the other disciples asked Jesus about the signs that would precede his coming and the end of the world. Jesus answers his questions in language taken, for the most part, from the Four Gospels. There is also some use of the Revelation of John, which must have suggested the writing of the *Revelation of Peter*. The day of judgment and the triumphal coming of Christ are described. The wicked will be punished in ways corresponding to their particular sins. Demons, led by Ezrael and Tartaruchus, will torment them with serpents, worms, and vultures, on fiery wheels, and in rivers of fire. Then follows a briefer description of the perfumed garden, full of beautiful trees and blessed fruits, where the redeemed will be found.

Short as it is, the *Revelation of Peter* is full of reflections of earlier Christian and Jewish writings. The Ezra Apocalypse in II Esdras (5:33–35), written probably about A.D. 100, is clearly reflected, but an even better *terminus a quo* is afforded by the writer's use of the Four Gospels, toward A.D. 120. The book cannot therefore be dated earlier than A.D. 125. On the other hand, it is evidently used in the *Epistle of the Apostles* (chap. 16), which can probably be dated between A.D. 140 and 160, where the coming of the Messiah is described in language much like that in the *Revelation of Peter*. It is also used in the *Acts of Paul*, especially in III Corinthians (*ca*. A.D. 160–70). These literary facts fix the date of the *Revelation of Peter* in the quarter-century between A.D. 125 and 150.

The *Revelation of Peter* is first mentioned in the Muratorian fragment, a Roman list of books that may be read in church, from about the end of the second century, where it stands after the Revelation of John, with the warning that "some of our people will not have it read in church." Clement of Alexandria, about the

same time, accepted it as the work of Peter: "Peter says in the
Revelation . . ." (Prophetic Extracts 41:2; 48:1). Early in the third
century it is quoted or paraphrased at some length in the Acts of
Thomas (chaps. 55–57). It stands at the end of the Clermont List,
representing Egyptian usage about A.D. 300, which closes with the
Revelation of John, the Acts of the Apostles, the Shepherd, the
Acts of Paul, and the Revelation of Peter. Early in the fourth century Methodius makes use of it, and Eusebius (A.D. 303) reckons it
among the rejected writings (Church History iii. 25. 4). Macarius
of Magnesia, early in the fifth century, mentions it and puts its
words into the mouth of his heathen adversary. Sozomen, in the
fifth century, says the Revelation was read every year on Good
Friday in some churches of Palestine (Church History vii. 19). In
the Stichometry of Nicephorus (ca. A.D. 850) it follows the Revelation of John among the disputed books. It is mentioned again by
name in an old Latin sermon of uncertain date on the ten bridesmaids. Its influence continued down the centuries, strongly
affecting Dante, in the Divine Comedy, with its accounts of heaven
and hell (A.D. 1300); and Gustave Doré's fearful pictures illustrating Dante owe much indirectly to the Revelation of Peter. There
is a far-off echo of the high esteem at first enjoyed by this little
book in the fact that it finally found refuge in the closing section
of the Ethiopic New Testament.

Although the Revelation of Peter is mentioned by this long
series of early Christian writers, the book itself had long since
disappeared when, in 1886, a part of it was discovered in a small
parchment manuscript in a tomb near Akhmim in Upper Egypt,
together with a considerable fragment of the Gospel of Peter, in a
hand not later than the fifth century. The old stichometrical lists
gave the length of the Revelation of Peter as from 270 (in the
Clermont List, A.D. 300) to 300 lines (in the Nicephorus list, A.D.
850), so that this discovery put into our hands almost one-half of
the little document, which must have been about four-fifths the
length of Galatians.

The contents of this fragment were later recognized in the so-
called Books of Clement,[4] which form an appendix to the New
Testament in Ethiopic manuscripts of it; and it was found that the
whole of the Revelation of Peter was actually imbedded in the

---

[4] The Books of Clement, extant also in Arabic, contain a series of revelations
supposed to have been communicated to Clement by Peter.

Ethiopic text, but that in the Greek fragment found at Akhmim the descriptions of heaven and hell had been transposed. The Greek gives the picture of the saved first and then that of the lost, whereas the Ethiopic has them in the reverse order. A comparison of the Ethiopic with the Greek suggests that the Greek fragment is from a condensed form of the book.

We also get some light on what the little book contained from some quotations from it in Clement of Alexandria (*Prophetic Extracts*), from the *Sibylline Oracles*, late second or early third century (2:190–338), from Methodius of Olympus, in the third century (*Symposium* 2:6), and from Macarius of Magnesia, about A.D. 400 (*Apocritica* 4:6, 7). There is also a small parchment leaf in the Bodleian Library containing twenty-six short lines of the Greek text, and a double leaf from the same codex, probably of the fourth century, in the Rainer Collection in Vienna. The discovery of the complete Greek text of this early apocalypse would be a great boon to the study of early Christian literature.

The Sibyl of Cumae (or elsewhere) was a Greek source of revelation mentioned, though with disapproval, as early as Heraclitus of Ephesus (500 B.C.). Early writers knew of but one Sibyl, but gradually a number came to be recognized, and shrewd sayings of a portentous character cast in Greek hexameters floated about the Greek world. Jewish writers took up the idea about the middle of the scond century before Christ, no doubt embodying not a little pagan material with their own, and continued to express themselves in connected Sibylline poetry on into the fourth Christian century.

Hermas, about A.D. 100, was the first Christian writer to mention the Sibyl, and Justin, Athenagoras, Theophilus, and many others did so after him. Christians were already introducing a Christian tone into the Sibylline books by interpolating passages of their own composing, for Celsus, about A.D. 177–78, in his *True Account*, Origen says, charged them with so doing (*Against Celsus* vii. 53; cf. v. 61). So the Sibylline books came to be a combination of pagan, Jewish, and Christian materials.

They eventually numbered fifteen, of which Books 9, 10, and 15 are lost. Although Celsus may be right in saying that Christians were already at work upon the Sibyllines by his day, most of the Christian expansions of and interpolations in them probably belong to the third century—the time when Christian hands, having previously colored the corpus of Jewish apocalypses known to us

as II Esdras by providing it with a Christian preface, were adding
to it a Christian conclusion.

The exact determination of the Christian additions to the Sibylline books is difficult; Books 1, 2, and 5 have undergone Christian
revision and expansion; Books 6, 7, and most of 8 (vss. 217–500)
are Christian compositions; the last section begins with the well-
known acrostic "Jesus Christ; Son of God, Saviour" (vss. 217–44).[5]
Books 11–14 also show strong Christian coloring.

The Christianized Sibyllines had small claims to literary character, being for the most part crude and unskillful in style—as pagan
critics observed. Although learned Christians often mentioned
them, their chief public was among the less educated parts of the
churches and may be compared to those who relish the prophecies
of Mother Shipton and her successors in modern times. They
played little part in the progress of Christian literature.

Gnostic writers, naturally enough, played a prominent part in
the production of new revelations. The most important example
of their work is to be found in the *Apocryphon* (or secret book)
of John, used by Irenaeus in his description of Ophite doctrines
(*Against Heresies* i. 29–30). Four Coptic versions of this document
have been published, one from the Berlin papyri[6] and three more
from the books discovered at Nag Hammadi.[7] The Berlin version
is similar to the one in Nag Hammadi Codex III, while a consider-
ably longer version is extant in Codex II and, though often fragmentary, in Codex IV. The book describes a vision of the Father,
the Mother, and the Son, which John was given after the ascension
of Jesus. It describes the nature of the supreme Being, the process
by which the world came into existence, and the true history of
mankind, "not as Moses said." The longer version contains the
names of many of the 360 or 365 angels who made the various
parts and activities of human beings, as well as a description of the
operations of Pronoia (Wisdom).

---

[5] *Iēsous Chreistos theou hyios sōtēr.* The initials of these words, *ichthys*,
spelled the Greek word for "fish" and led to the use of the fish as a Christian symbol.

[6] W. C. Till, *Die gnostischen Schriften des koptischen Papyrus Berolinensis
8502* (*Texte und Untersuchungen*, LX, 1955).

[7] M. Krause and P. Labib, *Die drei Versionen des Apokryphon des Johannes*
(Wiesbaden, 1962); also S. Giversen, *Apocryphon Johannis* (Copenhagen,
1963).

The contents of all the Nag Hammadi manuscripts could be called revelations; but Codex V of these books represents the material most relevant to the present discussion.[8] A brief description of four revelations from this codex follows.[9]

In Codex V the first revelation, which follows a fragmentary letter of Eugnostos the Blessed, is called the Apocalypse of Paul. According to this work, Paul met, on the way to Jericho, a little boy who told him that the Mount of Jericho was a place of revelation. Then the boy took him to the third and fourth heavens where the Holy Spirit spoke to him. He went upward to the fifth, sixth, and seventh heavens; in the last he saw an old man (possibly the Ancient of Days) brighter than the sun and told him that he was escaping from the "Babylonian captivity." In the eighth he saw the twelve apostles who went with him into the ninth and finally the tenth heavens.

Two revelations, both of which are called the Apocalypse of James, follow that of Paul. In the first one, the Lord described himself as an "image of the existent one" to his "brother" James. In a discussion of the Hebdomad the Lord said there were seventy-two heavens, and proceeded to delineate their inhabitants, and then predicted his departure. James went to the mountain of Gaugela (Galgale?) with his disciples, and when he prayed, the Lord appeared, kissed him, and explained that he had never suffered nor had the people harmed him; the meaning of the "sufferings" was spiritual. James and the Lord sat on a rock (*petra*) and the Lord predicted that James would suffer but would pass safely by the customs collectors above, by calling upon Sophia, the mother of Achamoth (cf. Iren. 1. 21. 5). James is designated "The Just" because he is a suffering servant. When he leaves Jerusalem war will immediately break out.

The second Apocalypse of James is a record of what James the Just said in Jerusalem to his father Theuda. These things, which were often spoken by James, were written down by Marion, one of the priests. As James was on the fifth step of the temple prepar-

8 See chap. 4 for a more complete discussion of these finds.

9 These descriptions are derived from the edition of A. Böhlig and P. Labib, *Koptisch-Gnostische Apokalypsen aus Codex V von Nag Hammadi* (Halle-Wittenberg, 1963).

ing to die, Jesus came to him and identified himself as his brother. He spoke of the Father and the inferior creator and of James' saving work; then he departed. James called upon his judges to repent and accept Jesus, the Lord of whom he is a helper. All, including the priests, propose to stone him and to cast him down as he expresses his confidence in God and salvation from the flesh.

The Apocalypse of Adam is the final revelation recorded in the fifth codex of the Nag Hammadi discovery. In Seth's seven-hundredth year Adam gave him a revelation describing his own original angelic state, higher than the god who created him and Eve. Their fall was due to the jealousy of this archon of the aeons. The eternal knowledge of the God of Truth was separated from them, and they were instructed in "dead works" in fear and bondage. Then Adam saw three men who told him and Eve, in spite of their creator's opposition, about their true origin and predicted the salvation of Noah, the division of the earth among Noah's sons, the attacks against the true Gnostics, and their salvation by Abrasax, Sablo, and Gamaliel, descending from above. In this context the archon of the aeons is designated as Sakla. Finally the luminary of Gnosis, Phoster, comes and gives fourteen warnings against their opponents. The people repent. A voice speaks against Michev, Michar, and Mnesinus, who are above holy baptism and living water but have misused them. This revelation is then described as "the hidden gnosis of Adam which he gave to Seth, the holy baptism of those who know eternal gnosis through the Logos-born and the eternal Phoster, those who have come forth from the holy Jesseus, [Maz]areus, [Jesse]dekeus . . . who are holy."

About the middle of the third century some Gnostic in Egypt composed the curious book known to us, through a Coptic recast found in the Askew codex, as the *Pistis Sophia* or *Faith Wisdom*. It portrays Jesus living with his disciples for eleven or twelve years after the Resurrection and telling them a great many things about sin and salvation, especially in response to the questions asked him by Mary Magdalene. The work consists of four books, although the fourth should perhaps be given another name as it is evidently earlier than the rest; it deals with matters immediately after the Resurrection.

In the earlier books, especially Books 1 and 2, Jesus' words have

to do with the experiences of Pistis Sophia, which evidently typi-
fies the human soul, in her efforts to reach heaven and find salvation. The book recalls passages in Epiphanius' account of certain
types of Gnostic teaching, for instance, *Heresies* xxiv. 3, 6; xxxvii–
xl. The writer was evidently a Valentinian or a Barbelo Gnostic,
of the Ophitic-Sethian type. Five of the *Odes of Solomon* are
quoted in his book.

4

GOSPELS

The Apocryphal Gospels

"The church," said Origen, "has four gospels, the sects very many, one of which is entitled 'According to the Egyptians,' another 'According to the Twelve Apostles.' Basilides dared to write a gospel and give it his name. . . . I know a gospel that is called 'According to Thomas,' and one 'According to Matthias,' and we have read many others."

The gospel is Christianity's first contribution to literary types. The primitive oral gospel may have originated the type, but its first written embodiment was the Gospel of Mark, from which every other gospel inside or outside the New Testament was directly or indirectly descended. To lose sight of this is to miss the originality of the gospel as a literary type, which is the most massive literary fact about the whole gospel literature.

The Fourfold Gospel

It was not so much the writing of the individual gospels of Mark, Matthew, and John, however, as the grouping of them with Luke in a collection, that stimulated the production of the uncanonical gospels. Luke-Acts was much more than a gospel, and the separation of its first volume from the second not only enriched the gospel corpus but left the Acts by itself, to form the pattern for the Acts literature that was to come. The collection of the Four Gospels showed the immense effectiveness of the gospel as a type of literature, and it seemed almost to invite the production of further gospels by its closing lines: "There are many other things that Jesus did, so many in fact that if they were all written out, I do not suppose that the world itself would hold the books that would have to be written."

Not that the writer of these lines intended to suggest the writing of further gospels; they are part of the epilogue of the Fourth

Gospel, perhaps added to anticipate any doubt or opposition that the new gospel might encounter by its very novelty, since few of the prospective readers of the combined gospels would have known more than one or possibly two of them before and might well be suspicious of the new, unfamiliar material another gospel would inevitably offer. But as soon as the churches became familiar with a plurality of gospels, this closing sentence might well suggest that the door was still open to new gospel narratives. Certainly a whole flock of Christian writers soon undertook to write new gospels, and none of them seems to have escaped the influence of one or more of the canonical gospels. Indeed, they were all in some degree imitators of them.

The idea that any early Christian anywhere might at any time have set out independently to write a gospel without ever having seen one loses sight of the fact that a gospel was by no means an inevitable thing, still less a commonplace or a matter of course. It was a definite literary creation for which no adequate literary precedents can be found. This is the distinction of the Gospel of Mark. It was soon improved upon and enlarged by the author of Matthew, and also imitated by Luke in his historical sketch of the beginnings of the movement. Independently—though we do not know how independently—John also made use of the gospel as a literary form. The existence of at least four written gospels obviously called the attention of Christians to the possibility of producing others—as did the words, already quoted, at the end of the Gospel of John. This situation undoubtedly lies behind the production of the uncanonical gospels.

The makers of the uncanonical gospels apparently aimed at unifying the gospels already in existence, ridding them of their repetitions and confusions, and at the same time enriching them from oral traditions and from creative imagination. The question at once arises whether or not they were in possession of any authentic material comparable in historical value with that in the earlier books. This question is hard to answer, for the canonical books necessarily provide the tests for authenticity, and it is therefore unlikely that we could recognize trustworthy materials not paralleled by those in the books generally accepted. Often we can see that the extra materials are based upon traditions already known to us; this is true about most of what we find in the *Gospel of the Hebrews* and the *Gospel of Thomas*. Sometimes, as in *Egyptians* and *Thomas*, we can see that a Gnostic or proto-Gnostic axe is being ground.

The Gospel according to the Egyptians

It was in beginning his first *Homily on Luke* that Origen said, "The church has four gospels, the sects very many, one of which is called 'According to the Egyptians.'" There seem to have been at least four uncanonical gospels that were well known in Egypt in the second century: the *Gospel according to the Egyptians*, the *Gospel according to the Hebrews*, the *Gospel of Peter*, and the *Gospel of Thomas*.

The *Gospel of the Egyptians* and the *Gospel of the Hebrews* were apparently so called because one circulated among the gentile Christians of Egypt and the other among the Jewish. Both were written in Greek, and we know them only from a few fragments. *Egyptians* was mentioned not only by Origen but, earlier at Alexandria, by Clement, at the very beginning of the third century. In his *Miscellanies*, Clement says that it was read and accepted by the ascetic sect of the Encratites, and quotes from it a conversation of Jesus with Salome, of a very ascetic character, discouraging the bearing of children: "For when Salome asked when what she had inquired about would be known, the Lord said, 'When you have trampled on the garment of shame and when the two become one, and the male with the female is neither male nor female'" (iii. 92). Again, when Salome inquired, "How long will death prevail?" the Lord replied, "As long as women bear." To this she answered, "Would I have done well, then, in not bearing?" (iii. 64, 66). According to the Gospel of Mark, Salome was a witness to the crucifixion (15:40) and to the empty tomb (16:1). She is fairly prominent in other apocryphal gospels.

As early as about A.D. 140 some of these words were quoted in the Roman sermon we know as *II Clement*, but we do not know whether or not the preacher derived them from *Egyptians*. It is clear enough, however, that in Rome at that time materials also employed in *Egyptians* were not regarded as suspect. By the time of Clement of Alexandria, however, some doubt was already arising, perhaps because of the enthusiasm with which Gnostics were viewing this kind of tradition, and a generation later Origen headed his list of heretical gospels with it. Hippolytus of Rome, in his *Refutation of All Heresies* (v. 7. 9), written about A.D. 235, says that the Naassene Gnostics support their doctrine of the "fluidity" of the soul by appealing to it. Later still, Epiphanius, toward the end of the fourth century describes the Sabellians as claiming its authority for their teaching that Father, Son, and Holy Spirit are "one and the same" (*Heresies* lxxii. 2). Although this was the central position of their founder Sabellius, it is not likely that he himself appealed to *Egyptians*.

The Gospel according to the Hebrews

The *Gospel according to the Hebrews* is believed to have been so called because of its use by the Jewish Christians of Egypt, but the name may really be no more than an inference from the very Jewish character of some of its contents. Jerome, writing about the end of the fourth century, says that he knew it only in Aramaic and himself translated it into Greek and Latin, but it was certainly current in Greek in the second century and was probably written in that language. We know it only from the quotations made from it by early Christian writers and from a few manuscript fragments which may, with some probability, be assigned to it.

Jerome declared that he found the book in Palestine, in use among the Nazarene Christians in Beroea in Syria, and that it was also preserved in the library of Pamphilus in Caesarea. The book was unfortunately confused with the supposed original Aramaic form of the Gospel of Matthew, and Jerome does not entirely escape this error. The fact is, the *Gospel of the Hebrews* borrowed so much from the Gospel of Matthew that they naturally had much in common, but such portions as appear in *Hebrews* are so manifestly elaborated and built up that there can be no doubt that it drew from Matthew, not Matthew from it. The influence of Luke may also be traced in the *Gospel of the Hebrews;* indeed, it is altogether probable that its writer knew the Fourfold Gospel. That he should have independently struck upon the gospel type of literature and created a written gospel without ever having seen one is in itself extremely improbable, and, when his manifest indebtedness to Matthew and Luke is observed, it becomes impossible.

The *Gospel of the Hebrews*, like that of the *Egyptians*, may have been written in the period between the publication of the Fourfold Gospel and its arrival at the status of scripture, that is,

the time when it came to be read in church side by side with the
Jewish scriptures, about the middle of the second century.
Hebrews was about seven-eighths the length of the Gospel of
Matthew, containing 2,200 *stichoi*, or lines of Homeric length,
against 2,500 in Matthew. It told of the baptism, the temptation,
the Lord's Prayer, the man with the withered hand, the rich in-
quirer, the parable of the talents, and the resurrection. In every
instance its accounts show literary development comparable with
those in the Four Gospels. Jesus is reluctant to go to John's baptism; he says he has no consciousness of sin. This carries the
account in Matthew a long step further. In Matthew, John suggests his freedom from sin; in *Hebrews*, Jesus claims it himself.
Mark's violent representation of the Spirit "flinging" or throwing
Jesus into the wilderness is heightened here: Origen quotes
Hebrews as saying, "My mother the Holy Spirit took me by one
of my hairs and carried me up to the great mountain Tabor"—
evidently for the temptation. This strange saying is usually explained by the fact that, in Hebrew, "Spirit" is feminine; and the
odd picture recalls the speculations of Jewish Christian theology
to which H. J. Schoeps and J. Daniélou have drawn attention.[1]
The vivid picture of Jesus being carried by his hair—indicating his
utter helplessness in the grip of the Spirit—recalls Ezekiel, seized
by a lock of his hair and carried to Jerusalem by the Spirit (Ezek.
8:3), and Habakkuk, lifted up by his hair by the angel of the Lord
and carried from Judea to Babylon with the speed of the wind so
that he could take food to Daniel in the den of lions (Bel and the
Dragon, 36).

Of the three men entrusted with the talents, in *Hebrews* the first
squanders his upon harlots and flute girls, the second increases his,
and the third hides his in the ground. This is evidently an effort to
improve upon the simpler story.

In dealing with the resurrection, according to Jerome, Hebrews
relates that Jesus said to Peter and those with him, "Feel of me,
and see that I am not a bodiless demon" (*On Illustrious Men* 16).
This curious saying, which recalls Jesus' words to the disciples in
Luke 24:39, occurs also in Ignatius, *Smyrnaeans* 3:2, and, according to Origen (*First Principles*, prologue 8), in the *Teaching* (per-

---

[1] Schoeps, *Theologie und Geschichte des Judenchristentums* (1949); Daniélou, *Théologie du Judéo-Christianisme* (1958).

haps meaning *Preaching*) *of Peter*. The question arises: In which
of these works did the saying first appear? It is sometimes assumed
that Ignatius was quoting the *Gospel of the Hebrews*. But there
are no other traces of *Hebrews* in Ignatius' letters, and it is equally
probable that both Ignatius and the compiler of *Hebrews* derived
the saying from earlier oral tradition. It is also possible that neither
Origen nor Jerome knew where the saying came from.

No less singular is the other resurrection incident which Jerome
found in this gospel (*On Illustrious Men* 2). It reads: "After the
Lord had given the linen cloth to the servant of the high priest, he
went to James and appeared to him, for James had sworn that he
would not eat bread from the hour when he had drunk the Lord's
cup until he should see him risen again from among those that
sleep." A little later it continues: "The Lord said, 'Bring a table
and bread,'" and then "He took bread and blessed it and broke it
and gave it to James the Just and said to him, 'My brother, eat
your bread, for the Son of Man is risen from among those that
sleep.'" This account is clearly intended to establish a direct relationship between Jesus and James of Jerusalem, the hero of
Jewish Christians and of some Gnostic groups. Just as Jesus had
sworn not to drink of the fruit of the vine until he drank it new
in the kingdom, so James takes a similar oath, and the Jewish
Christian eucharist is obviously based on Jesus' command to him.
According to I Cor. 15:7, the risen Lord appeared to James.

Eusebius in his *Church History* (iii. 39. 17) says that Papias,
who flourished in Asia Minor early in the second century, "related
another story about a woman who was accused of many sins before the Lord, which is contained in the *Gospel according to the
Hebrews*." This may refer to the incident about the adulterous
woman that, by the sixth century, had crept into manuscripts of
the Gospel of John in the seventh chapter and later found its way
into some manuscripts of Luke. On the other hand, the story
may have been a variant version of the account preserved in Luke
7:36–50. There is no way of telling.

Clement of Alexandria, writing at the end of the second century, quotes a curious saying of Jesus which, he says, is found in
the *Gospel of the Hebrews* (*Miscellanies* ii. 45; v. 96): "He will
not cease seeking until he finds; and when he finds he will be
amazed; and when he is amazed he will reign; and when he reigns
he will rest." Exactly this saying was found in the papyrus fragments of Jesus' sayings discovered at Oxyrhynchus in 1903; and

since these fragments belong to the *Gospel of Thomas* it is likely that *Thomas*, at least in part, was based upon *Hebrews*—or that both made use of common traditions.

One of the gospel fragments from Oxyrhynchus (*Oxyrhynchus Papyri* v. 840), a tiny parchment leaf, written in the fourth or fifth century, allies itself by its phraseology ("harlots and flute girls") with the *Gospel of the Hebrews* and, notwithstanding its disregard of temple arrangements and practices, may come from that gospel. Its diffuse style and evidently secondary character accord with this identification; and if, as we have argued, *Hebrews* was composed in Egypt, such ignorance of temple conditions would be natural enough. That it should have survived that long is not strange, for it seems to have contained nothing definitely heretical. The fragment tells of a conversation between Jesus and a chief priest about spiritual as against ceremonial purification.

The *Gospel of the Hebrews*, therefore, apparently originated in Egypt, in Greek, perhaps between A.D. 120 and 140. Eusebius implies that it was known to Papias of Hierapolis, about A.D. 120 and says that Hegesippus made some use of it in writing his *Memoirs*, A.D. 175–85 (*Church History* iv. 22. 7). Clement of Alexandria, soon after 200, quotes it with some respect, but Origen is dubious about it: "If any accept the *Gospel according to the Hebrews*" (*On John* ii. 4). In the third century, Christian opinion in Egypt was evidently going against it, as Origen shows, and the Greek form of it seems to have begun to disappear early in the fourth century, for Eusebius lists it among the "disputed books" (*Church History* iii. 25. 5). Jerome (toward the close of the century, could not find a Greek copy of it but saw an Aramaic text in Palestine, which, he says, he translated into Greek and Latin, probably meaning those parts he wished to copy or use in his works. This Aramaic version, so often regarded as the original, was probably made for the use of the Jewish Christian sects— perhaps the Ebionites, more probably the Nazarenes—who in the third century were using the book, and finally gave their name to it, so that it came to be known as the *Gospel of the Nazarenes*. Jerome's contemporary, Epiphanius (who died in 403), says in his Heresies that the "Nazaraeans," or Gnostic Jewish Christians, used a gospel resembling Matthew, which they call "According to the Hebrews" (xxx. 3). Probably in Jerome's days the tiny Oxyrhynchus copy, miserably written, was produced in some obscure quarter, since no Greek text of it came to his notice, only the Aramaic.

This is virtually the last appearance of *Hebrews*. What Theodoret (d. 458) says about it in the first half of the fifth century he derived from earlier writers. The *Gospel of the Hebrews* fades from sight, as the document of an obscure sect. The canon list known as the *Stichometry of Nicephorus* (*ca.* A.D. 850) lists it among the disputed books, along with the Revelation of John, the *Revelation of Peter* and the *Letter of Barnabas*. A copy of the *Gospel of the Hebrews*, either in its Aramaic version or its Greek original, is one of the desiderata of patristic study.

The Gospel according to Peter

The feeling that Jesus, being divine, could not have suffered a humiliating and agonizing death such as the gospels described led many Christians early in the second century to resort to the view that he only seemed to suffer but actually took refuge in another form, leaving his material body at the mercy of his executioners. This startling doctrine, as we have seen, was particularly opposed and condemned in the letters of Ignatius and the Gospel and Letters of John, which insist that Jesus Christ did indeed come in the flesh, that is, in human form (I John 4:2; II John 7).

On the other side, there arose the idea of writing a gospel to tell the story, at least of Jesus' passion, from the Docetic point of view. Probably in Syria, between A.D. 120 and 140, some Docetist produced such a book, assuming the great name of Peter and writing it in the first person: "I, Simon Peter, and Andrew my brother, took our nets and went off to the sea," as the one fragment of the book that has come down to us reads in its last lines.

Fifty years ago all that we knew of this book was gathered from the brief mentions of it in the writings of Serapion, Origen, Eusebius, and Theodoret. But in 1886, a fragment of it was discovered by a French expedition in a tomb at Akhmim, in Upper Egypt, and in 1892 it was published, along with a Greek mathematical papyrus, which in the eyes of the discoverers rather overshadowed it. But English and German scholars were not slow in discovering its extraordinary importance, for here at last was a veritable fragment of this long-lost gospel. It was written upon five leaves of a little parchment book, which contained also a portion of the *Apocalypse of Peter* and the first thirty-two chapters of the *Book of Enoch*, the first appearance of that work in Greek in modern times.

The fragment of the *Gospel of Peter* began abruptly with the handwashing incident at the trial of Jesus, continued with an account of the crucifixion and the resurrection, and broke off as Peter and some other disciples were setting out on a fishing expedition, evidently the one recorded in the epilogue of John. The use of every one of the canonical gospels, including John 21, is unmistakable. Their accounts are often heightened by slight touches, chiefly to enhance the guilt of the Jews, but there is little new material.

Jesus, while being crucified, held his peace as though he felt no pain, and on the cross he cries, "My power, my power, you have forsaken me," and is taken up.[2] After the entombment, two figures descend from heaven in the night and open the tomb and bring Jesus out. While their heads reach to heaven, his head overpasses the heavens, and a cross follows them. The cross declares that Jesus has "preached to them that sleep"—an allusion to the Descent into Hades, reflected in Ephesians and I Peter.

It is possible that the Oxyrhynchus gospel fragment 1224, a badly broken papyrus from the fourth century, refers to this gospel, which probably emphasized those portions of the gospel story in which Peter was conspicuous, such as his great confession of Jesus as Christ, his denial of him, and his conversation with him on the seashore (John 21:15–20) on the eve of which the Akhmim fragment breaks off. The Oxyrhynchus fragment is too small, however, for this guess to be confirmed.

Justin, who was converted at Ephesus about A.D. 135, and wrote his *Apology* at Rome, soon after 150, may have known the *Gospel of Peter*, for he occasionally uses its phraseology. But Serapion, who became bishop of Antioch toward the end of the second century (A.D. 191), is the first Christian writer to mention it by name. He had heard of its currency in the church at Rhossus, nearby, and took occasion to examine it. He wrote a letter about it, probably to that church, admitting that it contained much that

---

[2] This goes back to a different translation of the Hebrew of Ps. 22:1, which is quoted in Matthew (27:46) and Mark (15:34) in the Aramaic, the spoken language of Jesus' day. The Aramaic *Eloi* means "my God," but the Hebrew *Eli* was sometimes understood, as in the version of Aquila, to mean "my power."

was in accord with the accepted gospels, but pointing out the
heretical character of some of its contents. He recognized it as
a work of the Docetists. His letter is unfortunately lost, but an
important part of it is quoted in Eusebius' *Church History* (vi. 12).

Although Serapion's great Egyptian contemporary, Clement of
Alexandria, makes no mention of the *Gospel of Peter*, Origen, in
the first half of the third century, refers to it, along with the
Book of James, as supporting the idea that Jesus' brothers were the
sons of Joseph not by Mary but by a former wife (*On Matthew*
13:55). Eusebius, early in the fourth century (A.D. 326), mentions
the *Gospel of Peter* and records Serapion's investigation of it, but
it is doubtful whether he actually knew the book himself. He
classes it among the books cited by the schismatics in the name of
the apostles (*Church History* iii. 25. 6) and says that no church
writer has made use of it. Still later, Theodoret, a Mesopotamian
bishop early in the fifth century, refers to the *Gospel according
to Peter* as being used by the Jewish sect of the Nazaraeans, or
Nazarenes, but he does not seem to have known the book himself.

When the Akhmim parchment that preserves the fragment (174
lines) of its text was written, the gospel was already disappearing;
the little manuscript is complete as it stands and was evidently
copied from a fragment. The manuscript has been variously dated,
but closer study of its hand shows it is probably not later than
the fourth century. It was almost the only apocryphal gospel
written pseudonymously in the first person in the name of an
apostle, and one of the few that were produced to present sec-
tarian views in gospel form.

The British Museum Gospel

Sometime in the second quarter of the second century a Greek
Christian in Egypt wrote a gospel, or rather he condensed the
Four Gospels into one, omitting their numerous duplications of
material, which amounted to at least half their total length, and
combining with them some new units, either remnants of Palestinian tradition about Jesus and his work that had found their way
to Egypt, or new products of Christian reflection. He had no
heretical or schismatic axe to grind but was controlled by a practical purpose to produce a gospel which should be at the same
time shorter than the fourfold one and also richer. The possibility
of this must have been immediately apparent to the earliest users

of the Fourfold Gospel, as it has been to so many others—ancient, medieval, and modern. But unlike other combiners of the four, such as Tatian and his later successors, who, in interweaving the gospels into one, hesitated to add new elements of lesson or story, this Greek evangelist embellished his narrative with new details in the old stories and even added some altogether new stories. Since no one had yet come to think of the gospels as scripture, like the Law and the Prophets, and so not to be tampered with, the new gospel writer had no inhibitions of that kind. He saw how the Fourfold Gospel could be improved, as he thought, and so he blended the four into one.

Who he was we do not know, nor can we as yet identify his work with any of the numerous new gospels mentioned by early Christian writers. One would expect it to be the *Gospel of the Egyptians*, but it does not show the encratite or ascetic leanings which marked that book. And yet, the five columns of the work that came to light in 1935 in the British Museum are, of course, only a small fraction of the whole book, and other parts of it may have shown heretical bias of one kind or another; moreover, the *Gospel of the Egyptians* was not thought of as heretical for a long time. Neither can we identify it with the *Gospel of the Hebrews* or with that of *Peter*, although it must have been written in the same generation with them.

The writer of this British Museum gospel probably had the Fourfold Gospel in his possession and made use of every one of the four. He may not have used all they had to give him, but he did not hesitate to introduce some new material. There is very little probability that this was authentic Palestinian tradition from Jesus' immediate circle of followers. More probably, it was the product of Christian reflection, developed in the course of the century that had elapsed since Jesus' day. Its value, if we could recover it, would be for the light it would throw on the Egyptian Christianity in its earliest period.

For the fragments of five or six leaves of this old papyrus book that came to light in 1935 cannot have been written later than about 150, and the book of which they are a copy may well have been composed somewhat earlier. It is surprising to find the Four Gospels in circulation in Egypt at so early a date—although we must remember that the book, though found in Egypt, was not necessarily written there. Our evidence about the gospel usage in

Alexandria, at least, goes back to Basilides (about 117–38), and he seems to have known all four gospels, if not more. In various communities various books were doubtless favored. Another papyrus fragment published in 1935 comes from a leaf-book that was certainly copied in the first half of the second century. This is the Rylands papyrus that contains verses from the eighteenth chapter of John on both sides of the fragment. From their location we can calculate the size of the original book, which probably contained only the Gospel of John.

The contents of the British Museum fragments may be briefly outlined. Jesus tells the rulers that the scriptures bear witness to him, so that Moses becomes their accuser. They protest that they do not know whence Jesus comes. In a second fragment the rulers try to seize him, but he slips from their hands. In a third, a leper explains how he caught the disease by eating with lepers at an inn, and Jesus cures him. In another, the question of paying tribute to Rome is discussed. Another, badly broken and obscurely written, tells of Jesus on the bank of the Jordan.

The Infancy Gospel of Thomas

The existence of two different gospels ascribed to Thomas has led to considerable confusion. The older of the two is a collection of Jesus' sayings apparently edited by some Gnostic teacher and found in Coptic at Nag Hammadi in Egypt (see p. 61). This was mentioned by Origen (*Homily 1 on Luke*) and quoted by his Roman contemporary Hippolytus (*Refutation* v. 7. 20). The infancy gospel contains a story about Jesus' boyhood, which was also told by Marcosian Gnostics. "When the Lord was a boy learning his letters and his teacher said, as they do, 'Say Alpha,' he answered, 'Alpha.' But when the teacher told him to say 'Beta,' the Lord answered, 'First tell me what Alpha is and then I will tell you what Beta is.'" According to Irenaeus (*Against Heresies* i. 20. 1), this story was supposed to imply that Jesus alone knew the secret he revealed under the form of Alpha. We cannot be sure, however, that the infancy gospel of Thomas was the Marcosians' source, since the story occurs in several places, including the *Epistle of the Apostles*. The later form of this gospel contains many stories about Jesus' childhood wonders—shaping clay sparrows and making them come to life, striking dead those who annoyed him, covering his teachers with confusion, raising the dead, curing people of injuries, even making Joseph's mismeasurements in the carpenter shop come out right. As it stands, the crude little gospel reflects an ancient impulse to push Jesus' miracle-working power back into his boyhood.

The Traditions of Matthias

The Acts records the appointment by lot of a twelfth apostle to take the place forfeited by Judas (1:26); his name was Matthias. Nothing more is said about him in the Acts or anywhere in the New Testament, but sometime in the second century a work was written, probably in Egypt, which was given his name and called the *Traditions of Matthias*. There was apparently nothing particularly heretical about it, for Clement of Alexandria, writing probably about A.D. 190–210, quotes it with apparent approval three or four times in his *Miscellanies* (ii. 9. 45; iii. 4. 26; vii. 13. 82; and perhaps iv. 6. 35).

It is from Clement that we learn all that we really know about the work, although, it is true, he once speaks of the Gnostics as quoting it. Its title may have been suggested by Paul's use of the word in the plural, "traditions" (*paradoseis*), in I Cor. 11:2 and II Thess. 2:15, in a Christian sense, in such Christian instruction as he gave his converts. The work had a decidedly philosophical color, reminding Clement of Plato: "The beginning [of truth, or of the search for it] is to wonder at things, as Plato says, in the *Theaetetus*, and Matthias exhorts us in the *Traditions*: 'Wonder at what is present before you.'" The moral solidarity of the Christian society was strongly held in the *Traditions*: "If the neighbor of one of the elect sins, the elect man sins; for if he had behaved as the word [or, reason] enjoins, his neighbor also would have respected his manner of life too much to sin."

In a third quotation Clement records that the *Traditions* taught that the physical nature must be controlled and mortified and the soul made to grow through faith and knowledge (iii. 4. 26). This is the text quoted, Clement says, by the Gnostics.

The book was evidently written sometime before Clement wrote his *Miscellanies*, for Clement identifies its writer with "the apostle Matthias" (vii. 13. 82). It was probably written in the days when the Christian apologists were dipping into Greek philosophy, after the middle of the second century.

The *Secret Sayings*, which Hippolytus says the schismatic Basilides and his son Isidorus claimed Matthias had taught them privately (*Refutation* vii. 20), may well have been part of the *Traditions* Clement speaks of so respectfully, and they are perhaps to be identified with another book under his name, the *Gospel of Matthias*, mentioned by Origen along with the *Gospel of Thomas*, as among the schismatic gospels.[3] Nothing, however, is known of such a gospel except Origen's mention of it, although it is also spoken of as heretical by Eusebius (*Church History* iii. 25. 6), doubtless following Origen. It is mentioned among the apocrypha at the end of the *List of the Sixty Canonical Books* (seventh century or earlier) and in the so-called "Decree of Gelasius," really a product of the sixth century, although by these times the book must have disappeared, with only its name surviving. This is all that is known as yet of the *Traditions*, the *Secret Sayings*, and the *Gospel of Matthias*.

The Gospel of the Ebionites

Among the various Christian sects that arose in the second century, the most Jewish was the Ebionites, or poor. They seem to have been the successors of those Jewish Christians of Palestine, and especially of Jerusalem, who had not accepted Paul's views and letters but came to hold a modified Gnostic position, like that of Cerinthus who held that Jesus was the son of Joseph and Mary and that his messiahship,[4] or the Holy Spirit,[5] descended upon him at his baptism and departed from him before his death on the cross. They practiced circumcision but they did not accept the Pentateuch or practice animal sacrifice. We hear of them from Irenaeus in the second century, from Origen and Hippolytus in the third, and from Epiphanius in the fourth, when they had revived some of the ways and views of the old Jewish monastic order of the Essenes.

Toward the end of the second century the Ebionites produced a gospel embodying their views. It was written in the first person, singular or plural, Matthew being the spokesman in the singular, and the Twelve Apostles speaking in the plural.[6] This led to its

---

[3] *Homily 1 on Luke.*

[4] Irenaeus *Against Heresies* i. 26. 1; Hippolytus *Refutation* vii. 33.

[5] Epiphanius *Heresies*, xxviii.

[6] In this it resembles the *Gospel of Peter*, in which the apostles speak in the first person plural ("We the twelve disciples of the Lord wept and grieved"), and Peter speaks in the first person singular ("I, Simon Peter, and Andrew my brother took our nets and went away to the sea").

being called, especially by Epiphanius, by such a variety of names: "According to Matthew," "the Gospel of the Hebrews," "the Gospel of the Twelve," "the Gospel of the Ebionites." Only the last two properly designate its title, for the *Gospel of the Ebionites* was identical with the *Gospel of the Twelve* (Apostles), whereas the *Gospel of the Hebrews* was another book entirely.

The *Gospel of the Ebionites* was naturally strongly influenced at many points by the Four Gospels, which it was written to combat. It owed most to Luke and Matthew; the Paulinism of John would naturally repel its authors. Its great claim of representing the voices of Matthew and the Twelve was evidently made in opposition to the gentile Christian claim that the Four Gospels were the work "of the apostles and those who followed them," as Justin put it (*Dialogue* ciii. 8).

From the quotations from it preserved in Epiphanius, it is clear that the *Gospel of the Ebionites* opposed animal sacrifice and advocated vegetarianism. One of these quotations, with which this gospel may have begun, reads:

There was a man named Jesus, who was about thirty years of age, and he chose us. And he came to Capernaum, and went into the house of Simon who was called Peter; and he opened his mouth and said, "As I walked by the lake of Tiberias, I chose John and James, the sons of Zebedee, and Simon and Andrew and Thaddeus and Simon the Zealot and Judas Iscariot.[7] And you, Matthew, I called as you sat at the tollhouse, and you followed me. I wish you therefore to be twelve apostles for a testimony to Israel!

This gospel described the food of John as wild honey and "cakes made with oil and honey." In this way they made John a vegetarian simply by substituting the Greek word *enkris* ("oil cake") for *akris* ("locust") (Mark 1:6). It would seem that they not only used the Greek gospels in writing their gospel but actually wrote theirs in Greek, although it may have passed into Aramaic. Epiphanius is our chief informant on this gospel through his quotations from it in his *Heresies* (xxx. 13–22). These deal with John's preaching, the baptism of Jesus, the choosing of the Twelve, and the last Passover. They show that the *Gospel of the Ebionites* was not the *Gospel of the Hebrews*, for their accounts of the baptism

---

[7] Philip, Bartholomew, James the son of Alpheus, and Thomas seem to be omitted; perhaps their call had been related earlier in the story.

are very different. It was evidently written to promote the schismatic views of the Ebionite sect.

Symmachus, the first Christian translator of the Old Testament into Greek, in the days of Marcus Aurelius (A.D. 161–180), or (with Epiphanius and the *Paschal Chronicle*) under Severus (193–211), was an Ebionite; in fact, he made his translation for the Greek-speaking Jewish Christians of that sect. It is probable that these two literary products of Ebionism—the gospel and the Greek version of the Old Testament—were produced in the same region, the same period, and the same tongue. Symmachus left his books to a woman named Juliana, who lived in Caesarea in Cappadocia, and she turned them over to Origen, probably when he took refuge there from Maximin's persecution (A.D. 235–38).[8]

Origen is the earliest writer to mention the *Gospel of the Twelve*, as he called it (*Homily 1 on Luke*), and it was probably written in Greek in Asia Minor, perhaps fifty years before he visited Caesarea, or around 185. Our only other information about it comes from Epiphanius, in Cyprus, a century and a half later. Except for a few fragments preserved by him, the work has disappeared.

The Book of James

Around the middle of the second century the desire to set forth an account of the early life of the Virgin Mary and the birth of Jesus led some unknown Christian, probably in Egypt, to write a short story about these events. It was a rather small book, in Greek, consisting of no more than forty-nine pages; but it contained a whole series of striking narratives.

It begins with the conception and birth of Mary, in answer to prayer, and apparently miraculous, very much like the account of Samuel's birth in I Samuel. When she is three years old, she is taken to the temple and kept there through her childhood until her marriage at the age of twelve to Joseph, a widower with sons. The annunciation, conception, journey to Bethlehem, and birth of Jesus in a cave follow. The midwife who is summoned finds Mary still a virgin. At the moment of Jesus' birth all nature, animate and inanimate, stops transfixed. The Magi bring their gifts; Herod kills the infant children; the infant John is miraculously

---

[8] Eusebius *Church History* vi. 17; Palladius *Lausiac History* 147.

preserved, but Herod puts John's father, Zacharias, to death. In the closing lines James, meaning the Lord's brother, declares himself the writer, and Jerusalem the place of writing.

The story about the escape of John and the death of Zacharias is sometimes regarded as an addition to the little story; the abrupt appearance of Joseph as narrator—"Now I, Joseph, was walking, and walked not" (18:2)—may suggest that another source is being used (18:2—19:1); but literature produced by non-literary writers is not always fully coherent. The title of the work provided in a third-century Greek papyrus, "Revelation of James—Generation [genesis] of Mary," points to the notion that even early copyists found the book rather disjointed.[9]

The theory that *James* was written in Egypt is based primarily on the fact that Origen was the first to use it explicitly; he says that Jesus' brothers were the sons of Joseph by a former wife, basing this upon the *Book of James* (*On the Gospel of Matthew* 13:55). Clement of Alexandria, a few years earlier (A.D. 190–210), may have known the book, or at least part of its story, for he states that Mary, after she had brought forth, was found, when examined, to be a virgin (*Miscellanies* vii. 16. 93). This is exactly what is stated in chapters 19 and 20. Half a century earlier, Justin in his *Dialogue* (*ca.* A.D. 155–60) describes Jesus' birth as taking place in a cave near Bethlehem (chap. 78); but this may have been just a bit of current tradition and does not prove the *Book of James* as old as Justin's times. Justin also speaks of Mary as descended from David (*Dialogue* c. 3), as the *Book of James* does (10:1).

Epiphanius certainly knew the book (*Heresies* lxxix. 5), which he calls the story and traditions of Mary, and the "Decree of Gelasius," now assigned to the sixth century, repudiates it as heretical or schismatic along with a considerable list of such gospels, calling it the "Gospel under the name of James the Less."

We have seen gospels that were written to support heretical views; here is one written in support of views that were coming to be held as orthodox. The perpetual virginity of Mary, the doctrine that Jesus' brothers were sons of Joseph by a former marriage, and apparently even the idea that Mary herself was

---

[9] M. Testuz, *Papyrus Bodmer V: Nativité de Marie* (Geneva, 1958).

miraculously conceived are the views it was intended to promote. It also assumed the continuity of Christianity with Judaism.

But from a historical point of view the *Book of James* leaves much to be desired. No gospel is more completely fiction. The story of Mary's life in the temple from her third to her twelfth year, like that of some pagan vestal virgin, is altogether impossible; nothing could have been more repugnant to Judaism. The idea of all nature standing still at the moment of the Nativity is an obvious bit of folklore. The book is strongly influenced by the story of the birth of Samuel and shows the use of all four of our gospels as well.

This little work, about the length of a modern short story, has gone by a variety of names; the numerous late Greek manuscripts (there is no ancient Latin version) entitle it a narrative, or account; Origen calls it the "Book of James"; the "Gelasian Decree" calls it the "Gospel of James the Less." Its modern discoverer, Guillaume Postel, called it the "Protevangelium," or "Proto-Gospel."

Although often frowned upon by church authorities, the *Book of James* survived, largely unaltered, and had a wide literary influence. It became the source of the Coptic history of Joseph the Carpenter, of the *Gospel of the Pseudo-Matthew*, of the *Nativity of Mary*, and of the Arabic *Gospel of the Infancy*. It was summarized in the thirteenth century (A.D. 1275) in the *Golden Legend* (v. 96), and it has been drawn upon in a number of present-day gospel imitations, such as the Aquarian Gospel. Its scenes were richly illustrated by Italian painters—Giotto ("The Exclusion of Joachim from the Temple"), Raphael ("Betrothal of the Virgin"), Titian ("The Presentation of the Virgin in the Temple"), Ghirlandaio ("The Birth of the Virgin," "The Marriage of the Virgin"), and many others.

Two explicitly Gnostic gospels were fairly well known to some of the church writers. The first, the *Gospel of Truth*, was a product of Valentinus, according to Irenaeus (*Against Heresies* iii. 11. 9), who says that it shows no agreement with the "gospels of the apostles," and indeed is totally unlike them. Goodspeed rightly supposed that it was not a gospel at all but simply a presentation of Valentinian views, although in its time it may have stood fairly close to orthodoxy. It must have been written around the middle of the second century. The second, the *Gospel of Philip*, "the holy disciple," is mentioned by Epiphanius about 374 as being in use among Egyptian Gnostics of his day (*Heresies* xxvi. 13). He quotes a few sentences, beginning, "The Lord revealed to me what the soul must say as it goes up to heaven, and how it must answer each of the powers above." The answers to be given the powers follow. It is significant that in the *Pistis Sophia*, which contains supposed revelations made by Jesus to his disciples after his resurrection, it is Philip who is writing them down, and Philip, Thomas, and Matthew are named as the three witnesses who are to record these revelations (*Pistis Sophia*, 69 ff.). This suggests that the *Gospel of Philip* was written by this time and probably as early as the late second century.

Among the less well-known gospels produced in Gnostic circles we should first mention the *Gospel of Judas*, which Irenaeus tells us was used among the Cainites (*Refutation* i. 31. 1; see also Epiphanius, *Heresies* xxxviii. 1. 3). This group derived its name from its view that Old and New Testament personages who were hostile to the Creator—like Cain—were beloved by the heavenly Wisdom. Judas saw that Jesus was reluctant to be crucified; he therefore betrayed him, so that the mystery of redemption could be carried through. Other such works are the *Gospel of Eve*, from which Epiphanius quotes (*Heresies* xxvi. 2, 3), and the *Gospel of Perfection*, which he mentions in the same passage. From Nag Hammadi in Egypt comes the still unpublished *Gospel of the Egyptians or Book of the Great Invisible Spirit*. Enough is known of this book to show that it is not the *Egyptians* we have already discussed.

Mention of Nag Hammadi leads us to consider the most extensive discovery of Christian or pseudo-Christian literature in modern times. In 1945–46 there was found a jar that contained thirteen leather-bound books written on papyrus in Coptic—partly Sahidic, partly sub-Akhmimic—during the fourth and fifth centuries. These books constitute a Gnostic library unparalleled in importance. Accounts of them have been provided by various scholars, especially J. Doresse[10] and H.-C. Puech,[11] but relatively few of them have been published as yet. Those published come from the first five codices according to the new numbering system.

---

[10] *The Secret Books of the Egyptian Gnostics* (London, New York, 1960).

[11] "Les nouveaux écrits gnostiques découverts en Haute-Égypte," *Coptic Studies in Honour of Walter Ewing Crum* (Boston, 1950), 91–154.

The Gospel of Truth

For the present one can discuss only these published documents. First came the *Gospel of Truth*, which may be the Valentinian "gospel" of which Irenaeus spoke. It is certainly not a "gospel" in any conventional sense (indeed, the title may have been invented because of its opening line); instead, it is a mystical meditation or series of meditations on the meaning of salvation as given through Jesus. Its theological outlook is close to heterodox Judaism and heterodox Christianity; perhaps it was actually written by Valentinus toward the middle of the second century, but this hypothesis is most uncertain. W. C. van Unnik has shown that in it there are reflections of most of the New Testament books, including Hebrews and Revelation. If it comes from about 150 or even earlier such usage confirms the existence of a New Testament collection at an early date.

The Gospel of Thomas

Next came the *Gospel of Thomas*, which consists of nothing but sayings of Jesus—treated as secret sayings the risen Lord addressed to a few of his disciples. Sometimes they are similar to what is preserved in the *Gospel of the Hebrews* or the *Gospel of the Egyptians;* sometimes they are not paralleled elsewhere; more often they are strikingly similar to sayings preserved in the Synoptic Gospels and presumably come either from these gospels or from oral tradition or from a mixture of the two. The general outlook of the author-compiler is clearly Gnostic, although it cannot be identified as that of any one school. H.-C. Puech showed that the "sayings of Jesus" found in Greek among the Oxyrhynchus papyri actually come from this gospel, and that the book itself was probably used in the *Acts of Thomas* and among the Manichees.

The Gospel of Philip

The *Gospel of Philip*[12] is not really a gospel but an apparently miscellaneous collection of Gnostic ideas (principally Valentinian) related to the fall of man (the separation of Eve from Adam) and his redemption through Jesus (the restoration of the primal

---

[12] R. M. Wilson (trans.), *The Gospel According to Philip* (London, New York, 1963).

unity). The book frequently mentions the five Gnostic sacra-
ments: unction, baptism, eucharist, "redemption," and sacred
marriage. Oddly enough, it does not contain the one statement
that Epiphanius ascribes to it, although the statement does occur
in a Gnostic book not yet published.

Other Gospels

Among the Gnostic documents published by Till are the *Gospel
of Mary* and the *Sophia of Jesus Christ*.[13] The former, partly
preserved also in a fourth-century Greek papyrus in the John
Rylands Library, contains the risen Savior's revelations to Mary
Magdalene and shows how reluctant the disciples were to admit
that he could have revealed anything to a woman (his favorite
disciple according to the *Gospel of Philip*). The second, also
partly preserved in Greek in an Oxyrhynchus papyrus, has a
content close to that of the *Apocryphon of John*.

All these documents seem to be based on Greek originals, although in the course of transmission and translation some editing
undoubtedly took place. The order of the sayings of Jesus in
Thomas, for example, is somewhat different in Coptic from what
it is in the Greek fragments, and in *Philip* some sections are connected by plays on Coptic words, not Greek. On the whole,
however, it is likely that the documents reliably reflect the originals, which probably come from the second and third centuries.

We have already seen that Irenaeus ascribed the *Gospel of
Truth* to the Gnostic teacher Valentinus. In addition, Origen
specifically mentions a *Gospel of Basilides* (*Homily 1 on Luke*).
But there are no clear traces of such a book in the surviving
fragments which come from Basilides, a Gnostic teacher at Alexandria during the reign of Hadrian (A.D. 117–38), or his followers.
He did write a commentary, the *Exegetica* mentioned by Clement
of Alexandria (*Miscellanies* iv. 81), but it seems to have been
based on the church's gospels, not his own. On the other hand,
we know that his followers quoted some apocryphal sayings of
Jesus now found in the *Gospel of Thomas*, and that they held a
peculiar view of the crucifixion. According to them, Simon of
Cyrene was crucified in Jesus' place, while Jesus stood on the

---

13 *Die gnostischen Schriften des koptischen Papyrus Berolinensis 8502* (*Texte
und Untersuchungen*, LX, Berlin, 1955).

Mount of Olives and derided the authorities. This notion may have been based on a severely literal reading of Mark 15:21–25, or possibly on a work by Basilides himself. Origen also speaks of songs by Basilides (*On Job* xxi 11–12)—perhaps the "incantations" which Irenaeus says his followers used (*Heresies* i. 24. 5).

It seems likely that other gospels ascribed to heresiarchs, if not this one, owe their existence to the imagination of antiheretical writers. Epiphanius mentions a *Gospel of Cerinthus* (*Heresies* li. 7); Jerome, a *Gospel of Apelles* (*Preface to Matthew*). No traces of such works survive, whether or not they ever existed.

ACTS

Religious Fiction

Christian leaders of the second and third centuries, whether they held the standard or the schismatic type of belief, were alive to the values of fiction in religion. Not only was fiction useful in propagating their views of truth but it was valuable as a substitute for the romances current among Greeks and Romans. It is sometimes supposed that these romances were characterized by what we should call pornography, but generally speaking they were rather edifying narratives of love and adventure. The emphasis put on sex in their Christian counterparts is rather more impressive, in spite of—and partly because of—the enthusiasm of the heroes and heroines for asceticism. Many of the motifs of the Hellenistic romance recur in the Christian apocryphal acts.

If the Four Gospels seemed to their early readers to leave gaps in the life of Jesus which might be edifyingly filled, and so pointed toward further gospel writing, the Book of Acts left a mass of loose ends that invited literary effort. By the middle of the second century authentic memories of the apostles had largely disappeared, and the Gnostic sects were constantly appealing to apostolic authority for their special views—as was the church as a whole. What became of the apostles? What did they accomplish? What special teaching did they set forth? In the absence of authentic memories, imagination took the lead, and a group of religious novels resulted.

When the two-volume work of Luke, the Gospel and the Acts, was divided, and the gospel volume was taken out of it to form part of the collection of the Four Gospels, the second volume was left to go its own way. How soon it came to be called the Acts of the Apostles we do not know; we find it first called by that name in the Muratorian canon fragment about A.D. 200—the "Acts of All the Apostles." But it must have come by the name much earlier than that, for it bears a similar title in the writings of Clement of Alexandria, and it undoubtedly suggested the creation of the apocryphal Acts literature and gave it its name.

The Acts of Paul

The sequel most obviously demanded by the Book of Acts is some account of what became of Paul. Its narrative leaves him in prison, soon to go on trial for his life. Was he convicted or acquitted? The generation for which Luke wrote knew the answer perfectly well, but two generations later hardly anybody knew it. The letters to Timothy and Titus reflect the interest already felt in his subsequent movements, assuming his release from prison, and from composing such letters as might have been written on a later journey, it was a short step to describing the journey itself.

So it must have seemed to a Christian elder in Asia—we do not know his name—perhaps in Smyrna or Ephesus, who about A.D. 160–70 had come to feel that the Pastoral Letters exaggerated Paul's views on the place of women in the church and needed to be corrected. He also wanted to counteract the strong indorsement of marriage—". . . train the younger women to be loving wives and mothers" (Titus 2: 4, etc.)—and to recall the churches to ascetic views and the renunciation of marriage. So he wrote the *Acts of Paul*.

Paul had indeed said in I Corinthians that women were to keep quiet in church; they were not allowed to speak (14:34). I Timothy put this even more sharply: "I do not allow women to teach; . . . they must keep quiet" (2:12). Against these Jewish views of the role of women in religion some Christians in Asia felt that women should be allowed to teach and even to baptize. Montanus had already appeared as a prophet in A.D. 156, in Mysia, in the north-central part of the Roman province of Asia, and two women, Maximilla and Priscilla, were soon exercising the same prophetic gift. Women had long been prominent in Phrygian religion, and for twenty years this movement, Montanism, was most active in Phrygia, the eastern part of the province.

The *Acts of Paul* described one of Paul's women converts, Thecla, not only as teaching but as administering baptism unrebuked. Paul himself bids her go and teach the word of God. The author was clearly seeking to correct the antifeminism of I Timothy, which he flatly contradicts.

Tertullian relates (*On Baptism* 17) that when a few years later, the writer of the *Acts of Paul* was found out and made to admit the writing of this first Christian novel, he declared that he had done it out of love for Paul and was forthwith deprived of his office. But his book, although often officially condemned, achieved great popularity, and the story of Thecla, in particular, has never been forgotten. It exists in a number of Greek manuscripts and in half-a-dozen other versions. Its abrupt beginning turns out to be due to the fact that it is simply one episode in a large narrative.

For centuries that chapter was about all that was known of the *Acts of Paul*, and we did not even know that it was originally part of those *Acts*, so completely had they disappeared. The old lists of books of scripture, acknowledged and disputed, mentioned the book and gave its length as 3,560 lines, or more than twice that of the Gospel of Mark. Tertullian tells of its origin in Asia and of the elder who wrote it. Origen also mentions it. Hippolytus at Rome, early in the third century, shows it was highly regarded there in his day. "For if we believe," he writes (*Commentary on Daniel* iii. 29), "that when Paul was condemned to death, a lion, let loose upon him, fell down and licked his feet, how shall we not believe the things that happened in the case of Daniel?" [in the den of lions]. Eusebius, in A.D. 311, speaks of it as one of the books whose place in the New Testament was denied in his day.

But in 1896 a Coptic papyrus of the book was discovered that did much to clear up its story. It was unfortunately incomplete, but it showed that the *Acts* originally included not only the story of Paul and Thecla, but the two letters exchanged between Paul and the Corinthians which had once been extant in Syriac and in fact were actually included in Efrem's Syriac New Testament in the fourth century. A fourth-century papyrus leaf from Berlin and a parchment one of about the same age from Oxyrhynchus (*Oxyrhynchus Papyri* xiii. 1602) helped to build up the text in the original Greek. But more recently, the discovery at Hamburg in 1927 of eleven pages of the book in Greek, in a papyrus written about A.D. 300, has given us the concluding part of it in its original language.[1]

---

[1] Carl Schmidt and Wilhelm Schubart, *Praxeis Paulou: Acta Pauli* (Hamburg, 1936).

Course of the Narrative

As pieced together from these Coptic and Greek papyri and the famous chapter so long known as the "Acts of Paul and Thecla," the story of the *Acts of Paul* ran somewhat as follows:

1. Paul is at Pisidian Antioch. He restores a Jewish boy to life, and the boy's parents are converted, but the populace becomes incensed and Paul is driven from the town.

2. Paul reaches Iconium. This is the episode that has survived as the "Acts of Paul and Thecla." It always seemed to begin very abruptly: "As Paul was going up to Iconium after his escape from Antioch, Demas and Hermogenes the coppersmith were his fellow travelers." This apparent abruptness now disappears; it is just a natural transition from one scene to the next. Thecla is a Greek girl of position who becomes interested in Paul's preaching, breaks off her engagement, is converted and, although thrown to wild beasts in the arena, escapes and lives to teach others her new faith. Paul approves her doing this, in contrast with his reputed unwillingness that women should teach. Thecla subsequently visits Paul at Myra and later retires to Seleucia, where she dies. The leading interests of the book—aversion to marriage and indorsement of woman's place in teaching religion—appear most clearly in this romantic story, which not only survived in Greek and in many other versions but has been picked up and repeated in a number of modern forms of the life of Paul.

3. At Myra, where Thecla had left Paul, he cures a man of dropsy and thus incurs the enmity of the man's son Hermippus, who had hoped soon to inherit his father's property. The son is smitten with blindness but repents and is cured.

4. Paul proceeds by way of Perga to Sidon. There the people shut him and his friends up in the temple of Apollo, part of which collapses in the course of the night. This further incenses the people, who hurry Paul and his companions to the theater, but what happens there is lost.

5. Paul reappears at Tyre, where he heals the sick and discourses about Judaism.

6. He is next found at some mines, of unknown location, where a certain Frontina, who has been converted, is thrown from a cliff and killed, but Paul restores her to life and leads her home through the town, the people of which are at once won to Christianity.

7. Here belongs the story related by Nicephorus,[2] about 1320, of a visit to Ephesus, not mentioned in the Coptic fragments but now supplied in much detail by the newly discovered Greek text, which begins with this Ephesian episode. (The Coptic pieces comprise only about one-half the total length given in the medieval stichometry for the *Acts of Paul*, so that much is certainly missing from them.) At Ephesus, Paul is thrown into prison. Two women who are believers visit him in his prison, seeking baptism, and he escapes long enough to baptize them on the seashore. Next day, when a huge lion is let loose upon him in the stadium, it quietly curls up at his feet like a lamb. (This is the incident referred to by Hippolytus.) The lion speaks to Paul, and Paul asks if this is not the lion he had previously met and baptized. The lion replies that it is. The story of baptism of the lion (Jerome's fable of the baptized lion [*totam baptizati leonis fabulam*], which he not unnaturally rejected)[3] is told in detail in the Ethiopic *Epistle of Pelagia*, which goes on to relate the later encounter of Paul and the lion in the stadium, just as the new Greek portions describe it.[4] A great hailstorm comes on which kills many of the people and the animals and cuts off the governor's ear. The governor is converted. The lion escapes, and Paul is released and proceeds to Macedonia.

8. The next section, in Greek, is headed "From Philippi to Corinth," the stay at Philippi being passed over. The Coptic, however, relates that it was while in prison there that Paul received a short letter from the Corinthians, reporting the appearance among them of two false teachers, Simon and Cleobius. He writes a letter to the Corinthians in reply. (This is the letter accepted in ancient times by Syrian and Armenian churches as III Corinthians.) He takes leave of the Philippians; a local prophet and prophetess predict his work and fate in Rome.

9. The Greek proceeds with an account of Paul's stay in Cor-

---

[2] Nicephorus Callisti *Church History* ii. 25.

[3] *On Illustrious Men* 7. The story is obviously based on Androcles and the lion.

[4] This short martyrdom, which Goodspeed discovered in an Ethiopic manuscript in the British Museum many years ago ("The Epistle of Pelagia," *American Journal of Semitic Languages*, XX [1904], 95–108), offered the first explanation of the baptized and talking lion. See also Goodspeed's *Ethiopic Martyrdoms* (Chicago, 1931), pp. 92, 102.

inth. The brethren are grieved at his conviction that he must go on to Rome. He embarks on a ship the captain of which had been baptized by Peter.

10. On the voyage Jesus, walking on the water, appears to Paul, urges him on to Rome, and goes before the ship, guiding it on its way like a star. As Paul lands, Jesus again appears and says, "I am going to be crucified again." Paul is welcomed by the brethren at Rome and addresses them. He is tried, apparently before Nero, and executed with the sword, but later reappears to Nero and his attendants and declares that much evil will overtake him, in no long time, for the righteous blood he has shed. At this point in the Greek manuscript the title, *The Acts of Paul*, marks the end of the book.

This is perhaps two-thirds or three-fourths of the *Acts of Paul*. Jerome says, "The travels of Paul and Thecla, and the whole fable of the baptized lion we reckon among the apocryphal writings." Commodian, the fifth-century Christian poet, says of God's power, "For Paul, when he preached, he made a lion speak to the people with a God-given voice." In the Ethiopic *Epistle of Pelagia*, another of Paul's reputed converts, Paul meets a huge lion on a mountain. They become friends, and the lion asks to be baptized. Paul complies. Later when a woman named Pelagia is converted and leaves her husband, Paul is arrested and a huge lion is set upon him in the "theater." But it is the baptized lion, and he and Paul pray and converse. They let Paul go "with his lion," but Pelagia suffers martyrdom. It is now clear that the lion episodes are from the *Acts of Paul*; here are Jerome's baptized lion and Commodian's talking lion; they are one. The story of Pelagia also exhibits the same aversion to marriage that we find in the story of Thecla.[5]

The Asian elder who wrote the *Acts of Paul* was acquainted with the letters to Timothy and Titus; in fact, they evidently influenced him to write. From them he draws the names of Hermogenes and Onesiphorus; the latter's "household," twice mentioned in the Pastoral Letters, in the *Acts* becomes his wife Lectra and his children Simmias and Zeno. He also knew the Book of Acts, which gave him his model. His work is first mentioned by Tertullian in *On Baptism* 17, written at the beginning of the third century. So the *Acts of Paul* was probably written

---

[5] Goodspeed, *Ethiopic Martyrdoms*, pp. 100, 102.

between A.D. 160 and 170. Its feminist views repelled Tertullian, but Origen and Hippolytus used it without prejudice. It begins Eusebius' list of rejected writings. In the *Clermont List*, probably formed in Egypt about A.D. 300, it stands between the *Shepherd* of Hermas and the *Revelation of Peter*. In the *Stichometry of Nicephorus*, about A.D. 850, it leads the list of rejected books (apocrypha) under the title "Journey of Paul."

The Acts of John

Not long after the appearance of the romantic *Acts of Paul* (A.D. 160–70), some Docetist, probably in Asia, undertook to embody his views in an imaginative account of the wonders, discourses, and travels of John. He doubtless took his cue from the *Acts of Paul;* certainly he agreed with its author in his disapproval of marriage. John had been a comparatively neglected figure, of whom the Acts of the Apostles had little to say, but to whom tradition was already ascribing the Fourth Gospel and the Revelation. Who the writer of these *Acts of John* was we cannot say. Later writers spoke of him as Leucius Charinus. He certainly represented himself as a personal disciple of John, who accompanied him on his journeys and witnessed his wonders.

Clement of Alexandria in his *Outlines* (*On I John* i. 1), which may have been written as early as A.D. 189, quotes some sentences that are found in these *Acts*, ascribing them to the "Traditions." If he means the *Acts of John*, as he probably does, they must have been written about A.D. 170–80. The Nicephorus list, gives its length at 2,500 lines, or about the size of the Gospel of Matthew. The Greek *Acts of John* as we know it today, however, including the scattered fragments from various sources, is only about two-thirds that size. A good deal is evidently lost from the beginning (the first seventeen chapters, as ordinarily numbered, following the example of Bonnet's edition, are from a form of the Greek text very much later than the original), and there are places where gaps are apparent, as in chapter 37 and before chapter 58. A complete text of the *Acts* has yet to be found.

Chapters 18–55 describe John's journey from Miletus to Ephesus and his first stay there. In chapters 58–86 John returns from Laodicea to Ephesus for a second stay. In chapters 87–105 John tells of his first meeting with Jesus; of the transfiguration; of the strange hymn Jesus taught them (the English composer Holst set this to music); of the dance in which he led them; of the strange changes in his body, now hard, now soft, and again quite immaterial; of his appearance to John in a cave on the Mount of Olives, when his body was apparently being crucified across the valley outside Jerusalem; of Jesus' discourse about the cross; and of his ascension. At this point should perhaps be introduced some accounts of John's discourses and wonders preserved in other sources, chiefly Latin. John converts a philosopher, condemns wealth, raises a widow's son, drinks a deadly poison unharmed, and converts the heathen priest. The fourth-century Oxyrhynchus fragment (*Oxyrhynchus Papyri* vi. 850) must belong here; John is threatened with arrest by a soldier and receives a letter, probably a summons, from the emperor.

The Greek text of the *Acts* (chaps. 106–15) concludes with the peaceful death of John. He shows his disciples where to dig his grave, steps into it, and after a prayer lies down in it and quietly expires.

Although some of this may not have appeared in the *Acts of John* as they first existed, about A.D. 175 (the temple of Artemis in Ephesus, for example [chap. 42], did not fall until A.D. 262, when the Goths destroyed it), on the whole it is probably a fair picture of the work. It is clearly docetic, with its description of Jesus appearing to James as a little child, while John on the same occasion sees him as a full-grown man (chaps. 88 and 89), with its representation of his body as sometimes immaterial, and with his conversation with John on the Mount of Olives at the very moment of the crucifixion (chap. 97). At some points it sounds decidedly Gnostic, however; for example, the curious hymn before the betrayal:

> The number Eight sings praise with us. Amen.
> The number Twelve dances on high. Amen.
> The Whole on high joins in dancing. Amen.

This hymn, with its crude paradoxes (chap. 95), certainly reflects mystery forms of worship and Gnostic ideas:

> I would eat, and I would be eaten,
> I would hear, and I would be heard,
> I would be thought, being wholly thought.

The closing lines of the final prayer have a Gnostic sound too:

As I come unto thee, let the fire go backward, let the darkness be overcome, let the gulf be without strength, let the furnace die out, let Gehenna be quenched. Let angels follow, let devils fear, let rulers be broken, let powers fall, let the places of the right hand stand fast, let them of the left hand not remain . . . and grant that I may accomplish the journey unto thee without suffering insolence or provocation . . . [chap. 114].

It will be remembered that the Gnostics claimed to know the formulas that would turn aside the demons that beset the soul's way to God. The book is strongly ascetic; marriage is sternly rejected, and John in his dying prayer thanks God that he has been providentially kept from any union with a woman.

The story is full of marvels; and its author was eager to use sensational materials. When Drusiana died, in protest against the marriage relation, a disappointed admirer makes his way into her tomb to outrage her dead body. The author even makes some ponderous attempts at humor—in an abandoned inn a swarm of bedbugs is miraculously halted by the apostle's command (chaps. 60–61).

The story of John playing with the partridge or watching it playing in the dust probably also formed part of the *Acts of John*. There is some doubt about Domitian's having John plunged in boiling oil, apparently at Rome, although the episode appears in late forms of the *Acts*, and Tertullian was familiar with it, for in his book *On Prescription of Heretics* (chap. 36), written about A.D. 200, he speaks of Rome as the place "where the apostle John was first plunged unhurt into boiling oil, and then sent back to his island exile." Curiously enough this story has never been found in Greek, or in Greek writers, although the emperor's summons in the Oxyrhynchus fragment may have been leading up to it.

The story of St. John and the Robber Captain, whom he seeks out and leads to repentance, is as old as Clement of Alexandria (*What Rich Man Can Be Saved?* 42), but it has never been found in the *Acts of John*. It is difficult to believe that so good a story about the apostle did not form part of the original *Acts*.

Some scholars seek to date the *Acts of John* even before the *Acts of Paul*, but this loses sight of important literary facts: (1) The *Acts of Paul* forms a far more natural sequel to the Acts of the Apostles than does the *Acts of John*; when Acts breaks off, interest in Paul is at its height, while John is almost forgotten; he has long since disappeared from the narrative. (2) The *Acts of Paul* is conceivably a counterattack to the Pastoral Letters to

Timothy and Titus. It is the views they assert as Paul's that the *Acts of Paul* denies. (3) The *Acts of John* is more easily understood as suggested by the *Acts of Paul* than by the Acts of the Apostles; the sequence may have been: Acts of the Apostles, Pastoral Letters, *Acts of Paul*, *Acts of John*.

In the fourth century the *Acts of Paul* and the *Acts of John* were combined with those of Peter, Andrew, and Thomas into a collection by the Manicheans, who substituted them for the Acts of the Apostles because of their strong ascetic tone. Photius, the famous patriarch of Constantinople, who read and reviewed this collection about A.D. 890 in his *Bibliotheca* (cod. 114), says that they were all attributed to Leucius Charinus. Their order as known to Photius seems to have been Peter, John, Andrew, Thomas, Paul. The collection was entitled the "Travels [*periodoi*] of the Apostles."

In the first half of the fifth century, a *Life of John* was written under the name of his supposed disciple Prochorus that made much use of the *Acts of John*. This work often throws important light upon the Greek text of the *Acts*.

The *Acts of John* was condemned by the Second Council of Nicaea, A.D. 787, as it had been appealed to by the Iconoclasts, apparently because of its teaching about the immateriality of Jesus' body. It also has played a notable part in popular literature and Christian art; painters and sculptors have shown John holding the poison cup, while the poison leaps out of the cup in the form of a snake.

The Acts of Peter

The rise of the sects in the second century led the churches to return to the apostles as the true exponents of genuine Christian truth and had led to the organization of Catholic Christianity against the sects—Marcionite, Gnostic, and Montanist—about A.D. 175. We have seen that this increased regard for the apostles had found expression in such apostolic novels as the *Acts of Paul* and *Acts of John*.

The name of Peter had long been connected with the early history of the Church of Rome, as we have seen. II Peter, probably written after his death, alludes to a prediction of his martyrdom contained in the epilogue of the Gospel of John, 21:18, 19: "When you grow old, you will stretch out your hands and someone else will put a girdle on you and take you where you have no wish to go" (II Pet. 1:14).

A considerable body of apocryphal literature had already gathered about the name of Peter, and legend had been busy with it too. The rise of the *Acts of Paul* and of *John* made it inevitable that someone should write the *Acts of Peter*, especially in Rome, where he had suffered martyrdom and where his memory was therefore especially cherished. The Acts of the Apostles brought Paul to Rome, but not Peter. How did Peter come to visit Rome and how was their work there related? This was a question that would attract a Christian novelist.

Irenaeus of Lyons says in his treatise *Against Heresies* (iii. 3. 2, 3), *ca.* A.D. 185, that the Church of Rome had inherited her tradition from the apostles and had been founded and established by the glorious apostles Peter and Paul. The Gospel of Matthew contained a strong commendation of Peter from the lips of Jesus himself, who named him Cephas, or, in Greek, Peter—the Rock. "Your name is Peter, a rock, and on this rock I will build my church, and the powers of death shall not subdue it! I will give you [singular] the keys of the Kingdom of Heaven, and whatever you forbid on earth will be held in heaven to be forbidden, and whatever you permit on earth will be held in heaven to be permitted" (16:18, 19). The Roman bishop Calixtus (A.D. 217–22) ruled that persons who had been expelled from the church for grievous sins, even for murder, might, after due penance, be reinstated under these powers of the keys, as they were called, granted to Peter and, it was assumed, to his successors.

It was natural enough, then, for some Christian writer early in the third century (A.D. 200–220) to compose the *Acts of Peter*. Legend had already gathered thickly about the figure of the most picturesque and spirited of the Twelve. The writer had also a considerable library of Christian books. He shows knowledge of the Four Gospels and the letters of Paul, the Acts of the Apostles, the *Acts of Paul*, the *Acts of John* (in chap. 21), the *Preaching of Peter*, the *Apology* of Justin, II Peter, and probably the *Gospel of the Egyptians* (in chap. 38).

His purpose was to entertain and edify his Christian readers with tales of the words and wonders of the great apostle, upon whom Roman Christianity was more and more looking as its great founder and sponsor. He would also indorse asceticism and encourage women to separate from their husbands.

No complete text of these *Acts* has been found, but about two-thirds of it can be recovered from various sources—Greek, Latin, and Coptic. The Nicephorus list gives its length as 2,750 lines, or about that of the Acts of the Apostles.

From one source comes the story of Peter's daughter. Peter has a daughter who is stolen by a rich admirer; Peter prays God to protect her, and she is paralyzed. This story is preserved only in Coptic, but Augustine mentions it,[6] as well as the story of the gardener's daughter who fell dead at Peter's prayer for her. This story is told in the apocryphal *Letter of Titus*. The gardener wished her raised to life again, and when Peter complied, the girl was outraged by a slave and disappeared.

But the main part of the *Acts* is found in a Latin manuscript at Vercelli. It tells how Paul was released from his Roman imprisonment and set out for Spain. Simon Magus comes to Rome, and the church, left without a leader, is reduced to seven members. Peter, at Jerusalem, is warned in a vision that he is needed in Rome to resist his old enemy Simon (Acts 8:9–24). As the twelve years Jesus had told the apostles to remain in Jerusalem were over,[7] Peter sets out for Rome. The ship is becalmed, the crew is drunk, and the captain is converted. Peter goes down by a rope and baptizes him in the sea. They finally land at Puteoli and proceed to Rome. Peter rallies the believers. He knocks at Simon's door, but the porter pretends Simon is out. Peter sends his message in by the watchdog, which is suddenly endowed with speech. Seeing a dried herring in a shop, Peter puts it in water and brings it to life. He makes a seven-month-old baby speak. Peter tells how in Judea a woman had been robbed by Simon and his confederates, and how he had been enabled by a vision to uncover the crime and get back the stolen property.

A woman of bad character brings Peter a large sum of money. He is warned against accepting it, in view of her character; it was a case of tainted money. Peter laughs and says that in reality the money was a debt owed to Christ (chap. 30).

The senator Marcellus, who had entertained Simon, is shown his error by Peter and, after sprinkling his house with holy water, he offers it for use as a church or convent; the old women and widows are to come and pray, receiving a piece of gold for the

---

6 *Against Adimantus* xvii. 5.

7 According to the *Preaching of Peter*.

service. Peter finds the gospel being read in the dining-hall and preaches there. He relates the Transfiguration, and in a vision his hearers see Christ, who appears to some as an old man, to others as a young one, or, to some, even as a child (chap. 21; this rather docetic passage is taken from the *Acts of John*, chap. 87).

Platforms are erected in the forum, and great numbers of persons each pay a piece of gold to witness the contest between Peter and Simon. The prefect tells Simon to show his power by killing one of his pages; Simon obeys. Peter is then called upon to restore the boy to life, and other resurrections follow.

The rest of the *Acts* is preserved in Greek as well as in Latin. Simon, who has already amazed the Romans by flying over the city, announces that he will do it again. Peter prays that he may fall and break his leg in three places. He does so, disappears from Rome, and dies at Terracina.

Peter's success in prevailing upon wives to leave their husbands arouses leading Romans against him. He is warned and leaves the city but meets Jesus entering it. Peter asks, "Lord, where are you going?" (the famous "Domine quo vadis?"). Jesus replies that he is going into Rome to be crucified again. Peter accepts the rebuke and turns back into the city where he is crucified, at his request, with his head downward. This noble story of Peter's martyrdom goes far to redeem the trivial and even pagan elements that form so much of the book.

Origen says that the *Acts of Paul* contained the saying of Jesus, "I am going to be crucified again," and the newly discovered Greek *Acts of Paul*, as we have seen, contains those words. Evidently the *Acts of Paul* was used by the author of the *Acts of Peter*.

Peter's last words to his wife as she was being led out to martyrdom are recorded by Clement of Alexandria (*Miscellanies* vii. 11) and repeated by Eusebius (*Church History* iii. 30. 2): "They say that when the blessed Peter saw his own wife led out to die, he rejoiced because of her summons and her return home, and called to her very encouragingly and comfortingly, addressing her by name, and saying, 'O thou, remember the Lord.'" Clement does not refer this to the *Acts of Peter*, but it may later have formed part of them.

The idea that the apostles were told by Jesus to remain for twelve years in Jerusalem and then go forth into the world is drawn from the *Preaching of Peter* and was widely held in the early centuries. That there was in Rome a statue in honor of Simon Magus, with the inscription "Simoni deo Sancto" (chap. 10) probably comes from Justin, who in his *Apology*, about A.D. 150 or soon after, mentions it (*Apology* xxvi. 2). In fact, Justin is the first writer to suggest that Simon Magus visited Rome. The inscription was doubtless one in honor of Semo Sancus, an old Sabine deity; indeed in 1574 the base of a statue of him with such an inscription as Justin and the *Acts of Peter* describe ("Semoni Sanco deo fidio," etc.) was found at the spot Justin describes—"in the river Tiber [on the island] between the two bridges."

Eusebius quotes from the third book of Origen's lost *Commentary on Genesis* a few lines about the apostolic labors of Thomas, Andrew, John, Peter, and Paul that may imply that Origen knew *Acts* of all five of them (*Church History* iii. 1). The Genesis commentary was written in A.D. 220-30, so that the *Acts of Peter* would naturally fall between A.D. 200 and 220. Eusebius himself says the *Acts of Peter* was not accepted by the church (*Church History* iii. 3. 2), but it does not seem to have been definitely disapproved until sects like the Manicheans made so much of the ascetic elements in it. It is Peter's ascetic influence in relation to marriage especially that leads in the *Acts* to his execution. The groups of pious widows and virgins in the Roman church and the support given by the Christian Marcellus to the Christian poor, as described in the *Acts of Peter*, shows that the church is on the way to the state of things described by the bishop Cornelius (d. 253) when there were fifteen hundred in the Roman church in need of aid.

The earliest list of the heads of the Roman church that has come down to us is reflected in Irenaeus (*Against Heresies* iii. 3. 3) and names Linus as the first bishop. The Roman claim of primacy among the bishops for its head was made explicit under Victor (d. 198), progressed under Calixtus, who claimed the "power of the keys," and reached a peak under Stephen (A.D. 254-57), who professed to occupy the "chair of St. Peter."

The Liberian Catalogue of Roman bishops from Peter to Liberius dates from A.D. 354, and its earlier portions, from Peter to Pontianus, A.D. 231-35, have been shown to be derived from the *Chronicle* written about that time by Hippolytus. So by the time of Pontianus Roman writers were thinking of Peter as first bishop of Rome.

The *Acts of Peter* does not go so far as to call Peter the first bishop of Rome, and thus make him head a line of popes. It clearly contributes to the movement which was under way in the first half of the third century, however, and was probably written under Zephyrinus or Calixtus—that is, between A.D. 198 and 222.

The Acts of Thomas

Early in the third century some Christian novelist, probably at Edessa, wrote the thirteen *Acts of Thomas*, completing them with his martyrdom. Tatian had carried the gospel in Syriac into eastern Syria with his *Diatessaron*, or interweaving of the Four Gospels, about A.D. 172, and Bardaisan, A.D. 154–222, had developed some Christian Syriac literature with his poems. Whether the *Acts of Thomas* owes anything directly to him is questionable, but poems of Syriac origin have certainly been wrought into it, for it is rich in liturgical and poetical passages. Most scholars think it was written in Syriac, our numerous Greek manuscripts being a translation from that language, although James and Bonnet argue for a Greek original, now lost. The work, which seems to be complete, is much the most extended of all the really ancient apocryphal Acts. Besides the Syriac and Greek forms of it, it is preserved also in Latin, Ethiopic, and Armenian versions.

The *Acts of Thomas* is strongly ascetic, describing Thomas as laboring to separate wives from their husbands and to abolish the marriage relation. It is full of strange echoes of Gnostic, Mandaean, and Manichean religions. There is some reason to believe Christianity had reached southern India early in the third century, and some of the names in Thomas are known to history, such as King Gundafor (Hyndopheres), who ruled a part of India in the first Christian century; but there is no reason to suppose there is anything historical about these *Acts*. They are, in fact, full of the ancient popular religious vocabulary of demon and marvel. The dead are raised, animals speak, devils are cast out, relics cure.

Course of the Narrative

Although the *Acts of Thomas* abounds in long speeches, prayers, and hymns, there is a good deal of lively narrative, as a summary of its action will show.

1. The apostles draw lots for their mission fields. Judas Thomas draws India but refuses it. Jesus then sells him to a merchant from

India who wants a carpenter for the Indian king Gundafor, and gives him a regular deed of sale. (A king of this name, called Hyndopheres in Greek, is known to have reigned over part of India in the first century.) The merchant claims Thomas under the deed of sale and takes him to India. At Andrapolis the king's daughter is being married. At the wedding Thomas utters a mystic bridal song. He persuades the bride and groom to renounce marriage (chaps. 1–16).

2. Gundafor commissions Thomas to build him a palace and provides the necessary money. Thomas gives it to the poor and later explains to the king that he has built him a palace in heaven. The king is angry, but his brother dies and sees the palace in heaven. He is restored to life and tells the king about it.

3. A serpent has killed a woman's lover. Thomas makes the serpent confess this and all his crimes and also restore the man to life. He kills the serpent and converts the youth. The people of the city repent.

4. A colt blesses the apostle, who utters a hymn of praise to Christ (rather like the Oxyrhynchus Isis litany). He then converses with the colt and dismisses it. The colt drops dead.

5. A woman long tormented by a lustful devil begs the apostle's help. He rebukes the devil, and it departs in fire and smoke. Thomas utters a prayer to Christ and baptizes the woman and her companions and then administers the communion to them, marking the bread with a cross.

6. A young man confesses having murdered his mistress. The apostle restores her to life, and she tells of the punishments of the lost (chaps. 55–57), in words drawn from the *Revelation of Peter*. The apostle calls upon the people to repent, and they do so.

7. A captain asks Thomas to come and cure his wife and daughter who are harassed by devils; he sets off with him.

8. As they travel, the animals drawing their car gives out, and the apostle summons four wild asses to take their places. On reaching the house, Thomas sends one of the asses in to call the demons out. The women come out, and the apostle assisted by the wild ass completes their cure. The apostle sends the four wild asses back to their pastures.

9. A woman of position named Mygdonia is converted and leaves her husband, Charis (or Charisius). He is incensed and has Thomas imprisoned. In prison Thomas utters the Gnostic Hymn

of the Soul, or of Redemption, the finest and most perplexing of the many liturgical pieces that distinguish the *Acts of Thomas:* a prince goes down to Egypt to recover a pearl, but, once there, he forgets his errand, until a letter from his own country rouses him to obtain it, to resume his royal attire, and return home.

10. The apostle leaves the prison long enough to baptize Mygdonia. The king Misdai (or Misdaeus) releases him with orders to reconcile Mygdonia to her husband.

11. But now Misdai's wife Tertia is converted and decides to leave her husband.

12. The king's son, Vazan (or Iuzanes), joins the disciples of Thomas and follows him back to prison, where the apostle preaches and prays. (But the great prayer, chaps. 144–48, probably belongs in the martyrdom, after chap. 167, where some manuscripts have it.)

13. Thomas' leading converts join him in the prison. They all go to Vazan's house, and Vazan and the others are baptized and are given the communion.

These thirteen *Acts* are followed by the martyrdom of Thomas. Misdai condemns Thomas to death. He is taken up into a mountain and killed with spears. Misdai himself is afterward converted.

The *Acts of Thomas* probably belongs to those Acts which Efrem says were written in Syriac and Greek by the followers of Bardesanes, and it is possible that it was put forth in both languages, as Harnack suggests. The conception of the work seems to be Greek, while some parts of it, like the Hymn of the Soul, are in all probability of Syriac origin. Its use of the *Revelation of Peter,* in chapters 55–57, and of the *Acts of John* (chap. 22), in chapter 53, rather favors a Greek original, for we do not know that these works were so anciently known in Syriac versions. The long series of honorific titles piled up in the prayer in chapters 10 and 39 recalls the style of the Isis litany discovered at Oxyrhynchus (*Oxyrhynchus Papyri* xi. 1380) and of the hymn near the end of Clement's *Tutor.* There are traces of the use of the *Gospel of the Hebrews* ("they do rest, and resting do reign," chap. 136) and of the *Gospel of the Egyptians* ("him that was inward have I made outward and the outward inward," chap. 147)—or more probably of the *Gospel of Thomas,* which contains both sayings.

There are even touches of humor in the *Acts of Thomas,* as when Thomas refuses to obey Jesus and go to India, and so Jesus without his knowledge sells him into slavery to the Indian merchant (chap. 2); or when Thomas draws a plan for a palace for the king but gives the money to the poor and explains to the king that he has built him his palace in heaven (chap. 21). When Thomas' ascetic habits were reported to the king, "he rubbed his face with his hands and shook his head for a long time" (chap. 20).

This can hardly be the *Acts of Thomas* that Eusebius intimates Origen knew, for it described Thomas' field as Parthia, not India. The *Acts* was used by the Gnostics and, according to Epiphanius, by the Encratites and the Apostolics (*Heresies* 47, 61). Augustine says it was used by the Manicheans, and Turribius, by the Priscillianists. It entered into the Manichean corpus of apostolic Acts described by Photius (*Bibliotheca* cod. 114) and into the *Apostolic History* of Abdias. It was also revived in a paraphrase by Nicetas of Thessalonica in the twelfth century.

The ascetic ideal of the *Acts* is presented in the description of Thomas himself: "He continually fasts and prays, and eats only bread, with salt, and drinks water, and wears the same garment in fine weather and winter, and accepts nothing from anyone, and gives what he has to others" (chap. 20). This, with Thomas' renunciation of marriage, sums up the monastic ideal of later days. Indeed it goes beyond it in its abstinence from meat and wine. The estimate of the length of the *Acts* ("Travels") *of Thomas* in the Nicephorus list as 1,600 lines accounts for hardly more than half our present *Acts of Thomas* and is either a mistake or represents an abbreviated form of the work.

The Acts of Andrew

About the middle of the third century, perhaps as late as A.D. 260, some Christian, probably in Greece or Asia Minor, wrote a story of the wanderings, wonders, and discourses of Andrew, ending with his martyrdom. Its chief purpose seems to have been to discourage marriage and to lead women converts to forsake their husbands; it falls into line with the other apocryphal *Acts* in their aversion to marriage. It was probably not heretical, though highly ascetic, and also exhibited some Gnostic echoes.

Little remains of the *Acts of Andrew*, and what there is mostly relates to the efforts of a woman named Maximilla to escape from her husband Aegeas or Aegeates, the proconsul of Greece, and

Andrew's encouragement of these efforts. His encouragement is successful, and the proconsul has him crucified. On reaching the place of execution, Andrew utters an address to the cross, reminiscent of Peter's rhapsody before his cross. He lingers for three days on the cross, refuses release, and dies.

In his famous chapter on the New Testament canon (*Church History* iii. 25. 6) Eusebius speaks of *Acts of Andrew* and of *John*, which he describes as heretical. His reference in iii. 1. 1, 2, to Origen's account, now lost, of the labors of these apostles, John in Ephesus and Andrew in Scythia, may imply that Origen knew the *Acts* of each of them. But Eusebius is the earliest writer to mention them, and we cannot be sure that Origen knew them or that they existed in his day.

Gregory of Tours (A.D. 538–94) came across the Greek *Acts of Andrew* and produced a Latin epitome of them, frankly omitting the tedious parts (the discourses were probably fairly long) and emphasizing Andrew's miracles. This epitome is in the main embodied in the Andrew section (Book 3) of Abdias' *Apostolic History*.

The scene of the story is not Scythia, north of the Black Sea, which Eusebius said was the field of Andrew's labors, but Pontus, Bithynia, Macedonia, and Greece, where Andrew finally suffers martyrdom at Patrae, the modern Patras. Gregory prefaced his account of it with a summary of the Egyptian *Acts of Andrew* and of *Matthias* (or Matthew) among the cannibals, who kept any strangers who fell into their hands for thirty days and then ate them, tagging each one with the date of his arrival so as to make no mistake. (This verges on the *Odyssey* and the *Arabian Nights*.) On a ship steered by Jesus himself, Andrew comes and rescues Matthias and the other victims. A sequel to this episode is supplied by the *Acts of Peter and Andrew*, in which Peter causes a camel to go through the eye of a needle. But these were not part of the third-century *Acts of Andrew*. All that we really possess of it is (1) the story in Euodius (*On Faith, against the Manicheans* 38) around A.D. 400 about Maximilla's efforts to escape from her husband; (2) a Vatican Greek fragment, telling of Andrew's discourses in prison, especially those encouraging Maximilla to leave her husband; and (3) the martyrdom of Andrew.

Epiphanius (d. 403), in *Heresies* 47, says that the *Acts of Andrew*, as well as those of John, Thomas, and others, was appealed to by the Encratites, who were vegetarians and total abstainers and renounced marriage and private property (chap. 61), and by the Origenians or eunuchs (chap. 63). Innocent I, in his letter of A.D. 405, according to some manuscripts, condemns the *Acts of Andrew*, stating that they were written by "the philosophers Neochares and Leonidas," perhaps a miswriting of Leucius Charinus, the reputed author of the *Acts of John*.

The Clementine Recognitions and Homilies

The impulse toward Christian fiction, which had found expression in the second and third centuries in the *Acts* of the individual apostles—Paul, John, Peter, Thomas, and Andrew—in the early years of the fourth century probably between 313 and 325, resulted in two considerable works, the *Recognitions* and the *Homilies* of Clement. The *Homilies* have come down to us in Greek, but the *Recognitions* are preserved in full only in a Latin translation by Rufinus.

The *Recognitions*, in ten books, ostensibly written by Clement of Rome in the first person, describes a journey of Clement to Palestine, his meeting with Peter, and his life with him; the discussions they had about all sorts of religious and doctrinal matters; and the marvelous way in which Clement's long-lost parents and brothers are restored to him. It is to this feature of the narrative that it owes its name, the *Recognitions*.

The twenty *Homilies* relate extended conversations between Peter and Clement, in which spiritual matters are discussed very much as in the *Recognitions*. Both works seem to rest on an earlier piece of fiction about Clement, a sort of Clement romance, written probably about A.D. 260, but now lost; and this in turn probably drew upon two conflicting sources, one Jewish-Christian and Gnostic in color, the other Catholic and anti-Gnostic—the latter probably the *Acts of Peter*, which had so much to say about Simon Magus who also appears prominently, especially in the *Recognitions*. Such sources would explain the strange mixture of heretical and orthodox elements that the *Clementines* exhibit. The author was no doubt a Catholic Christian, and probably unconscious of the heretical character of some of his materials. The *Homilies* are introduced by letters from Peter and Clement to James of Jerusalem, designed to give them credibility.

6

HYMNS, HOMILIES, AND EXEGESIS

Most of the literature with which we have thus far been concerned consists of writings like those in the New Testament or those intended for particular occasions. From this literature it is difficult to get much of an impression about the life of the early Christian communities, although the *Didache* (see chap. 2) offers a notable exception. We are fortunate, therefore, in possessing a few scattered examples of other kinds of materials such as hymns, homilies, and fragments of a book containing what seems to be biblical exegesis.

The Odes of Solomon

From the very beginning of the Christian movement, hymns and songs were part of its life. These were at first the psalms of Judaism; at the end of the Last Supper, Jesus and the disciples "sang the hymn"—the second part (Pss. 115–18)—of the Hallel. Paul recommends the use of psalms, hymns, and sacred songs to the Colossians (3:16). In the canticles of Luke—the Magnificat, the Benedictus, the Gloria in excelsis, and the Nunc dimittis—we begin to see the dawn of a Christian hymnology, and we catch other glimpses of the same movement in the great arias, antiphonies, and choruses of the Revelation.

Nothing like a collection of early Christian hymns seemed to have survived, however, until J. Rendel Harris, the discoverer of Aristides, in 1909 found, among some Syriac manuscripts gathered in the neighborhood of the Tigris, a group of Christian hymns he soon identified as the so-called *Odes of Solomon*, mentioned in the *Synopsis of Holy Scripture* that goes under the name of Chrysostom, which may be as late as the sixth century, and also in the *Stichometry of Nicephorus* (*ca.* A.D. 850). In both these lists the *Odes* appear not by themselves but as the *Psalms and Odes of Solomon*, and in *Nicephorus* their length is given as 2,100 lines. It is interesting to observe that in Harris' manuscript the *Psalms of Solomon* accompany and follow the *Odes*.

The *Psalms of Solomon* are the well-known Pharisaic hymns, composed in the last century before Christ and extant in Greek in a few manuscripts. They once stood at the end of the fifth-century Codex Alexandrinus, after the New Testament and the two *Letters of Clement*, for they are listed in its table of contents, although they have long since been lost from the manuscript.

But the *Odes of Solomon* had never been found in modern times until Harris discovered them in his Syriac manuscript on January 4, 1909. A second manuscript of the *Odes and Psalms* was soon after identified by F. C. Burkitt in the British Museum. Neither manuscript is entirely complete, however. The *Pistis Sophia*, a Coptic product of Egyptian Gnosticism of the Ophite or Sethite type, about A.D. 250–300, quotes five of the *Odes*, the first of which is missing in both Syriac manuscripts. The nineteenth ode is quoted by Lactantius in his *Divine Institutes* 4:12 (A.D. 311). He introduces his quotation with the words, "Thus Solomon speaks."

The *Odes*, forty-two in number, are followed in the Syriac manuscript by the eighteen *Psalms of Solomon*, which are numbered continuously with them, from 43 to 60. The *Odes* introduce us at once to a very well-marked religious atmosphere which pervades them all but is utterly unlike that of the *Psalms of Solomon* that follow them. The *Odes* are spiritual, mystical, imaginative, and boldly, even harshly, figurative, a trait they share with the *Letters of Ignatius*, with which they have other affinities. They sometimes recall characteristic touches in the Gospel and Letters of John, and, of course, they owe much to the Hebrew Psalms. They also remind one of the meditative psalms found at Qumran. In fact, some scholars regard them as Jewish hymns made over by revision and expansion to serve Christian purposes; but the Christian strain in them is probably too pervasive to be thus explained. "Love," "light," "life," and "truth" are words often employed by the odist, and the combination seems Christian, although admittedly they are also present in late Judaism.

Why were these hymns of devotion and aspiration ascribed to Solomon? Probably for the same reason that the Song of Songs and the Psalms of the Pharisees were—among the Hebrews Solomon was credited with five thousand songs (I Kings 4:32). Cer-

tainly their amalgamation with the Psalms of the Pharisees which
went by his name carried the fiction of his authorship with it.
Judaism had long enjoyed these sweeping literary verdicts—all the
Law by Moses, all the Psalms by David, all the Proverbs and Wisdom writings by Solomon. The closing of the Psalter turned new
song writers to Solomon, in view of his record in that field
announced in Kings. Such verdicts were, of course, no more than
dedications or gestures of respect to great figures of the past.

Who really wrote these *Odes* no one can say. They have come
to light only in Syriac, and some scholars have thought they might
be the work of the Syriac poet Bardaisan (Bardeisanes), A.D. 154–
222. But they were almost certainly written in Greek some time
near the middle of the second century, before Christian theology
had begun to assume something like fixity of form. What may well
be the Greek original of one of them—the eleventh—has been discovered among the Bodmer papyri and was edited in 1959 by M.
Testuz. It is entitled "Ode of Solomon" and is almost identical
with the Syriac version. The use of the *Odes* in the *Pistis Sophia*
shows that they were acceptable to some groups of Gnostics but
does not prove that they were of Gnostic origin, although what
looks very much like Gnostic influence can be traced here and
there in them. Probably some imaginative and devout Greek Christian, perhaps of Ephesus (the Johannine atmosphere) or even
more probably of Antioch (for they sometimes make us think of
Ignatius), poured out his soul in them. Certainly they seem to be
all from the same hand.

Soon after Harris discovered these *Odes*, he described them in a
letter as being "redolent of antiquity and radiant with spiritual
light." It would be difficult to characterize them more vividly.

In the same volume of Bodmer papyri Testuz published a liturgical hymn; O. Perler suggested that it might be a hymn for the
Easter vigil by Melito of Sardis, although the grounds for assigning it to Melito are not very strong.[1] The hymn reads as follows:

(a) Hymn the Father, ye saints;
    Sing to the Mother, ye virgins.
(b) Let us hymn them and exalt them highly, ye saints.

---

[1] M. Testuz, *Papyrus Bodmer X–XII* (Geneva, 1959); O. Perler, *Ein Hymnus zur Ostervigil von Meliton?* (*Paradosis* XV, 1960).

(c) Be ye exalted, brides and bridegrooms,
   For ye have found your bridegroom, Christ.
   Drink of the wine, brides and bridegrooms.

This hymn, perhaps preserved only in part, recalls the fragmentary hymns of the New Testament (for example, Eph. 5:14)
and looks forward to the more elaborate compositions found in
the writings of Clement of Alexandria. There are also a few
hymns among the early Gnostic remains; we may mention the one
called "Harvest" which Valentinus wrote (Hippolytus, *Refutation*
vi. 37. 7).

II Clement

Another prominent feature of early Christian worship was the sermon, of which examples are imbedded in New Testament writings, especially in the Epistle of James. The oldest complete sermon we possess is what has survived as the *Second Letter of
Clement*—obviously not a letter at all and probably not by
Clement. But it follows the *Letter of Clement* both in the Greek
manuscripts of that work and in the Syriac one, although not in
the Latin or Coptic versions of it. Eusebius is the first writer to
mention *II Clement* (*Church History* iii. 38. 4), but he is careful
not to acknowledge it as actually being a letter of Clement. Irenaeus may have used it, but he did not refer to the work.

This sermon is an appeal to its hearers to repent and serve God
with their whole hearts, live pure and holy lives, and cling to their
hope of the resurrection of the body. Its true character as a sermon is plain from some words in 17:3: "Let us not merely seem to
believe and pay attention now, while we are being exhorted by
the elders, but also when we have gone home let us remember the
commandments of the Lord, and let us not be dragged aside by
worldly lusts, but let us try to come here more frequently, and to
make progress in the commands of the Lord." It is evidently, like
James, a sermon that has come to be treated as a letter—a letter of
Clement of Rome.

It evidently owes this connection with Clement to the fact that
it was preserved at Corinth, which was the destination of *I
Clement*, the genuine letter of the Roman church to the Corinthians, written about A.D. 95. It must either have been preached in
Corinth or sent there for some purpose. At any rate, it came to be
associated with the *Letter of Clement*, which was preserved there

and perhaps occasionally read in church, as Dionysius of Corinth says in his letter to Soter, bishop of Rome, about A.D. 165–75. He is replying to a letter from Soter recently received by the Corinthians and indicates their purpose to preserve it and read it from time to time. "From it," he writes, "whenever we read it, we shall always be able to draw advice, as also from the former epistle, which was written to us through Clement" (Eusebius *Church History* iv. 23. 11). This prompt associating by the bishop of Corinth of Soter's letter with Clement's led Hilgenfeld and Harnack to think that *II Clement* was probably Soter's letter and that immediately on its arrival in Corinth it had been filed with the *Letter of Clement*, making two letters from the church at Rome to that at Corinth from which the Corinthians could read from time to time for their edification. This is an attractive suggestion, for it solves two problems: How did *II Clement* ever come to be grouped with *I Clement?* What has become of the letter from Soter, which Dionysius said the Corinthians would keep and read with the *Letter of Clement?*

The difficulty with this view is that *II Clement* is not really a letter but a homily or sermon and conveys nothing in the way of a message from Rome to Corinth that might not have been sent from any church to any other. In fact, it does not sound like a church letter at all. That it lacks the name of Soter does not matter; *I Clement* has no mention of Clement. It is, of course, hard to see why the church of Rome should send a sermon, of no particular applicability, to the church of Corinth, except as a gesture of interest and good will; that is perhaps, in view of Dionysius' words to Soter, the best explanation of it.

This difficulty led scholars like Lightfoot to the view that the homily was really written in Corinth, perhaps at a time when crowds were gathering for the Isthmian games, and that these are reflected in chapter 7: "Many are landing for the corruptible contests." It may have been a favorite sermon with the Corinthians which was kept and read occasionally in church, like *I Clement*, and so came to be associated with it.

Others have thought *II Clement* might have been of Alexandrian origin, partly because of its use of something like the *Gospel of the Egyptians*, especially in 12:2: "For when the Lord himself was asked by someone when his kingdom would come, he said, 'When the two shall be one, and the outside as the inside, and the male with the female neither male nor female.' " This closely resembles Jesus' words to Salome, as quoted by Clement of Alexandria from the *Gospel of the Egyptians* (*Miscellanies* iii. 92). Other curious sayings ascribed to Christ in the sermon are derived either from oral tradition or from that gospel, but the writer is also familiar with the Four Gospels, the principal letters of Paul, and I Peter. This list of Christian books with which Clement is acquainted, especially his knowledge of the *Gospel of the Egyptians*, brings the date of the sermon well into the second quarter of the second century. From another curious book, which he does not name, but merely describes as "the word of prophecy," he quotes a strange saying:

Miserable are the double-minded who doubt in their hearts and say, "These things we heard long ago, and in the days of our fathers, but we have waited from day to day and have seen none of them." You fools! Compare yourselves to a tree; take a vine; first it sheds its leaves, then there comes a bud, after that an unripe grape, then a full cluster. . . .

This passage appears also in *I Clement* (23:3, 4), but in *II Clement* it is carried a sentence further, so that the writer is not quoting *I Clement* but the word of prophecy from which it drew, possibly the mysterious *Book of Eldad and Modat*, which is mentioned in Hermas (*Vision* ii. 3, 4). Hermas quotes from it the saying, "The Lord is near those who turn to him," and described Eldad and Modat as those "who prophesied to the people in the wilderness" (Num. 11:26).

Nothing is really known of this work, although it is mentioned in the *Stichometry of Nicephorus* among the Old Testament apocrypha.[2] But, at any rate, *II Clement* is certainly quoting the same book as *I Clement*, and that suggests that both were written in the Roman church. If the book they quoted was the *Book of Eldad and Modat*, mentioned and quoted in Hermas, the link between *II Clement* and Rome becomes still stronger, for Rome would appear to be the one place where that little apocryphon was known and valued. But of this we cannot be certain.

Although the place of *II Clement*'s origin remains uncertain, its

---

[2] There is also a somewhat dubious reference to it in the *Targum of Jonathan*, on Num. 11:26–27. The *Stichometry* gives its length as 400 *stichoi*, or about that of Galatians.

value as a piece of Christian preaching from the second quarter of the second century is considerable. For the time of its origin is reasonably clear; traditions like those in the *Gospel of the Egyptians* are current but not yet suspected as heretical. As to place, it must certainly have been written in a circle remarkably well provided with Christian books—five gospels, the principal Pauline letters, I Peter—and the "book of prophecy," now lost. This points to one of the major Christian centers of the time, such as Antioch, Alexandria, Ephesus, Corinth, or Rome. And while the *Gospel of the Egyptians* is mentioned by Clement of Alexandria and by Origen, it is also discussed by the Roman Hippolytus, about A.D. 230, so that it was obviously known far beyond the borders of Egypt, and its use does not necessarily connect *II Clement* with Alexandria. *II Clement* was translated along with *I Clement* into Syriac, but it did not follow it into Latin and Coptic versions, so that *I Clement* must have begun to circulate widely before *II Clement* became attached to it.

After the time of *II Clement* we encounter other sermons, of course. The most important are those by Melito of Sardis, Clement of Alexandria, and Origen. Sermons provide one means of giving interpretation to the biblical texts. Another is that of writing books of exegesis—a practice already current not only among Jews like Philo but also among Greek and Roman commentators on the poets.

Papias of Hierapolis

The oldest Christian writer to give exegesis of this kind was one named Papias, who lived at Hierapolis in Phrygia early in the second century. Papias lost no opportunity to meet and talk with any older Christian who came his way who might have known anyone who had heard the apostles. For from such living witnesses to Jesus' words and doings Papias felt he could learn more than from Christian books. And out of such interviews with his elders, about A.D. 120, or a little later, Papias produced a work of his own, in five books, which he called the *Interpretations of Sayings of the Lord*.

This work has disappeared, but Irenaeus and Eusebius knew it and made use of it, and what they and later writers quoted from it shows that it contained traditions of the utmost value about the beginnings of Christian history and literature. A long list of

Christian writers use or mention Papias other than Irenaeus (A.D. 181–89) and Eusebius (326)—Jerome (d. 420), Philip of Side (*ca.* 430), Andreas of Caesarea (late sixth century), Maximus the Confessor (d. 662), Anastasius of Sinai (d. *ca.* 700), Georgius Hamartolus (*ca.* 842), and Photius (890). There are also scattered references to him in anonymous pieces.

It is from Papias that we learn the early Christian tradition about the origin of the Gospel of Mark:

Mark having become the interpreter of Peter wrote down accurately everything that he remembered, without however recording in order what was either said or done by Christ. For neither did he hear the Lord speak nor did he follow him, but afterwards, as I said, attended Peter, who adapted his instructions to the needs of his hearers, but had no design of giving a connected account of the Lord's oracles. So then Mark made no mistake while he thus wrote some things as he remembered them, for he made it his one care not to omit anything that he heard, or to set down any false statement therein.

This statement, obscure as it is, has proved of great value in dealing with the vexed question of the origin of Mark. Much more perplexing is Papias' statement about Matthew: "So then Matthew composed the Sayings (*logia*) in the Aramaic language, and each one translated them as best he could." The only possible meaning of this is that Matthew the apostle was believed to be the author of the oral gospel.

Eusebius calls Papias a man of very limited understanding, but this is perhaps due to Papias' crass millennialism, which rather attracted Irenaeus but so repelled Eusebius:

The days will come in which vines shall grow each having ten thousand shoots, and on each shoot ten thousand branches, and on each branch again ten thousand twigs, and on each twig ten thousand clusters, and on each cluster ten thousand grapes, and each grape when pressed shall yield twenty-five measures of wine. And when any of the saints shall have taken hold of one of their clusters, another will cry, "I am a better cluster; take me, bless the Lord through me!"

Such millennial calculations—more modestly paralleled in 2 Bar. 29:5—outrun current population figures, but under them lay the dream of a time when nature would respond freely and richly to man's needs.

Papias did not agree that Judas hanged himself and died, as

Matthew reported (Matt. 27:5), but held that, like the traitorous Nadan, in the Story of Ahikar, he swelled to a hideous size. This tradition of his fate is reflected in Acts 1:18. He speaks of Aristion and the Elder John as disciples of the Lord who were among his informants (so Eusebius and Jerome say). He quoted the daughters of Philip, mentioned in Acts (21:9), as saying that Barsabbas, who was called Justus—the man mentioned in Acts 1:23 as nominated to take Judas' place—"when challenged by unbelievers drank serpent's poison in the name of the Lord and was shielded from all harm." He says that some persons raised from the dead by Christ lived on until the time of Hadrian, who became emperor in the summer of A.D. 117. He also says that John and James were killed by the Jews. These statements are preserved in Philip of Side, who wrote about A.D. 430; the last one is also reported by Georgius Hamartolus, about A.D. 842.

Papias is quoted by Andreas of Caesarea as the earliest witness to the Book of Revelation, and as time went on he was pushed further and further back toward John the Evangelist, becoming in the Middle Ages not only his disciple but the scribe to whom John dictated his gospel. Most of these writers indicate in which of the five books what they report from Papias is found, so that it is fairly clear that his work was still in existence at the end of the ninth century. Of all the early Christian books now lost, Papias' *Exegeses* is one we should most like to recover. Some of his interpretations may underlie those given by Irenaeus, but recovering them is a task unlikely to lead to complete satisfaction.

7

THE FIRST APOLOGIES

As Christianity gradually separated from Judaism and came to feel its individual character as a new faith, competing with various ethnic, philosophic, and mystery religions in the Roman world and meeting objection and persecution, it began to be conscious of itself and to frame answers to the criticisms and attacks that were made upon it. This was the beginning of the Christian apologetic literature that soon took shape in a series of apologies and dialogues in defense of the new religion.

Christians were mostly persons of little distinction or position, and some things about them and their proceedings aroused suspicion and hostility. They were suspected of incest, cannibalism, atheism, disloyalty to the state, and even setting fire to the capital. Their views, too, were ridiculed, especially their worship of a man who had been crucified.

Jewish writers, seeking to command their religion to Greek readers, had already produced such books as the Wisdom of Solomon, Philo's treatise *On the Contemplative Life*, and Josephus' two volumes *Against Apion*, all written in the first century. Christian gropings toward such expression begin to appear in Luke's account of Paul's address in Athens in Acts 17:22–31. But the earliest Christian book or booklet in this field was the so-called *Preaching of Peter*.

The Preaching of Peter

Peter appears in the Acts as the first Christian preacher, and it was natural for a Christian writer, setting up a pattern of Christian preaching to be followed in carrying the gospel about the Greek world, to think first of him. In his name, therefore, about the beginning of the second century, or very early in it, the *Preaching of Peter* was written. The little book itself has long since disappeared, but quotations from it in Clement of Alexandria and in Origen give us some substantial information about it.

It attacked, on the one hand, the prevalent idolatry of its times—the Greek ways of worshiping God—and, on the other, the Jewish ways of worship, with their angels and archangels and their sacred days and seasons, which were governed by the changes of the moon. Christians worshiped God in a new way and, in contrast with Jews and Greeks, formed a third race. For twelve years the apostles were to labor among the Jews; then they were to go out into the world to preach to all men the one God and salvation through faith in Christ. Jesus is both "Law" and "Word." In the writings of the prophets the coming of Christ and his sufferings, death, and resurrection would be foretold.

These teachings of the *Preaching of Peter* are reported in Clement of Alexandria. Origen, a generation later, seems to be using the same book (in his *On First Principles*, prologue 8) under the name the *Teaching* (or *Doctrine*) *of Peter* (the passage is preserved only in Latin) when he writes that in that book the Savior is represented as saying to the disciples, "I am not an incorporeal demon." This saying appears in Ignatius' *Letter to the Smyrnaeans* 3:2 (A.D. 110–17) as evidence that Jesus appeared in a material body after the resurrection. The way the saying is introduced in Ignatius ("When he came to Peter and his companions, he said to them, 'Take and handle me, and see that I am not an incorporeal demon'") sounds very much as though it were drawn from some document associated with Peter's name. Jerome says that this saying stood in the *Gospel of the Hebrews* (*On Illustrious Men* 16), but there is no difficulty in supposing that both Ignatius and that gospel derived it from the *Preaching of Peter*.

If the *Preaching* is quoted in the *Gospel of the Hebrews* (A.D. 120–30) and in Ignatius (A.D. 110–17), it must have been written in the opening years of the second century, A.D. 100–110. Its primitive character accords reasonably well with this date. Its reference to the worship of cats, dogs, and apes has been taken to suggest an Egyptian origin, since idols with the heads of cats and dogs were worshiped in Egypt. Jewish apologetic had been particularly active there, too, in the Wisdom of Solomon, the work of Philo, the *Letter of Aristeas*, and in such attacks on idolatry as the story of Bel and the Dragon and the Letter of Jeremiah in the Apocrypha.

Some of our earliest mentions of it are also from Egypt—Clement of Alexandria, who accepts it and quotes it as Peter's, and Origen, who has found the book quoted in a work of Heracleon's but is very skeptical about its genuineness as a work of Peter. Heracleon was a pupil of Valentinus and flourished between A.D. 145 and 180. Clement says that he was the most distinguished of the followers of Valentinus and quotes some of his comments on the Gospel of Luke. Heracleon wrote a commentary on the Gospel of John, of which Origen made a good deal of use. Hippolytus locates Heracleon in Italy, and so the first reflections of the *Preaching* are widely scattered: the *Apology of Aristides* in Athens and the *Gospel of the Hebrews* in Egypt in the second quarter, and Heracleon in Italy in the third quarter. On the whole, the evidence rather favors Egypt as the place of origin.

The *Preaching* may have been the model for a larger Christian apology, that of Aristides, written in Greece probably between A.D. 138 and 147, for much of what we have of it is reproduced in that book. The belief that Jesus instructed the apostles to remain in Jerusalem for twelve years after his departure before going out into the world to preach reappears, as we have seen, in the *Acts of Peter*, chapter 5, and seems to have influenced Eusebius to date the Gospel of Matthew in A.D. 41, when Matthew would, according to this belief, be ready to leave Jerusalem and would write his gospel to leave behind him. The Catholic tradition of Peter's twenty-five years' ministry in Rome also rests upon it.

In his work *On First Principles* (prologue 8), Origen says that the *Teaching of Peter* is not by Peter or anyone else inspired by the spirit and is not counted among the books of the church. Eusebius in his *Church History* (iii. 3. 2, A.D. 326) groups the *Preaching* with the *Acts of Peter*, the *Gospel of Peter*, and the *Revelation of Peter* as not accepted by standard Christianity and not appealed to by church writers.[1] Indeed, of all the works claiming the name of Peter, Eusebius accepted only the first epistle as his work (*Church History* iii. 3. 1).

The *Preaching of Peter* is chiefly significant as the first of the Christian apologies. It is another book of which a complete copy may someday be found.

The Apology of Quadratus

The early Christians were indeed in a most difficult position. Under Roman administration religions had to be recognized—"li-

---

[1] Although Clement of Alexandria accepted the *Preaching* and the *Revelation of Peter* as genuine and quoted from both.

censed"—by the state before they could be lawfully practiced. But Christians practiced an unlicensed religion; in fact, Christianity did not obtain the necessary state recognition until early in the fourth century. Christian meetings had sometimes to be covertly, almost secretly, held, and this occasioned suspicion and criticism. Christian ways of describing their proceedings—eating Christ's flesh and drinking his blood—led the uninitiated to think some cannibalistic rites were observed by them. It was easy to think of them as haters of the human race, as Tacitus put it (*Annals* xv. 44), and to charge them with the burning of Rome. So to the official hostility of the government were added the suspicion and detestation of the public.

It was natural that intelligent Christians should undertake to repel these attacks and defend themselves against the hostility of the empire. A beginning in this direction was made in Egypt, very early in the second century, in the *Preaching of Peter*. But a more formal appeal to the emperor himself was soon after written by a Greek named Quadratus and presented to the emperor Hadrian, perhaps at Athens when Hadrian visited that city in A.D. 125 or later in 129. Eusebius, who gives us all the information we possess about Quadratus (for Jerome seems to have simply repeated what he had read in Eusebius about him), connects the presentation of the apology to the emperor with the year 125. He quotes a sentence from the little book, which is all that has been preserved of it:

But the works of our Savior were always present, for they were genuine; those who had been cured, those who had risen from the dead, who were seen not only when they were cured and raised, but on all occasions when they were present; and not only while the Savior was on earth, but also after his departure, they were alive for some time, so that some of them lived even to our day (*Church History* iv. 3. 2).

This little fragment comes from the oldest Christian apologetic we possess, apart from the sermon in Acts 17 and—perhaps—bits of the *Preaching of Peter*. It seems to contrast the works of "our Savior" with the works of someone else, possibly someone else's Savior. Our Savior's works were lasting because they were real; presumably, therefore, someone else's works were not lasting because they were not real. It would appear that Quadratus is making a statement about the history of religions. He may well imply that pagan gods are deified dead men. When their unreal cures and raisings have been unmasked because they do not last, the gods are recognized as merely human in origin. Jesus, on the other hand, is rightly recognized as Savior because of the permanence of his works. At any rate, similar lines of argument occur among the philosophical theologians of Quadratus' day.

Eusebius says that when he wrote, this book of Quadratus' was still in the hands of a great many of the brethren; but no copy of it is now known to exist. Dom Andriessen has propounded the ingenious theory that Eusebius' fragment is just what is now missing from the *Epistle to Diognetus* (7:6),[2] but it is extremely improbable (though not impossible) that Eusebius omitted what the copyist of the letter preserved and the copyist omitted exactly what Eusebius preserved. Moreover, if the fragment means what we have suggested it does, it does not fit the gap in *Diognetus*.

The Apology of Aristides

The writing of apologies for Christianity emerges into clearer light with the figure of Aristides. He was a Christian philosopher of Athens and addressed a defense of the new faith to the emperor Antoninus, probably between A.D. 138 and 147, since Marcus Aurelius is not mentioned in the address as co-emperor. A century ago all that was known of this book was what Eusebius said of it in the *Church History* iv. 3. 3. We cannot be sure that even he had actually seen it, although he says it was still in existence and widely circulated in his day. But in 1878 an Armenian fragment of it, from the tenth century, was published. This confirmed the statement of Eusebius that it was addressed to the emperor Hadrian. In 1889, however, J. Rendel Harris discovered in St. Catherine's on Mount Sinai an almost complete text of the book in a Syriac version. This gave the title of the emperor addressed more fully: "To the Imperator Caesar Titus Hadrianus Antoninus Augustus Pius," which means Antoninus Pius, although it might easily have suggested Hadrian to Eusebius (who sometimes got other emperors confused) and to the Armenian translator. Harris showed his find to his friend J. Armitage Robinson, who soon after came across large parts of it in Greek in the medieval romance of *Barlaam and Joasaph* (or Josaphat), the writer of which had evidently worked

---

2 *Vigiliae Christianae* I (1947), 129-36.

practically the whole apology into his book. This romance (written in the seventh or eighth century) is the story of a prince of India named Joasaph who is converted by a Christian monk. The monk, Barlaam, is later called upon to defend Christianity before the king and his court, and the defense that is offered is the ancient *Apology of Aristides*.

In 1922 a few lines of chapters 5 and 6 were published from a Greek papyrus leaf of the fourth century in *Oxyrhynchus Papyri* xv. 1778. Another fragment, covering Aristides 15:6—16:1, was published by H. J. M. Milne in 1923.[3] The sources for the text of the Apology are therefore the Syriac version, the Greek recast of the work employed in *Barlaam and Joasaph*, the Greek fragments from Oxyrhynchus and those in the British Museum, and three short Armenian fragments preserving the opening lines. The Greek, of course, promises to be the truest witness to the text, but it has been alternately expanded and condensed for the immediate purpose in the medieval story, so that in the absence of more ancient materials the textual problem is almost insoluble.

The apologist begins with an account of the Christian idea of God. He then presents the Chaldean, the Greek, the Egyptian, and the Jewish ways of worshiping God, showing the weaknesses of each.[4] The Chaldeans worship the elements—sky, earth, water, fire, air, sun, and moon. The Greeks worship gods like men, as beings full of frailties and crimes. The Egyptians worship plants and animals—crocodiles, cats, dogs, and snakes. The Jews are too fond of angels and holy days. Finally he presents the Christian way, which he strongly commends, although he speaks of the Christians as well as of the other four groups in the third person. The closing chapters, 15–17, give a fine picture of early Christian practices and morals.

The influence of the Four Gospels is clearly seen in Aristides' account of the Christians; indeed, he probably refers to them when he invites the emperor to examine the Christians' books (16:3, 5). Aristides is also strongly influenced by the *Preaching of Peter*, as we have seen. He sees in the Christians a new race, as the author of the *Preaching* did. He seems to have known the Acts and probably Romans and I Peter. His way of referring to the

---

[3] *Journal of Theological Studies* XXV (1923), 73–77.
[4] In the Syriac the groups are barbarians, Greeks, Jews, and Christians.

writings of the Christians as his sources suggests the possession of a larger Christian library.

The book was current in Greek in the fourth century, as Eusebius and the Oxyrhynchus fragment show; it passed early into Syriac and later into Armenian, and its Greek form was used in the seventh or eighth century in the romance of *Barlaam and Joasaph*. We may still hope that a complete Greek text of it will sometime come to light.

Aristo of Pella; the Christian Dialogue

The dialogue was a Greek literary device for making philosophy easy, and about A.D. 140 Aristo, a man of Pella, in Palestine, laid hold of it for Christian purposes. Pella was the city in Perea in which the Christians of Jerusalem were warned to take refuge when the Roman armies gathered about Jerusalem to besiege it in A.D. 66–70 (Eusebius *Church History* iii. 5. 3). It was one of the ten cities that formed the league known as the Decapolis. Aristo may have been a descendant of those Jerusalem refugees. At any rate, his writings, probably this very dialogue of his, supplied some material to Eusebius on the subject of the Bar-Cochba rebellion against Rome (A.D. 132–35), and Eusebius mentions Aristo as the source of some of his information about it (*Church History* iv. 6. 3).

The dialogue was represented as taking place between a Christian named Jason and a Jew named Papiscus and became the model for a whole series of such Jewish-Christian dialogues. The first mention of it is in the famous *True Discourses* which Celsus, about A.D. 178, directed against Christianity. This work has long since disappeared, but Origen in his answer to it (*Against Celsus,* A.D. 248) quoted from it so extensively that we can recover a good deal of it.

Celsus says he knows a *Dialogue of Jason and Papiscus* and that it deserves not so much to be laughed at as to be pitied and hated. Origen finds nothing hateful about the book but defends it as showing how the Jewish prophecies of the Christ apply to Jesus (*Against Celsus* iv. 52).

A few years after Celsus and before Origen, Clement of Alexandria mentioned the book in the sixth book of his *Outlines*. The *Outlines* are now lost, but Maximus the Confessor in the seventh century reports Clement's mention of the *Dialogue*.

Jerome in his *Commentary on Galatians* (3:13) remembers that he has read in the *Dialogue of Jason and Papiscus* that he who is hanged is a reproach of God. This was Aquila's translation of a sentence in Deut. 21:23, which is familiar from Paul's quotation of it in Gal. 3:13. Aquila flourished, according to Epiphanius, in A.D. 128–29, so that his translation of the Hebrew scriptures cannot be much earlier than A.D. 130–35. Taken with Aristo's report of the Bar-Cochba War, which ended in A.D. 135, this suggests that Aristo cannot have written before A.D. 140. Jerome also says that the *Dialogue* said: "In the Son God made the heavens and the earth."

Toward the end of the fifth century another man named Celsus made a Latin translation of the *Dialogue*. This has disappeared, but the preface he wrote for it has survived and informs us that Jason was a Jewish Christian and Papiscus an Alexandrian Jew who was finally converted by Jason's arguments.

Maximus the Confessor, a Greek writer of the seventh century already mentioned, is the first reader of the *Dialogue* to tell us that it was the work of Aristo of Pella. He reports that it spoke of seven heavens, and, as we have seen, we owe to him our knowledge that Clement of Alexandria mentioned it in the sixth book of his *Outlines*.

In the sixth century another Greek dialogue between a Jew and a Christian—the *Dialogue of Papiscus and Philo*—appeared, and, since it uses the name of one of Aristo's debaters, it is natural to suppose that it made use of Aristo's book; but we cannot be sure of this. Certainly Aristo's idea of using the Greek dialogue as a medium for arguing out the rival claims of Christianity and Judaism was acted upon by a whole series of Christian apologists,[5] beginning almost immediately with Justin's *Dialogue with Trypho*. This exhausts our present knowledge of Aristo's dialogue, a complete text of which, in either Greek or Latin, would help much toward the recovery of early Christian apologetic.

---

[5] E.g., the *Dialogue of Simon the Jew and Theophilus the Christian*, a fifth-century work, by the monk Evagrius.

8

THE AGE OF JUSTIN

Justin Martyr

Both the early forms of apologetic, the dialogue and apology, were employed by Justin, about the middle of the second century, in defense of Christianity. Justin was a native of Flavia Neapolis, in Palestine, the ancient Shechem, the modern Nablous. He was not a Jew but traveled into the Greek world to complete his education. He visited various philosophical schools—Stoic, Pythagorean, Peripatetic, and Platonist—but found no complete satisfaction until at Ephesus he met a Christian who introduced him to the Jewish prophecies and showed him how they were fulfilled in Christ. This was probably about A.D. 135. A few years later he became a Christian teacher, and by 150 found himself in Rome, where he wrote the only books of his that have survived, his *Apology*, written about 150, an appendix to it, and the *Dialogue with Trypho*, written between 155 and 160. He suffered martyrdom in Rome between A.D. 163 and 167.

Eusebius (*Church History* iv. 18) lists eight works of Justin—two *Apologies*, *Against the Greeks*, the *Refutation*, *On the Sovereignty of God*, *Psaltes* (perhaps a hymnbook), *On the Soul*, and a *Dialogue against the Jews*. Eusebius also mentions a work of Justin, *Against Marcion* (iv. 11. 8), but, when he proceeds to quote from it, he quotes from what we know as the *Apology*. But Justin's contemporary Irenaeus also mentions *Against Marcion* and quotes from it a sentence that is not found in the *Apology:* "Justin well says in his work against Marcion that he would not have believed the Lord himself if he had preached another God besides the Creator" etc. (*Against Heresies* iv. 6. 2; Eusebius *Church History* iv. 18. 9). Eusebius also mentions elsewhere (*Church History* iv. 11. 10), in Justin's own words, a work *Against All Heresies*, which he had probably never seen. This work is now lost.

Another list of Justin's writings is given by Photius, about A.D. 890, in his *Bibliotheca* (cod. 125), but for the most part it is taken from Eusebius and adds nothing of value. He does not seem to have seen any of the genuine works of Justin. In general, almost everything said about Justin after the time of Eusebius seems to have been drawn mostly from what he had said in the *Church History* about him.

Of all the works with which Justin has been credited, only two have reached our day: the *Apology* and the *Dialogue*. They are preserved in two manuscripts dated in 1364 and 1541, the latter being a copy of the former. There is also a fifteenth-century fragment, containing *Apology* chapters 65–67.[1] The manuscripts, it is true, offer two apologies, perhaps under the influence of Eusebius, but what they count as the first may have been an appendix to the other one. It is doubtful if there ever was really a second.

The *Apology* is addressed to the emperor Antoninus and his colleagues and asks the emperor to examine the charges made against the Christians and to satisfy himself that they are really a decent, law-abiding body who should not be condemned simply for the name they bear. They are not atheists, even though they are not idolators. Christ taught a higher morality, and his life and work were foretold by the Hebrew prophets. Persecution and error are the work of the demons. The religious practices of the Christians are pure, pious, and simple. In closing, Justin quotes a letter of Hadrian to Minucius Fundanus, which he thinks favorable to the Christians.

Justin was the most voluminous Christian writer up to his time, and his *Dialogue* was probably the longest Christian book thus far written. It describes the discussion, begun on one day and continued on the next, between Justin, speaking in the first person, and a Jew named Trypho, a name perhaps suggested by a well-known Jewish rabbi named Tarphon. Justin makes a great deal of the argument from prophecy. His contention that the Jewish prophecies are fulfilled in Christ is so contrary to the position taken by Marcion in his *Antitheses*, or *Contradictions*, that the *Dialogue* may be regarded as a counterblast against Marcion's book. Justin naturally allegorizes the Jewish scriptures in the manner of interpretation customary with Jews, Greeks, and

---

[1] These chapters are also preserved in two Latin manuscripts of the sixteenth century.

Christians in antiquity. In the end, while Trypho is not converted, they part, with courtesy and good feeling. This irenic note is characteristic of Justin, whether he deals with Jewish prophecy or Greek philosophy.

In the *Apology* (xxvi. 8) Justin speaks of his treatise *Against All Heresies*, which may have been the work *Against Marcion* which Irenaeus mentions and quotes and which Eusebius had confused with the *Apology*. Justin is frequently mentioned by later Christian writers, beginning with his own pupil Tatian, who speaks of him as the "most admirable Justin" and refers to his martyrdom as brought about by the Cynic Crescens, who may have reported him to the authorities.[2] His *Apology* manifestly influenced later apologists like Athenagoras, Theophilus, Tertullian, and probably Minucius Felix. Hippolytus (*Refutation* viii. 9 [Gr. 16]), and other Roman writers knew his work, although Clement and Origen do not mention him. How far he may have influenced subsequent writers on the heresies we cannot certainly say, but, beginning with his contemporary Hegesippus, they probably owed much to his lost work *Against All Heresies*. Eusebius quotes a dozen passages from his *Apology*, and Methodius, about A.D. 300, in his book *On the Resurrection*, describes him as a man "neither in time nor virtue far removed from the apostles."

Justin flourished in what Harnack called the blooming time of the sects, the middle of the second century, and it was natural that he should be the first to undertake a literary counterattack upon them which led to such notable works as those of Hegesippus, Irenaeus, Hippolytus, and Epiphanius. He also laid hold of both apology and dialogue in the service of Christian truth. Not only the bulk but the breadth of his literary work gives him importance. In seeking to bring Greek philosophy to the aid of his Christian faith, he is a forerunner of the Alexandrian theology.

We are most grateful to Justin for his account (*Apology* 65–67) of early Christian worship as practiced in the church at Rome in the middle of the second century, when the memoirs of the apostles or the writings of the prophets (67:3) were read to the congregation as long as time permitted. Even after his conversion, he continued to wear the philosopher's cloak, which drew

---

[2] *Address to the Greeks* 18:2; 19:1.

Trypho's attention to him, in the opening scene of the *Dialogue*, and, like Aristides, he was called a "Christian philosopher," which seems to have been a sort of primitive Christian honorary degree.

But, notwithstanding all his influence and fame, Justin's works have for the most part disappeared, and even those we have rest on the slenderest manuscript tradition—a single fourteenth-century manuscript and a copy made from it in the sixteenth century. Even this is, for the *Dialogue* at least, somewhat dilapidated, for there is a manifest break at 74:4, where one leaf or more was missing from the text from which our oldest manuscript was copied. What follows seems to belong to the second day of the debate, 78:6, and so forth. So for Justin, too, we should welcome new manuscripts of his works, whether extant or lost.[3]

In addition to the works of Justin himself, we are fortunate enough to possess an account of his martyrdom that seems to be based on an actual report of his trial, along with that of several other Christians, before the Roman prefect Junius Rusticus (prefect between 163 and 167). This account, preserved in four Greek manuscripts of which the earliest comes from the tenth century, constitutes the oldest of the Greek martyr-acts—with the possible but improbable exception of the *Martyrdom of Polycarp*.

Out of a number of works preserved in Greek manuscripts under the name of Justin, but quite certainly not written by him, three may be mentioned here. The *Exhortation (Cohortatio) to the Greeks* appeals to the Greeks to turn from Homer and the poets to Moses and the prophets and to accept the truth of Christianity. It shows the use of the *Chronography* of Julius Africanus (A.D. 221) and was probably written in the latter part of the third century, somewhere about the Aegean.

In the *Address (Oratio) to the Greeks*, a Greek who has become a Christian offers a justification of his course, exposes the immoralities of Greek mythology and of pagan festivals, and urges the Greeks to follow him into the Christian faith. It is probably a work of the early years of the third century.

On Sovereignty makes use of quotations from the Greek poets

---

[3] The older of the two Justin manuscripts, Paris. 450, was a corpus of twelve works ascribed to Justin and included such pieces as the *Letter to Zenas and Serenus* and the *Exhortation to the Greeks*, ending with a work *On the Resurrection*, really written by Athenagoras, but here evidently regarded as a work of Justin.

to show the truth of monotheism. Justin is said to have written a work on the *Sovereignty of God*, but his method of proof was rather different, as he sought to establish it from the scriptures as well as from the books of the Greeks—so Eusebius tells us (*Church History* iv. 18. 4). The present work gives little evidence of its date, but it may be as early as the closing years of the second century. Six other works have come down to us under the name of Justin, but all except possibly the *Letter to Diognetus* are as late as the fifth century.

It may be that the fragments of a treatise *On the Resurrection* ascribed to Justin in the eighth-century *Sacra Parallela* are actually his.[4] P. Prigent has argued that one can recover Justin's earlier *Syntagma* from his *Dialogue* and *Apology* and that the work *On the Resurrection*, also based on the *Syntagma*, was written by Justin himself.[5] The differences, however, in vocabulary, style, and thought between this treatise and the demonstrably genuine works remain striking.

The Letter to Diognetus

In a Strassburg manuscript of some Greek writings falsely ascribed to Justin that was destroyed in the burning of the cathedral library during the siege of 1870, there stood a *Letter to Diognetus*. It has never been found in any other manuscript, nor has any reference to it been identified in Christian literature. The text is broken at two points (7:6 and 10:1), and the final chapters (11 and 12), are evidently from another work altogether, perhaps from a homily of Melito of Sardis or someone belonging to his circle, although some have thought them a fragment from Hippolytus.

Diognetus was the tutor of Marcus Aurelius, and he may be the individual ostensibly addressed in the opening lines: "Since I perceive, most excellent Diognetus, that you are exceedingly zealous to learn the religion of the Christians." The ten or twelve short pages of the *Letter* proper reveal a decidedly rhetorical style, which sometimes seems to be more the concern of the writer than

---

[4] K. Holl in *Texte und Untersuchungen* XX, 2 (Leipzig, 1899), nos. 107–10. On the fragments in general see R. M. Grant in *Biblical and Patristic Studies in Memory of R. P. Casey* (ed. J. N. Birdsall and R. W. Thomson, Freiburg, 1963), 182–88.

[5] *Justin et l'Ancien Testament* (Paris, 1964), 50–68.

what he has to say. It bristles with antitheses; in short, it is so full of art that it verges on the artificial. The letter reflects the increasing concern of Christian writers with matters of literary style and belongs with such documents as the paschal homily by Melito of Sardis or the *Protrepticus* by Clement of Alexandria. Its author follows traditional apologetic patterns in attacking pagan idolatry and Jewish sacrifices, but develops more original ideas in describing the mission of Christ and the work of Christians in the world; their relation to the world is analogous to that of soul and body. H.-I. Marrou has convincingly dated the work in the late second century or the early third.

Tatian

Soon after the middle of the second century a rhetorician from the East, Syria or Assyria, journeyed westward to Athens and Rome in the pursuit of his studies. His name was Tatian. He says he came from Assyria, but Clement of Alexandria calls him a Syrian (*Miscellanies* iii. 81). He claims to have traveled widely about Greece, although his apparent familiarity with Greek works of art may be owing to his use of some Greek book describing them. In Rome he met Justin and became a Christian, although he was not among the group arrested at the time when Justin was martyred (A.D. 163–167). Later he returned to Syria, and it was probably there, about A.D. 167, or perhaps a decade later, that he wrote his *Address to the Greeks*. It is usually classed as an apology, but it is just as much a bitter attack upon Greek pretensions to leadership in arts and letters. Tatian declares that all the great inventions really came from the barbarians, with whom he identifies Jews and Christians. He points out the disagreement among philosophers and ridicules Graeco-Roman plays and athletics. He declares, and tries to prove, that Moses is more ancient than Homer and dwells upon the immoralities celebrated in Greek sculpture. With all this polemic he interweaves a sketch of Christian views, especially about demons and morals and declares himself a champion of this barbarian philosophy.

Tatian is a sprightly, if somewhat intemperate, writer, and he certainly does not share Justin's favorable attitude toward many aspects of Greek thought. But it must be remembered that he wrote under great provocation, for his teacher had been executed under a philosopher-emperor, and another persecution was begin-

ning. In addition, he combines his acceptance of Christianity with
a kind of cultural primitivism not uncommon among rhetoricians
even in Greece. He writes with the utmost rhetorical vigor and
shows a keen satirical delight in exposing what he regards as the
foibles and faults of Greek philosophy, art, and religion.

After the death of Justin, Tatian broke with the church and
returned to the East, where he became the leader, if not the
founder, of the Encratite sect, discouraging marriage and denying
the salvation of Adam. Irenaeus discusses his heretical views in the
Refutation i. 28; some of them are either anticipated or hinted at
in the *Address*. Eusebius tells us that Tatian left a great multitude
of writings, but most of these are unknown. He himself refers in
the *Address* (15:2) to a book *On Animals*, of which nothing is
known except what is repeated in the *Address*—examples taken
from natural history to show that unredeemed man is not superior
to the beasts that perish. He also seems to refer to a treatise *On
Demons* (*Address* 16) and to a future work to be called *Against
Those Who Have Discussed Divine Things* (40). Eusebius had
also heard that Tatian had ventured to paraphrase certain utterances of Paul to improve their style. Perhaps this rumor should be
connected with the book of *Problems* mentioned by Tatian's former pupil Rhodo; in it Tatian promised to explain the obscure and
hidden parts of the scriptures.[6] Clearly Tatian was deeply concerned with exegesis of the New Testament, as we learn from
the one fragment of his book *On Perfection according to the
Savior* which has been preserved (Clement, *Miscellanies* iii. 81).
Here Tatian takes the anti-ascetic verses of I Cor. 7:3–6 and
twists them in an Encratite direction. No doubt he thought he
was improving Paul's style. Rufinus' statement that Tatian wrote
a *Chronicon,* or chronological work (*Church History* vi. 11)
probably arose from confusion over the concluding chronological
chapters of the *Address*.

Tatian's great work, however, was his *Diatessaron,* or interweaving of the Four Gospels into one continuous narrative. This
was probably written in Greek, for a Greek fragment of it, written probably early in the third century, was discovered at Dura-

---

[6] Rhodo, converted to Christianity by Tatian, wrote *Against the Heresy
of Marcion* and a commentary *On the Six Days' Work of Creation;* he
considered writing a book of *Solutions* of Tatian's *Problems* (Eusebius,
Church History iv. 13).

Europos on the Euphrates in 1933 and was published by C. H. Kraeling two years later; but its chief significance was in the Syriac version into which Tatian immediately put it, apparently for missionary use in Syria. It had a remarkable success, became the first Christian scripture of the Syriac-speaking Christians, and was not displaced from their scriptures until the appearance of the Peshitto New Testament in A.D. 411. Tatian with his Syriac *Diatessaron* seems to have been the founder of Syriac Christianity. Eusebius and Epiphanius both mention Tatian and the *Diatessaron*, but our best glimpse of it comes from Theodoret, who was bishop of Cyrrhus, west of the Euphrates. In his *Epitome* of heresy written about A.D. 453 he relates (1:20) that he found more than two hundred copies of the *Diatessaron* held in honor among the churches, which he gathered up and replaced with the gospels of the four evangelists. This process was probably generally followed after the introduction of the Peshitto version in 411, and the result is that, although Peshitto manuscripts are numerous, not a single copy of the *Diatessaron* in Syriac has yet been found.

It has survived, however, in an Arabic version, published by Ciasca in 1888, and a Latin form of it in the Vulgate text takes the place of the Four Gospels in the Codex Fuldensis, A.D. 541–46. Efrem (d. 373) wrote a commentary on it in Syriac; this work has recently been found,[7] and a sixth-century Armenian version of it was published in a Latin translation by Moesinger in 1876. An Old German version of the Fuldensis Latin and a Dutch version made from the Syriac itself have also appeared. The recent discovery of a small Greek fragment at Dura-Europos has already been mentioned and encourages the hope that substantial parts at least of the early Greek or Syriac forms of this remarkable work may yet be found.

Tatian must have been a strong personality, as not only Rhodo but Clement of Alexandria seem to have been among his pupils; for when, at the beginning of the *Miscellanies* i. 1. 11, Clement speaks of his teachers, the first of them, whom he describes as born in Assyria and heard by him in Greece, is generally identified as Tatian. In the so-called *Little Labyrinth* Hippolytus mentions Tatian as an apologist. But numerous writers refer to him as a heretic—Irenaeus, Clement of Alexandria, Tertullian, Origen, Eusebius, and the author of the *Acts of Archelaus*. What the Fa-

---

[7] Cf. L. Leloir in *Biblica* XL (1959), 959–70.

thers found most unpardonable in Tatian was his idea that Adam was not saved—a view that he was said to have originated, although later writers, like the author of the *Acts of Pilate*, held that Adam was saved when Christ descended into Hades and preached the gospel to the dead (24:2). Medieval miniatures show Christ emerging from Hades, leading Adam by the hand.

Marcion

One of the most dynamic characters in Christian history in the second century was Marcion. Although he wrote little himself, books were written about him and against him, and for a time he seemed to bid fair to dominate the Christian movement and to reshape its scripture, organization, and views. Certainly in organization and scripture, standard Christianity learned much from Marcion, and his influence can be traced in the later effort to organize Christianity into one great body and to add the letters of Paul to its scripture. Marcion was the first man, as far as we know, to attempt these things.

Marcion was the son of the bishop of Sinope in Pontus. He was born about A.D. 85 and grew up to be a man of affairs, a well-to-do shipowner of Sinope. He felt the incongruity between the picture of God the Creator in the Jewish scriptures, which were the Bible of the churches, and the merciful and loving Father revealed by Jesus. He concluded that they were different beings and, since the Jewish Bible was so largely concerned with the Creator, that it should be dislodged from its place in Christian worship and replaced by really Christian books—the Gospel of Luke and the ten letters of Paul. He went to Rome about A.D. 138 and gave money to the church there, but left the church about 144, although he continued his efforts to prevail upon the western churches to unite upon his platform. He almost succeeded, for Justin, writing in Rome some ten years later, says that Marcion was still at work and had attracted followers from every race (*Apology* 26:5; 58:1).

Marcion wrote but one book, his *Antitheses*, or *Contradictions*. It was written about the middle of the second century or soon after. In it he sought to show how different Christianity was from what the Jewish prophets had foretold; how history and prophecy had, in fact, contradicted each other. (This idea had been broached as far back as the writing of Matthew, which was written in part to meet it.) The Law and the Gospel were set forth as irreconcilable opposites. Passages in Jewish and Christian writings were set up in contrast to each other and probably interpreted, but not by the allegorical method then so popular, for Marcion strongly condemned it. Justin's *Dialogue with the Jew Trypho*, written in Rome within five or ten years after Marcion's book, has this position in mind in its insistence that Jewish prophecy was fulfilled in Christian history. In fact, the *Dialogue* may be regarded as a counterattack to Marcion's *Antitheses*, so directly does it oppose the central idea of Marcion's book.

Marcion was also immediately opposed, as we have seen, by Justin, who presumably dealt with him faithfully in his book *Against All Heresies* and may have written a special treatise, *Against Marcion*. Theophilus of Antioch, who flourished about A.D. 181–90, wrote a treatise, *Against Marcion*, which is mentioned by Eusebius (*Church History* iv. 24. 3) and was very probably made immediate use of by Irenaeus, but is now lost. Irenaeus tells of Marcion in the same decade (A.D. 181–89) in his books *Against Heresies* (i. 27. 2; iii. 3. 4) and more than once declared his intention of writing a special treatise against him (i. 27. 4; iii. 12. 12). Eusebius quotes this promise, *Church History* v. 8. 9, and in iv. 25 speaks as though Irenaeus had written such a work; but, if he did so, nothing is known of it, and Eusebius may be referring to his treatment of Marcion along with the other schismatics in the *Refutation*. He associates him with an otherwise unknown Philip of Gortyna, who "wrote a most elaborate work against Marcion," and a certain Modestus, who, Eusebius says, "exposed the man's error more clearly than the rest." He also mentions Rhodo, a convert of Tatian's, as writing a book *Against Marcion*, probably at Rome, about A.D. 180–90, but now lost (*Church History* v. 13. 1).

Few fragments of Marcion's book have been identified, but among them is its opening sentence. Marcion is speaking of the Gospel: "O wealth of riches! Folly, power and ecstasy!—Seeing that there can be nothing to say about it, or to imagine about it, or to compare it to!"[8] It was evidently a book rich in paradox and fraught with strong emotion.

---

[8] From a Syriac and Armenian "Exposition of the Gospel," especially the Parables, published by J. Schaefer (1917); as revised by Harnack, *Marcion: Das Evangelium vom fremden Gott* (2d ed., Leipzig, 1924), p. 256, and Burkitt, *Journal of Theological Studies*, XXX (1929), 279-80.

What with Justin, Rhodo, Theophilus, Irenaeus, Philip, and Modestus there was evidently a whole barrage of books against Marcion. That none of them survived was partly caused by the decline of Marcion's movement and hence of zeal for its correction, but perhaps also by the massive and satisfying way in which Tertullian dealt with it. For Tertullian devoted one of his major works to him—the five books *Against Marcion*, the first edition, in three books, written about A.D. 200 (198–202). This was soon revised and then again revised ten or twelve years later, a fact which suggests its popularity and influence. This book remains our best source of information about Marcion, of whom Tertullian characteristically inquires, "What Pontic mouse ever had such gnawing powers as he who has gnawed the gospels to pieces?"

Hippolytus, about A.D. 230, deals with him briefly in his *Refutation* (vii. 17; x. 15), bracketing him with Cerdo, the Syrian Gnostic who had come to Rome a little before him and influenced him a good deal, although Marcion never became a complete Gnostic; he was too devoted to Paul and his doctrine of faith for that. Clement of Alexandria occasionally mentions Marcion, always to oppose his views. Origen, too, assails him now and then, as in *Against Celsus* vi. 53. Eusebius has a good deal to say about Marcion, principally about the controversial literature he provoked.

Marcion's book and his sect continued to flourish with some success for two centuries after his death. His influence upon orthodox Christianity, however, has often been exaggerated. No reader of Ignatius' letters can suppose that Marcion was responsible for the idea of a world-wide church, or for the idea of treating either the gospels or the Pauline epistles as scripture—such a notion would neglect the use of the gospels as scripture in *Barnabas* and *II Clement*, to look no farther. Harnack once remarked that in the second century Marcion was the only man who tried to understand Paul—and he misunderstood him. This remark is unfortunate because it not only assumes that Paul should be understood apart from the context of the church but also neglects the obvious influence of central Pauline ideas in *I Clement* and Ignatius.

9

THE SUCCESSORS OF JUSTIN

Melito of Sardis

The Lydian city of Sardis, in Asia, was the seat of a Christian church before the end of the first century, as the Revelation shows (3:1–6), and in the time of Marcus Aurelius its bishop was one of the ablest and most prolific writers of his day—Melito of Sardis. He is credited with having written eighteen and perhaps twenty works, chiefly on the evidence of Eusebius, who in *Church History* iv. 26. 2 gives this list: *On the Passover* (two books), *On the Conduct of Life and the Prophets, On the Church, On the Lord's Day, On the Faith of Man, On His Creation, On the Obedience of Faith, On the Senses, On the Soul and Body, On Baptism, On Truth, On the Creation and Generation of Christ, On Prophecy, On Hospitality, A Key* (to the scriptures), *On the Devil and the Revelation of John,* and finally, the *Apology*. He later mentions the *Extracts* (iv. 26. 13), or *Selections from the Old Testament,* of which Jerome says there were six books. Eusebius preserves the opening paragraph of this work. It was addressed to a brother Onesimus and gives the list of the Hebrew scriptures as current in Palestine.

The *Apology* was written probably between A.D. 169 and 176, certainly by 180. Three passages from it, making about a page in all, are quoted by Eusebius (*Church History* iv. 26. 5–11). Another small fragment—a part of a sentence—is preserved in the *Paschal Chronicle*. Melito points out to the emperor that the church had proved a benefit to the empire and should be regarded as a bulwark and ally of it, not as a hostile force. Even these are enough to show that Melito's *Apology* influenced Tertullian's.

Small fragments of at least six other works have been recovered from various sources, the longest, of little more than a page, from the work *On Baptism*. One is preserved in Origen and two in

112

Anastasius of Sinai, altogether a meager record of so copious a writer.[1]

Anastasius of Sinai, in the seventh century, credits Melito with a work *On the Incarnation of Christ* in three or more books. He also mentions a work *On the Passion*, from which he quotes a single line: "God suffered under an Israelitish hand." It is an extraordinary thing that this homily of Melito should have gone unmentioned until the seventh century and in 1940 should have come to light, almost entire, in Greek. For among the papyri obtained from Egypt by A. Chester Beatty and the University of Michigan is one written in the fourth century and preserving no less than seventeen pages of its text, mostly in good condition, and headed with the name of Melito. In it we find almost the very words quoted by Anastasius (sec. 96): "God has been murdered! The king of Israel has been slain by an Israelitish hand!"[2]

This extraordinary discovery at last provided one substantial work of Melito, and it was buttressed by the detection of three additional fragments of the same homily, one in Greek (*Oxyrhynchus Papyri* xiii. 1600, a fifth-century leaf, covering secs. 57–63), one in Coptic (fourth century, now in the British Museum, covering secs. 12–14), and two in Syriac in the British Museum.

In 1958 another copy of Melito's homily—actually *On the Passover*, not *On the Passion*—was published by Michel Testuz from a third-century papyrus in the Bodmer collection. In addition, there are Latin paraphrases of the homily,[3] and a Coptic version which belongs to the University of Mississippi.

It has been maintained that Hippolytus and Origen were the first orthodox Christian preachers to make full use of Greek rhetorical techniques in their sermons, but that distinction must now go to Melito.[4] He revels in the ornate artificialities of Greek

---

1 The so-called *Apology of Melito* current in Syriac is now recognized as a Syriac composition, having no connection with Melito.

2 Campbell Bonner, *Homily on the Passion by Melito, Bishop of Sardis* (*Studies and Documents*, Vol. XII [London, 1940]).

3 M. Testuz, *Papyrus Bodmer XIII: Méliton de Sardes: Homélie sur la Pâque* (Geneva, 1960); H. Chadwick in *Journal of Theological Studies* XI (1960), 76–82. On the fragments of Melito see R. M. Grant in *Biblical and Patristic Studies in Memory of R. P. Casey* (ed. J. N. Birdsall and R. W. Thomson, Freiburg, 1963), 192–201.

4 E. Norden, *Die antike Kunstprosa* (Leipzig, 1898), II, 547; cf. Bonner's ed., p. 20.

rhetoric—exclamation, apostrophe, antithesis, rhetorical questions, startling forms of statement, dramatic impersonations, beginning sentence after sentence in the same way, etc. These overconscious habits of style weary the modern reader, and yet the earnestness and power of the preacher can still be felt, after all these centuries of oblivion. And, as a matter of fact, these same traits appear in the familiar fragment, a page long, from the work *On Baptism,* which has long been included among Melito's literary remains.[5]

The homily interprets the Passover, in the usual early Christian way, from Paul down (I Cor. 5:7), as symbolic of the redemptive death of Christ. Melito relates the slaying of the firstborn in Egypt and the preservation of the Hebrews; explains the Jewish Law as simply a temporary sketch or model for Christianity, which is the true and enduring work of the Great Artist; finds the sufferings of Christ foreshadowed in those of many Old Testament worthies; and bitterly condemns the Jews for their responsibility for his death.

Like most Asian bishops, Melito was a Quartodeciman; he celebrated the Passover on the fourteenth of Nisan, whatever the day of the week, so that this would be comparable to a Good Friday sermon today. His work *On the Passover* was evidently a contribution to the debate over the date of Easter, which so divided the church. It was written, as its opening lines indicate (they are quoted by Eusebius' *Church History* iv. 26. 3), in A.D. 167–68. Polycrates of Ephesus, writing to Victor of Rome when the controversy was resumed about A.D. 190, speaks of Melito as no longer living (*Church History* v. 24. 5, 6), so that his literary work as far as we can trace it fell between A.D. 167 and 190.

The new use of Greek rhetoric made by Melito in introducing it into non-schismatic Christian preaching (the Gnostics were already using it in theirs) was soon taken up by Hippolytus and Origen, and Bonner has traced the influence of this particular homily upon the work of Melito's contemporary Apollinaris of Hierapolis *On the Passover,* and upon the work of Hippolytus *On the Passover,* recently identified by Charles Martin in a sermon long erroneously ascribed to Chrysostom.[6] Clement seems to have

---

[5] Printed as No. viii among the remains of Melito in Goodspeed, *Die aeltesten Apologeten* (Göttingen, 1914), pp. 310–11.

[6] *Mélanges Franz Cumont* (Brussels, 1936), pp. 321–63.

written his work *On the Passover* (now lost) in reply to Melito's. Jerome says that Tertullian derided the declamatory elegance of Melito's style, although Tertullian was even more addicted to that sort of thing himself and should have recognized a kindred spirit in Melito. We have noted the influence of Melito's *Apology* upon Tertullian. That he influenced such men as Tertullian, Clement, and Hippolytus is sufficient proof of Melito's powers.

It is very evident that if the discovery of one fairly complete work of Melito can so alter the picture of one phase of early Christian literature, the finding of the whole library of his writings might change it a good deal more. But, as yet, probably nineteen-twentieths of his work remains lost.

Athenagoras

The defense of Christianity against misrepresentation and persecution took a variety of forms; Justin had done it in one way, and Tatian in quite another. The friendly and understanding way that Justin had tried to take was followed even more successfully by Athenagoras of Athens, who is described in the title of his book as a Christian philosopher. Athenagoras holds that Christians should be entitled to the same liberty to practice their faith that is enjoyed by other miscellaneous groups that make up the population of the empire and appeals to the emperor Marcus Aurelius to see that justice is done them.

Athenagoras repels the stock charges of atheism, cannibalism, and incest that were brought against the Christians; shows that their worship and teaching are more reasonable and moral than those of their accusers; and appeals again and again to Greek philosophers and poets in support of his claims. Indeed, over and over again Athenagoras by his quotations preserves to us a few lines of Greek poetry that have nowhere else survived, thus contributing a whole series of precious items to the Greek anthology. He is better versed in Greek literature and thought than his predecessors in Christian literature. He writes earnestly and competently and in good temper, not as an advocate but as a reasonable man.

He produced his *Apology*, or *Appeal on Behalf of Christians*, perhaps at Alexandria, between A.D. 177 and 180. Both the work and its author went unmentioned for a long time in Christian antiquity; Methodius, early in the fourth century, is the first writer to speak of him, quoting freely a passage from the *Apology*.

Philip of Side (*ca.* A.D. 430) also mentions him as flourishing in the times of "Hadrian and Antoninus" and addressing to them an apology for the Christians. But the *Apology*—the Greek manuscripts call it *Presbeia*, or *Embassy*—shows by its opening lines that it was addressed to Aurelius and Commodus, as joint emperors, a state of things that existed only in A.D. 177–80.

In A.D. 914 Arethas, the learned bishop of Caesarea, the reviser of the commentary of Andreas on the Revelation, had a manuscript written which proved of great importance. The scribe was Baanes, but Arethas himself revised and corrected the text, and the book is known as the Arethas Codex. This manuscript, now in Paris,[7] although it contained other items as well, was practically a corpus of early Christian apologies; it contained works of Clement, Justin (as was supposed), Tatian (now lost from it but preserved in the three copies early made from it), Eusebius, Athenagoras (*Apology* and *On Resurrection*), and Eusebius again. It seems to have been copied from a seventh-century manuscript and was itself the parent of three copies made from it in the eleventh, twelfth, and fourteenth centuries, portions of the Arethas manuscript having disappeared in the meantime. From each of these, further copies were made in later centuries, the whole relationship constituting one of the clearest manuscript genealogies known. This fact, together with the unique importance of its contents and the scholarly care taken in its preparation, gives the Arethas Codex great significance.

The treatise *On the Resurrection of the Dead* which accompanies the *Apology* of Athenagoras in the Arethas manuscript exhibits somewhat the same philosophical attitude that appears in the *Apology*. Athenagoras presents the reasons for believing in resurrection, basing his argument on general considerations, rather than on the narrative of the gospels about the resurrection of Jesus. Athenagoras argues not only for the possibility and actuality of resurrection but for its necessity.

Zahn suggested that Athenagoras was the philosopher of that name to whom Boëthus of Alexandria dedicated his work on Plato, not long after A.D. 180. Although this is possible, it cannot, of course, be established.

---

[7] Paris. Graec. 451.

Theophilus of Antioch

Among the notable Christian writers who sprang up in such numbers in the last third of the second century was Theophilus, the sixth bishop of Antioch (Eusebius *Church History* iv. 20). He wrote a number of books of varied character. He describes himself as being of Eastern origin, coming from near the Tigris and Euphrates (*To Autolycus* ii. 24), and indicates that he had grown to manhood before he became a Christian. Eusebius gives a short list of his works: three "elementary" works addressed *To Autolycus*, one *Against the Heresy of Hermogenes*;[8] some catechetical books—that is, instructions for those wishing to enter the church—and, finally, a discourse *Against Marcion* (*Church History* iv. 24. 1–3). Jerome (*On Illustrious Men* 25) adds a gospel harmony, or a commentary on Proverbs,[9] and from Theophilus himself we learn (iii. 30) that he had also written a work *On History*.

Of all these, the only one that has survived is the defense of Christianity, in three books, addressed to Theophilus' pagan friend *Autolycus*. As it refers to the death of Marcus Aurelius (iii. 27), which took place in A.D. 180, it must have been written after that time. But the earliest mention of it is in Lactantius, a Western writer who died about A.D. 325, who in his *Divine Institutes* i. 23 speaks of such a work of Theophilus addressed to Autolycus and quotes from it (iii. 29). The work is preserved in an eleventh-century manuscript and in two copies made directly or indirectly from it.

The three books are really independent of one another and belong to different literary categories. The first is a direct personal address, put as though Theophilus and Autolycus were face to face. It deals with the existence of God, the frailties of heathen gods, and the absurdities of idolatry and offers some analogies for the resurrection. The second is a treatise. It continues the attack upon pagan religion and contrasts the contradictory doctrines of Greek writers with the messages of the prophets. The Genesis accounts of the Creation and Fall are taken up and explained. The

---

8 The heresy of Hermogenes was that God created the world not out of nothing but out of matter eternally existent like himself; so Tertullian and Hippolytus described it.

9 *Epist. ad Algasiam* 121.

third book begins like an ordinary Greek letter: "Theophilus to Autolycus, greeting." It shows the superiority of Christianity to paganism, exposes the immorality of pagan writers and the falsity of their charges against the Christians, and gives evidence for the antiquity of Moses and the Jewish religion, of which Christians felt they were the true heirs.

Theophilus shows a good deal of familiarity with Greek literature, quoting numbers of poets and philosophers, as well as the Sibylline books, which, of course, were really more Jewish than Greek. He is also familiar with Greek rhetorical devices and uses them freely. He had a deep reverence for the Jewish Bible—the Holy Scriptures, as he often calls it. He also had a high regard for the gospels and once definitely coordinated them with the Law and the Prophets, "because they all spoke inspired by one spirit of God" (iii. 12). Theophilus gives us the first express quotation of one of the gospels that has come down to us; it is from the Gospel of John, which he describes as inspired (ii. 22).

Eusebius is the first and only Eastern Christian writer to mention Theophilus, as far as our information goes, but Theophilus' contemporary Irenaeus seems to make use of the second book (chap. 25 and 26), in which Theophilus alludes vaguely to Marcionites, although it is possible that Irenaeus was really using the lost work of Theophilus *Against Marcion* instead. Indeed, it has been argued that not only Irenaeus but Tertullian, Adamantius, Minucius Felix, Clement, Hippolytus, Julius Africanus, and Novatian were all influenced by one or another of the works of Theophilus (*Against Hermogenes, Against Marcion*); but, until further discoveries bring more of his writings to light, the extent of his contribution to Christian thought cannot be determined. Even the rather shadowy picture of his work that we possess shows that Theophilus must have been a many-sided writer—commentator, apologist, opponent of heresy, and religious teacher. But probably four-fifths of the writings of Theophilus have yet to be found.

10

ANTIHERETICAL WRITERS OF THE LATE SECOND CENTURY: IRENAEUS AND HEGESIPPUS

The Catholic Church

About A.D. 180 Christian leaders, hard pressed by nearly a century of schismatic movements, Gnostic and non-Gnostic alike, launched an intensified literary campaign against these minority groups. It is sometimes supposed that this campaign marks the creation of the "universal" or Catholic Church, but the term as such goes back to the days of Ignatius (*Smyrnaeans* 8:2) and is used to differentiate the Church as a whole from sectarians in the *Martyrdom of Polycarp*. To imagine that something new was created toward the end of the second century is to misunderstand the traditional ideals of such a writer as Irenaeus.

Irenaeus is important because he binds together the Eastern and Western Christianity of his day; he was born in Asia Minor and spent his youth in Smyrna, where he saw Polycarp and heard him speak. He tells of this in a letter that was virtually a treatise *On Sovereignty* (that of the one God), addressed to his sometime friend Florinus, a Roman ex-presbyter inclined toward the views of Valentinus. Irenaeus' middle and later life was spent at Lyons, in Gaul, where he succeeded the aged Pothinus as bishop and carried on an active mission among the Gauls, preaching to them in their own tongue. While still a presbyter at Lyons, when Montanism was at its height, he was sent to Rome with a letter of introduction to the bishop Eleutherus from the confessors who had survived the persecution of A.D. 177. Irenaeus thus knew Christianity East and West—Asian, Gallic, and Roman; he participated in the controversies over Gnosticism, Montanism, and the Quartodeciman question.

Against Heresies or Refutation

Irenaeus was not only an active missionary churchman; he was also one of the leading Christian writers of his day, and his work describing and attacking the heretical movements of his times is the most important work of its kind that has come down to us from the second century. (We do not possess Justin's treatise *Against All Heresies* or the writings of Theophilus *Against Marcion* and *Against Hermogenes*.) He set out, it is true, to deal with the Gnostic heresy and called his book a *Refutation of Gnosticism* ("Gnosis falsely so called," cf. I Tim. 6:20, where the same phrase is used). But, as he advanced, the work grew under his hand, and, before he had finished, he had covered not only Gnosticism in its various forms (Books i and ii) but had presented the sound Christian position as he understood it (Books iii–v).

Irenaeus appeals to the fact that some churches of apostolic foundation had maintained an unbroken tradition of sound Christian teaching and so should, when he wrote, be trustworthy centers of the faith as the apostles had taught it. As he was writing in the West, he pointed to the Roman church as such a center and appealed to its tradition of Christian truth through an unbroken line of bishops in support of the standard type of Christianity (*Haer.* iii. 3. 2). He gives a list of these Roman bishops reaching down from the days of the apostles to his own contemporary Eleutherus (iii. 3. 3), in whose episcopate, A.D. 175–89, he evidently wrote his third book, and probably all five books, of his work.

Irenaeus also appealed to a Christian scripture, not only an Old Testament and the Four Gospels (iii. 11. 8) but the Acts (iii. 12. 15) and the letters of Paul. In fact, Irenaeus is the first Christian writer who can be shown to have had something like what we understand by the New Testament, at least in its earliest form of twenty-two books—four gospels, the Acts, thirteen letters of Paul (including the three Pastorals, to Timothy and Titus), I John and I Peter, the Revelation of John, and the *Shepherd* of Hermas. With Irenaeus, Christians began to call these books "scriptures" just as they did the Jewish books of our Old Testament.

In these more constructive books of his *Refutation*, Irenaeus still has his eye on the heretics, for he occasionally deals with the positions of Marcion, the Ebionites, and others. His book has been well described as a treasure house from which later writers on the heresies drew. He himself was indebted for material to Justin, from whose book *Against Marcion* he quotes (iv. 6. 2), to Hegesippus, and probably to Theophilus. His own work, on the other hand, was later used by the anti-heretical writers Hippolytus and Epiphanius. He was the most important anti-Gnostic writer of antiquity. His practice of quoting characteristic passages from the writings of leading schismatics that have since disappeared makes him an invaluable source of information about them, although of course he is writing polemic, not dispassionate descriptions. And the positive statement of Christian views that forms more than half his great book reveals him as a notable definer and developer of Christian thought.

It is a curious fact that so important a book as Irenaeus' treatise should have disappeared, but in its original Greek form it has nowhere been found; except for quotations from it in later writers, our knowledge of it is largely dependent upon an early Latin translation of it, which is extant in numerous manuscripts. There is also an Armenian version of Books iv and v,[1] besides fragments of a Syriac translation. Some portions of the Greek original are known, quoted in the pages of Hippolytus, Eusebius, and Epiphanius or unearthed in fragmentary papyri now chiefly at Jena. But one, found at Oxyrhynchus, is believed to have been written in the late second or early third century, so that it is almost contemporary with Irenaeus.[2]

Other Writings

In addition to his major work, Irenaeus wrote a number of other books. Eusebius mentions one *On Knowledge*, "written against the Greeks," as he says (*Church History* v. 26. 1). Jerome mistakenly thought this was two books (*On Illustrious Men* 35). Eusebius also mentioned a book dedicated to a certain brother named Marcianus, entitled *In Demonstration of the Apostolic Preaching*, and a "book of various dissertations." This *Demonstration*, long lost, was discovered in 1904, at Eriwan, in Armenia, in an Armenian translation, and published with a German translation in 1907.[3] The book is a short one, of seventy-five or eighty pages, and was designed to give the intelligent Christian a sum-

---

[1] *Texte und Untersuchungen*, XXXV, 2 (1910).

[2] *Oxyrhynchus Papyri* iii. 405; iv, p. 264.

[3] *Texte und Untersuchungen*, XXXI, 1.

mary of the Christian positions and the grounds for them. It gives new evidence of Irenaeus' debt to Justin Martyr but shows the advance Christian thought was making in the hands of men like Irenaeus.

Irenaeus also wrote a number of letters that, to judge by their names, must have been almost treatises. Eusebius mentions one to Blastus *On Schism*, one *On the Ogdoad*, and one to Florinus *On Sovereignty* (*Church History* v. 20. 1). From this he quotes an important passage bearing on Polycarp, and on Irenaeus' memories of him (*Church History* v. 20. 2–8).

Irenaeus himself says that he intends to write a book devoted to exposing the errors of Marcion (i. 27. 4; iii. 12. 12), and Eusebius (*Church History* iv. 25) lists him among the writers against Marcion. The others he mentions are Philip of Gortyna and Modestus, and, of the three, he declares Modestus the most effective. But all these works on Marcion have disappeared.

Irenaeus participated in the paschal controversy, so bitter in his day, between Polycrates and Ephesus and Victor of Rome. The important letter written by Polycrates to Victor on the subject is preserved in part in *Church History* v. 24. 2–8. Victor replied by excommunicating all the churches of Asia, which were represented by Polycrates. Irenaeus sought to calm the storm with a letter to Victor, pointing out that the East had long differed from the West in this matter, and yet the churches had respected and tolerated these differences of practice, and urging that they continue to do so. Parts of this wise and temperate letter are preserved in Eusebius (*Church History* v. 24. 12–17). Eusebius adds that Irenaeus corresponded with most of the other Christian leaders of his day on this matter. He rightly held that Victor should not excommunicate whole churches of God.

A few other fragments of Irenaeus have been discovered in later writers like John of Damascus, A.D. 675–749, but some of the fragments ascribed to him have been found to be modern forgeries, in particular those published in the middle of the eighteenth century by C. M. Pfaff (d. 1760).[4] It is evident that it would greatly

---

[4] See Harnack, *Texte und Untersuchungen*, XX, 3 (1900), 1 ff. On the fragments see R. M. Grant, "The Fragments of the Greek Apologists and Irenaeus," in J. N. Birdsall and R. W. Thomson (eds.), *Biblical and Patristic Studies in Memory of Robert Pierce Casey*, 179–218.

serve the study of early Christian literature to find any one of
the works of Irenaeus in the original Greek.

The Memoirs of Hegesippus

Luke's two volumes on Christian beginnings had pointed the way
for the Christian historian, but for a long time little was done to
carry on the work of a history of the church. The first writer to
take any steps in that direction was Hegesippus. He came from
the East, and his knowledge of Aramaic and Hebrew led Eusebius
to think he must have been of Jewish birth, but this is more than
doubtful. Probably he was a gentile Christian of Syria. He traveled from the East to Corinth, and spent some time there, pro-
ceeding thence to Rome, perhaps about A.D. 155–60, and later returning to the East to write, or at least to finish, his book, which
he completed while Eleutherus was bishop of Rome (A.D. 174–89),
probably about A.D. 180.

The real motive of Hegesippus in writing his five books of
Memoirs was polemical rather than historical. He wrote to prove
the superior claims of Christian apostolic tradition against the
vagaries of the sects. Agrippa Castor, about A.D. 135, had begun
the literary warfare against Gnosticism, with his *Refutation*,
which was particularly directed against Basilides (*Church History*
iv. 7. 6–8). Later Justin carried on the fight in his lost book
Against All Heresies, and Dionysius, bishop of Corinth (*ca.* A.D.
170), wrote a letter to the church of Nicomedia, in Bithynia,
attacking Marcion's views, as Eusebius informs us (*Church History* iv. 23. 4). Eusebius reports a whole series of books entitled
Against Marcion about this time, as we have seen in connection
with Justin and Tatian.

Hegesippus was widely traveled and knew the East as well as
the West, and he made use of a variety of historical materials,
most uncritically, of course, in championing apostolic Christianity
as he understood it against the sects. He said that on his journey
to Rome he met many bishops and received the same doctrine
from them all (*Church History* iv. 22. 1). Hegesippus gives a list
of the Christian sects and describes the Marcionites and Gnostics as
arising from a Jewish sect, the Masbotheans. He lists the seven
Jewish sects, as Justin had done (*Dialogue* lxxx. 4), but agrees
with Justin in only four of the seven named. But it is likely that

he made use of Justin's book *Against All Heresies*, which had appeared some twenty-five years before (*ca.* A.D. 150).

The *Memoirs* have unfortunately disappeared, but Eusebius made a good deal of use of Hegesippus, especially valuing the pieces of Christian Palestinian tradition that he supplied. He often quotes him at length, his most notable use of Hegesippus being the latter's account of the life and martyrdom of Jesus' brother James, who was thrown from the pinnacle of the temple and then stoned and beaten to death by the Jews (*Church History* ii. 23. 3–18). Of almost as much interest is his story of Domitian and the grandsons of Jesus' brother Jude. He says that the emperor was seeking out any descendants of David, as possible leaders of insurrection, and his agent found two grandsons of Jude who were farmers, cultivating a little farm of thirty-nine acres. They showed their toilworn hands, and were so manifestly harmless peasants that the emperor let them go (*Church History* iii. 20. 1–8). So, however careless Hegesippus was, his book would be of great interest to students of primitive Christianity if it could be found.

The *Memoirs* were used almost immediately by Irenaeus, A.D. 181–89, in his great work against heresies, or *Refutation of Gnosticism*, and by Clement of Alexandria, in his lost *Outlines*, as Eusebius' references to the two writers show (*Church History* ii. 1. 3, 4; 23. 3). Neither Clement nor Origen actually mentions Hegesippus, in such of their writings that are extant, but Eusebius owed much to him, perhaps even more than he credits him with. Indeed both historical and polemical writers were indebted to Hegesippus. But his work does not seem to have long survived; as the sects disappeared, books about them, like those of Justin, Hegesippus, Irenaeus, and Hippolytus, likewise disappeared; they were no longer of interest. Jerome and Sozomen (*ca.* 440) probably knew Hegesippus only from Eusebius' account of him. But Philip of Side made use of his work in his *Christian History*, written about A.D. 430 but now for the most part lost;[5] and Photius, about A.D. 890 (*Bibliotheca*, cod. 232), quotes a passage from Hegesippus that he had found in the work of Stephen Gobarus, now lost.

---

[5] Philip said that Hegesippus gave the names of Jesus' relatives called before Domitian as Zoker and Jacob.

It would be difficult to name a lost book of early Christian literature that would be more warmly welcomed than the five books of the *Memoirs* (*Hypomnemata*) of Hegesippus. They may possibly be preserved somewhere under the name of Josephus, which was sometimes confused with that of Hegesippus in the Middle Ages.[6]

---

[6] Cf. also N. Hyldahl, "Hegesipps Hypomnemata," *Studia Theologica*, XIV (1960), 70–113; W. Telfer, "Was Hegesippus a Jew?" *Harvard Theological Review*, LII (1960), 143–53.

11

THE ALEXANDRIANS: CLEMENT

The First Christian School

The first school established by Christians of which we have any knowledge was at Alexandria, designed to instruct converts from paganism in Christian truth. Just when it was instituted we do not know, but it must have been in operation soon after the middle of the second century. For a long time it was headed by Pantaenus, a man of piety and force, but a teacher rather than a writer in the Christian cause. To this school came probably about A.D. 180 a young man named Titus Flavius Clemens, who took up his studies with such vigor and ability that he became the assistant of Pantaenus and finally his successor. His later career as teacher and writer was so identified with Alexandria that he came to be known as Clement of Alexandria.

Pantaenus

Most of what we know of his master Pantaenus we learn from Clement, who seems to refer to him when he speaks of the "blessed presbyter"; he very rarely mentions his name. Alexander of Jerusalem, Origen, Pamphilus, and Eusebius all mention Pantaenus and speak of him with respect. Eusebius and Jerome went so far as to credit him with a good deal of writing, probably through a misunderstanding of what Clement had said. Clement himself shows that Pantaenus left no writings behind him (*Miscellanies* i. 1. 11).

It was Pantaenus who taught Clement that Paul was the author of Hebrews (*Church History* vi. 14. 4), and it was through Clement that this idea became established in the Eastern church and extended finally, two centuries later, to the West as well. Alexander of Jerusalem was another of his pupils and admirers (*Church History* vi. 14. 8). Lightfoot suggested that Pantaenus might have been the author of the work from which, he thought, the last two chapters of the *Letter to Diognetus* were taken and pointed out that such language on the part of Pantaenus might have led Photius (*Bibliotheca* 118) to say, quite erroneously of course, that Pantaenus had heard the apostles preach.[1] But Clement clearly implies in *Miscellanies* i. 1 that he had to depend on his notes and his memory for the teachings of his masters, the elders, or presbyters, as he calls them; and in *Selections* 27 he distinctly says, "The elders did not write." Of course, if Tatian was actually one of Clement's teachers, Clement certainly did not have him in mind when he wrote this.

Pantaenus was the last of Clement's teachers and the one who gave him most satisfaction. "When I came upon the last (he was first in power), having tracked him out, concealed in Egypt, I found rest. He, the true Sicilian bee, gathering the spoil of the flowers of the prophetic and apostolic meadow, engendered in the souls of his hearers a deathless element of knowledge."

Origen appeals to the practice of Pantaenus in defense of his own custom of dealing with the teachings of the philosophers as a proper part of Christian studies (*Church History* vi. 19. 13). Both Eusebius and Jerome say that Pantaenus went on a mission to India (*Church History* v. 10. 3; *On Illustrious Men* 36).

Clement

Clement was himself a native of Athens and was probably of pagan parentage. He traveled widely about the world, pursuing his studies under a series of masters, of whom he speaks half playfully, but most obscurely, in the opening pages of his *Miscellanies*, which were in part at least the result of years of diligent note-taking.

Now this work of mine is not a writing artfully constructed for display, but my notes are stored up for old age, as a remedy against forgetfulness, an image without art, and a rough sketch of those powerful and animated discourses which it was my privilege to hear, and of blessed and truly remarkable men.

Of these, one was in Greece, an Ionian; another in Magna Graecia; another of them from Coele-Syria, and another from Egypt. Others were in the East, one born in Assyria, and another, a Hebrew, in Palestine.

[1] J. B. Lightfoot and J. R. Harmer, *The Apostolic Fathers* (2d ed.; London and New York, 1893), pp. 488–89.

Clement seems to have had six teachers before he found his way to Pantaenus, but it is difficult to name any of them, except probably the Assyrian, who must have been Tatian. That Tatian's later views were very objectionable to Clement does not conflict with this.

Clement probably began to assist Pantaenus about A.D. 190, and actively taught at Alexandria until about 202, doing most of his writing in these twelve years. The outbreak of the persecution of Severus drove him from Alexandria, and apparently he never returned. When Alexander (later bishop of Jerusalem) wrote his letter from prison to Antioch, A.D. 211, he sent it by Clement (*Church History* vi. 11. 6), so that Clement was still alive at that date, but we cannot trace him after that time. Alexander tells of the useful work that Clement (also called "the blessed presbyter") has been doing for the church at Caesarea in Cappadocia while its bishop, Alexander himself, was in prison. In another letter, written to Origen not later than A.D. 217, Alexander speaks of Clement as deceased (*Church History* vi. 14. 9). Clement's death must therefore have occurred not far from A.D. 215. Our last glimpse of him is in Cappadocian Caesarea in A.D. 211, strengthening and building up the church there.

It is interesting to observe that although Alexander of Jerusalem speaks favorably of both Pantaenus and Clement when he writes to Origen, Clement is not mentioned in Origen's reply—or indeed in any of his works. Scholars have rightly pointed out that the official church school of Alexandria began with Origen, not with Clement. Furthermore, it would appear that Origen actively disapproved of Clement. Forty years after the persecution of the year 202, in which Origen's father was a martyr, he still looked back to the period as a golden age of faith and devotion, but Clement had avoided martyrdom by leaving Alexandria!

Clement had traveled and studied widely; he seems to have visited Ionia, Middle Syria, Palestine, southern Italy, and Egypt in his pursuit of learning. And he had studied well. His firsthand acquaintance with scripture and classics exceeds that of any Christian writer before him, and of this lore he made good use in his literary efforts to propagate the gospel.

For Clement was not content, like his master Pantaenus, with lecturing to his pupils; he committed his views to writing and expressed himself in the form of books, and books on a grand scale.

Whether he planned a great cycle, after the threefold organization of the pagan mysteries—Purification, Instruction, Revelation—may be doubted. Certainly such a plan was never completed, if he ever contemplated it.

Eusebius gives a long list of Clement's works:

The *Miscellanies (Stromateis)*, in eight books
The *Outlines* (of holy scripture), in eight books
The *Address to the Greeks* (the *Protrepticus*)
The *Tutor* (the *Paedagogus*), in three books
What Rich Man Can Be Saved?—a tract, or sermon
On the Passover
On Fasting
On Evil-speaking
On Patience, a discourse to the newly baptized
Against the Judaizers, on the rule of the church

Besides these ten works listed by Eusebius, Clement wrote one *On Providence* (two books) of which some fragments exist, and one, Palladius says,[2] *On the Prophet Amos*, but of this there are no remains.

Of these twelve books, the majority have almost entirely disappeared, but three of Clement's major works survive: The *Miscellanies*, the *Address*, and the *Tutor*. We have also the tract or sermon, *What Rich Man Can Be Saved?* and part of the *Outlines*. All these books seem to have been written while Clement was still at Alexandria, that is, by A.D. 202.

The *Protrepticus*, or *Address*, was directed to pagan readers and designed to clear the way for the presentation of Christianity by showing the folly of idolatry and the failure of their old faiths and philosophies to bring them the salvation they needed. The immoralities of Greek mythology, the prostitution of Greek art, and the vagaries of the philosophers are unsparingly set forth, with an extraordinary amount of direct quotation, often of Greek classics now lost. Yet these philosophers, Clement goes on to say, sometimes did find the truth and spoke by divine inspiration—Plato and Socrates and Cleanthes and Pythagoras. In the Greek poets, too, Clement often finds divine truth expressed. But the true teaching is to be found in the prophets. Clement calls upon the pagan Greeks to repent and accept the salvation offered them through

---

[2] *Lausiac History* 139.

Christ. The *Address* is a spirited, richly illustrated, penetrating, and moving appeal.

The *Tutor*, the second book in Clement's sequence, for to that extent at any rate, his sequence did extend, frankly regards its readers as children in spiritual matters and proceeds to teach them in the name of Jesus, the divine Instructor. "We are the children," says Clement. The true basis of morality is set forth and intemperance, extravagance, frivolity, luxury, matrimonial relations, dress, and personal habits are frankly and fully dealt with. Incidentally, an extraordinarily bold and detailed, almost photographic, picture emerges of ancient life, its vanities, foibles, and fashions, as the background against which a Christian morality was being developed. Modestly, frugality, simplicity, and decency are to be the Christian practice. Clement shows how the Christian is to dress, walk, talk, look, and even laugh, and what his attitude should be to jewelry, cosmetics, amusements, and public spectacles. After a veritable volley of scripture texts bearing on the good life, Clement closes with an extraordinary hymn, addressed to Christ. The hymn is uttered ostensibly by children, but really, of course, by all believers, thought of by Clement as children. It may have formed part of the liturgy of the Alexandrian church and, with its string of disconnected epithets, twelve of them at one time, recalls the Isis litany found some years ago at Oxyrhynchus.[3] It marks another step in Christian hymnology already being developed, as we have seen, in the *Odes of Solomon*.[4] It has been made the basis of a modern children's hymn, widely used, beginning "Shepherd of tender youth."

If Clement meant to produce a trilogy culminating in a *Didascalus*, or *Teacher*, as some have thought, he never reached his goal, although his tract called *What Rich Man Can Be Saved?* has been thought to be possibly a part of such a work—without much plausibility. In this short work Clement argues that it is not the possession of wealth so much as its misuse that is to be condemned. Still less can the *Miscellanies* be identified as such a third book.

The *Miscellanies*, or *Scrapbooks* (*Stromateis*) disclaims any literary or orderly intention. It does this in its very title: "Scrap-

---

[3] *Oxyrhynchus Papyri* xi. 1380.

[4] Cf. H. Jordan, *Geschichte der altchristlichen Literatur* (Leipzig, 1911), pp. 458–59.

books of Gnostic Notes after the True Philosophy." Into it
Clement crammed things he wished to say or at least to preserve.
The fact that the book does not seem to come to an end accords
well with this; he kept putting things into it perhaps as long as he
lived or kept at work. The eighth book has a very different air. It
begins with a fragment on logic, which Westcott thought was
part of the introduction to the lost *Outlines*. It includes also the
Excerpts from the Valentinian Theodotus[5] and the *Selections*
from the Prophets that are evidently incomplete notes and materials Clement never found time or inclination to write up. His
method seems to have been to deal with an occasional sentence,
allegorically or doctrinally.

The *Miscellanies* have been well described as "a heterogeneous
mixture of science, philosophy, poetry, and theology," controlled
by the conviction that Christianity can satisfy man's highest intellectual yearnings.[6] Clement is a great reconciler of the intellectual
with the religious, as his hospitality to truth wherever he met it
among the writings of the philosophers shows. He argues for the
greater antiquity of Moses as against Homer and tells, in language
evidently drawn from Tatian,[7] what the Greeks owed to other
peoples. Like Tatian, too, he speaks of Christianity as a barbarian
philosophy. He thinks that philosophies and in a sense even heresies help on the finding of the truth (vi. 15). Clement is not afraid
to describe the true Gnostic, who attains gnosis (knowledge)
through virtue and does right because he loves what is right, as the
perfect man. Clement's wide acquaintance with books and his
numerous quotations from all sorts of sources come out most
strongly here, as do his breadth of view, his tolerance, and his
genial good will. The *Miscellanies* makes a decidedly positive impression, but interwoven with its argument is an undercurrent of
apologetic and also of antiheretical polemic, as Clement seeks to
regain the honorable title of Gnostic from the sects that had
appropriated and abused it.

In the *Outlines*, Eusebius says, Clement gave concise accounts

---

[5] Edited with commentary by R. P. Casey, *Excerpta ex Theodoto of Clement
of Alexandria* (*Studies and Documents*, Vol. I [London, 1934]), more adequately by F. M. Sagnard, *Clément d'Alexandrie: Extraits de Théodote*
(Paris, 1949).

[6] A. C. McGiffert, *Eusebius* (New York, 1890), p. 259.

[7] *Address*, chaps. 1, 31.

of the whole scriptures, "not passing over the disputed books;—I mean Jude and the rest of the Catholic letters and Barnabas and what is called the Revelation of Peter." It was in the *Outlines* that he declared Hebrews to be the work of Paul and quoted the authority of "the blessed presbyter" Pantaenus for that view. This book, which would be of the utmost interest, has never been found, but a considerable fragment, covering I Peter, Jude, and I and II John, is preserved in a Latin translation by Cassiodorus, under the name of the *Adumbrations of Clement.* Smaller fragments are found in Eusebius and others. Photius says that irreligious and fabulous passages occurred in them (*Bibliotheca* 109) and this may have led to their disappearance.

Of the homilies *On Fasting* and *On Evil-speaking* no pieces have been found, but there are fragments of the works *On the Passover* (called forth by Melito's book of that name), *On Patience*, and *Against the Judaizers.* There are also traces of some of his letters, the most important of which is a copy of his *Letter to Theodore* which Morton Smith discovered in 1960 at the monastery of Mar Saba near Jerusalem. Written in an eighteenth-century hand on the flyleaves of a seventeenth-century book, the letter agrees perfectly with Clement's style and vocabulary and almost certainly comes from him. In it he warns Theodore about the Carpocratians' appeal to their own secret gospel of Mark but admits that the Church of Alexandria also possesses a secret gospel that Mark wrote after he had produced the ordinary gospel at Rome and had gone to Alexandria. Clement provides a few quotations to show the way in which the secret gospel differs from the ordinary one. This secret gospel, he says, is available only to those initiated in "the greater mysteries" at Alexandria. In the course of his writings Clement indicated his intention to write five other books, on various subjects, and some of these he may have written; but, if so, they have disappeared.

Clement saw in Christianity the true philosophy and found in the works of Greek philosophers and poets an armory for its defense. It was not the least of his distinctions that he abandoned the types of Christian writing that had been customary and in the *Address* and the *Tutor* cast his views and arguments in literary forms more familiar to the Greek paganism he was seeking to reach.

Clement's liberality was illustrated in his Christian scripture, to which he admitted not only Hebrews, but *I Clement, Barnabas,* the *Shepherd* of Hermas, the *Revelation of Peter,* the *Preaching of Peter,* and the *Teaching of the Twelve Apostles;* at any rate, he quotes these books as scripture. In fact, he goes further and sometimes quotes as scripture works now quite unknown. "Take away from you the heavy yoke, and take up the easy one, says the scripture." "Ask, says the scripture, and I will do; think and I will give." "The scripture exhorts us, Be ye skilful money-changers."

Clement sometimes quoted the Sibylline books and spoke of the Sibyl as a prophetess: "Let the Sibyl prophetess be the first to sing to us the song of salvation" (*Address* 8). He knew the *Gospel of the Hebrews,* the *Gospel of the Egyptians,* and the *Traditions of Matthias,* and, although he did not accept them as scripture, he did not dismiss them as heretical.[8]

We are fortunate in possessing, almost complete, three of his major works; the beginning of the first book of the *Miscellanies* is missing, and the so-called eighth book, as we have seen, is a group of unrelated pieces, plainly unfinished. Of the *Outlines* we have little more than what Cassiodorus has left us in his translation, as the *Adumbrations.* Whatever the value of Clement's lost minor works might be, the recovery of the *Outlines* would have the utmost value for many phases of biblical study.

---

[8] On his Bible see R. M. Grant, *The Formation of the New Testament* (London and New York, 1965), pp. 164–69.

THE ALEXANDRIANS: ORIGEN

His Voluminous Writings

Origen was the greatest Christian scholar and the most prolific Christian writer of antiquity. Epiphanius declared that he wrote six thousand works, doubtless meaning rolls, or scrolls, of ordinary length, about as long as Matthew or Acts. Rufinus laughed at this and called Epiphanius a crazy old man (*delirus senex*), but Jerome rather took his side: "Which of us," said Jerome, "can read all that he has written?"

Origen was a native of Alexandria, where he was destined to carry the great tradition of Pantaenus and Clement to its peak. He was born in (A.D. 184–85. His father was a Christian teacher and suffered martyrdom in the persecution of Severus, A.D. 202, which had driven Clement from the city. Origen, then sixteen or seventeen, undertook to support his widowed mother and his six brothers and sister by teaching, and a year later, in 202–3, Demetrius, the bishop, put him at the head of the catechetical school, when he was hardly eighteen years old. For a dozen years he carried on that work with marked success.

This was his first Alexandrian period. In the course of it he traveled to Rome, visited the church there, and heard Hippolytus preach. He was also summoned to Arabia by the governor there for an interview (*Church History* vi. 19. 15). In A.D. 215 Caracalla's furious attack upon the Alexandrians interrupted Origen's work at the school and drove him from the city.

He took refuge in Palestine and lived for perhaps two years in Caesarea, preaching in the churches at the request of the bishops of Jerusalem and Caesarea. As he was not ordained, this offended his old friend Demetrius the bishop of Alexandria, and he called Origen back to resume his conduct of the school, probably about A.D. 217. About this time Origen found an able assistant in Heraclas, whose lectures later drew Julius Africanus to settle in

Alexandria for a time to hear them (*Church History* vi. 31. 2). It was in this second Alexandrian period, which lasted for thirteen years, that Origen's real work of writing began.

In 230 he traveled to Greece on some church business and, stopping at Caesarea on his way, was ordained a presbyter by Theoctistus, the bishop there. When Demetrius heard of this, he felt that his authority had been flouted, and, on Origen's return, Demetrius assembled a synod that decreed that Origen should no longer teach or live in Alexandria. Only the bishops of Palestine, Phoenicia, Arabia, and Greece stood by Origen. In this most unhappy way his work in Egypt, which was destined to prove so historic, was ended.

Origen now removed to Caesarea, where he prosecuted his studies and his work of teaching, preaching, and writing. His fame spread over the East. The emperor's mother, Julia Mamaea, invited him to visit Antioch so that she might hear him preach (*Church History* vi. 21. 3, 4). He also revisited Athens and Arabia in these years. The persecution of Maximin, A.D. 235–38, may have driven him to take refuge in Caesarea in Cappadocia and spend two years there, as Palladius says (*Lausiac History* 64), although this is not altogether certain. But in the Decian persecution, Origen was imprisoned and suffered tortures in consequence of which he soon afterward died, probably in Caesarea, but perhaps in Tyre, A.D. 254, at the age of sixty-nine.

About the time of Origen's return to Alexandria, in A.D. 217, or soon after, he made a great friend in Ambrose, a man of means and position whom he had won over from Valentinian views. Ambrose became his friend, patron, and publisher. Eusebius' account of this connection gives us the clearest picture of an ancient writer and his publisher that has come down to us anywhere. It is doubly important not only for showing one early Christian publishing house actually at work, but for the light it throws upon the immense literary output credited to Origen by ancient writers.

Eusebius says that Origen "began his commentaries on the divine scriptures being urged thereto by Ambrose, who employed innumerable incentives, not only exhorting him by word, but furnishing abundant means. For he dictated to more than seven amanuenses, who relieved each other at appointed times. And he employed no fewer copyists, besides girls who were skilled in elegant writing. For all these Ambrose furnished the necessary ex-

pense in abundance" (*Church History* vi. 23. 1, 2). It will be seen
that Ambrose not only expedited the publication of books thought
of and written by Origen but urged further undertakings upon
him, in particular his commentaries on the scriptures. "To the
management and support of Ambrose," said Harnack, "we owe a
great part of the works of Origen."[1] Origen long refused to have
his sermons taken down stenographically, but after he was sixty
he allowed this to be done. It is clear that all that ancient methods
could do was done to encourage Origen to produce, and to circulate his product. So urgent did Origen's publisher sometimes become in his demands for new books that Origen once humorously
described him as his taskmaster, or slave-driver (*ergo-dioktes*).

This great body of Origen's writings may be conveniently divided under five heads: textual studies, interpretation, theological
studies, apologetics, and letters.

On Text

Ever since the founding of the Alexandrian Museum more than
four centuries before, Alexandria had been the home of textual
study, especially of Homer, and Origen now turned a scholar's
eye upon the text of the Greek Old Testament, which formed so
great a part of the Bible of the early church. He knew it was a
translation from the Hebrew, so he obtained a Hebrew Bible, in
his day of course a mass of rolls, and learned Hebrew. The standard Greek form of the Old Testament among the churches was the
Septuagint version, but other translations had been made in the
second century by Aquila, Theodotion,[2] and the Ebionite Symmachus. Origen sought for still others and found them, one at
Nicopolis, near Actium. He also found three more translations of
the Psalms, one of them, Eusebius says, in a jar in Jericho.

Origen conceived the magnificent idea of setting out these four
versions side by side, with the Hebrew and a Greek transliteration
of it in parallel columns, to facilitate their study. This enormous
work, which could obviously be at least six times the size of the
Old Testament, seems to have been actually copied out but could
hardly have been published. This was Origen's celebrated Hexapla, his "sixfold" Old Testament, a work which, judging from the

---

[1] A. Harnack, *Geschichte der altchristlichen Litteratur* (3 vols.; Leipzig,
1893–1904), I, 328–29.

[2] Theodotion's work was really for the most part a revision of the Septuagint
version.

size of the Vatican manuscript, written a century later, must have
reached nine thousand pages.[3] It does not seem likely that it was
ever recopied, but the original passed into the hands of Origen's
admirer Pamphilus and remained for many years in the library
that he gathered in Caesarea to enshrine the memory of Origen.

The great Sinaitic manuscript of the Greek Bible, now in the
British Museum, has notes in a hand of about A.D. 600, at the end
of Esther and of Esdras (Ezra-Nehemiah), that state that the
manuscript had been compared with a very ancient one which in
turn had been corrected in prison by the martyr Pamphilus with
the aid of Origen's own copy of the Hexapla. Jerome consulted
the Hexapla in the library at Caesarea toward the end of the
fourth century. The library, with the Hexapla in it, seems to have
existed until the Saracens took Caesarea early in the seventh century (A.D. 638), for in 616–17 Paul of Tella, a Syrian bishop, translated the Septuagint column of it into Syriac, retaining Origen's
critical marks; and his translation, about half of which is preserved
in an eighth-century manuscript, is now the best window through
which we can observe the textual work of Origen.

Interpretation

Origen must have been a man of prodigious energy, for he worked
with titanic force in every field of Christian literature. Besides
pioneering in the textual study of the scriptures, his work in interpretation covered every book of the Old and New Testaments.
This ranged all the way from his scholia, or brief notes on difficult
or decisive texts, through homilies, prepared or ex tempore, to
those full-size commentaries which Ambrose prevailed upon him
to undertake. His homilies or expository sermons numbered twenty-eight on Numbers, twenty-six on Joshua, thirty-two on Isaiah,
forty-five on Jeremiah, twenty-five on Matthew, thirty-nine on
Luke, twenty-seven on Acts, and so on; these are only a few of the
items given in a long list of the works of Origen found in a letter
from Jerome to Paula and Eustochium. Not until he was sixty, it
must be remembered, would Origen permit his homilies to be
taken down when he delivered them. The list reaches at least 444
for the Old Testament (a few figures for individual psalms have
been lost) and 130 for the New. But, of these, only 21 have survived in the Greek original and only 186 in the Latin translation.

---

[3] Eusebius *Church History* vi. 16. 1–4; Jerome *On Illustrious Men* 75.

Even more important for interpretation, of course, were his commentaries, which ran to twenty-five books on the Minor Prophets, twenty-five on Matthew, thirty-two on John, fifteen on Romans, fifteen on Galatians, and so on; Origen held that each text had an inner, spiritual, mystical sense, in addition to its literal and historical meanings. Like most ancients, pagan, Jewish, or Christian, he made much use of allegory in interpretation; it was, of course, by the use of allegory that the Stoics had succeeded in making Homer the Bible of the Greeks.

In Jerome's list, which is probably far from complete, the commentaries ran to at least 177 books (rolls) for the Old Testament, and 114 for the New, or 291 in all; of these, only 16 books are preserved in Greek. It is safe to say that they represent no more than five per cent of the total bulk of the commentaries; nineteen-twentieths of them have disappeared. Even in Latin we have less than half the commentary on Matthew, and Rufinus' recast of the one on Romans and part of the one on the Song of Songs.

It must be added that no small amount of Origen's exegetical work survived piecemeal in the catenas—those collections of valuable observations found in early writers. These began to be made very early, and by A.D. 500, in the hands of Procopius of Gaza, were in full swing.

Theology

On the theological side Origen's principal works were his two books *On the Resurrection* and his four books *On First Principles* (*De principiis*). The latter is perhaps the greatest of Origen's works and marks a long step toward the formulation of Christian theology, even though to the modern reader Origen seems over-influenced in some of his thinking by philosophy and appears more Greek than Christian. In this work he followed the path Clement had taken before him, and sought to bring Greek philosophy and Christian teaching together. Unfortunately, the original Greek form has disappeared, except for a number of fragments, and we are dependent for our knowledge of it upon a free Latin translation published in Rome in A.D. 398–99 by the diligent Rufinus, the friend and then the enemy of Jerome. It was, in fact, Rufinus' unguarded reference in his preface to Jerome's admiration for Origen that offended Jerome. Jerome himself later made a more faithful translation of the book, of which only a score or so of fragments survive. The book *On the Resurrection* has also perished, except for some fragments; it called forth a reply from Methodius of Olympus (311), which is itself extant only in an Old Slavonic version but adds to our knowledge of what Origen's book contained. The book *On the Resurrection* may be regarded as a prelude to the larger work *On First Principles*. Jerome's list of Origen's works mentions also two dialogues *On the Resurrection* now lost.

Like his teacher Clement, Origen left behind him his *Scrapbooks*, or *Miscellanies (Stromateis)*, in ten books. But, except for a few small fragments, these too have been lost.

With Origen's doctrinal works may be grouped two highly practical writings of his, one *On Prayer*, written at the request of Ambrose, and one *On Martyrdom*, addressed to two Christian leaders, urging them not to flinch from it in the persecution of Maximin then just beginning (A.D. 235). Both are fortunately extant in Greek.

Apologetics

In the apologetic field Origen's great work was his reply to Celsus. That pagan thinker had directed a searching attack against Christianity, some two generations earlier, under the name of the *True Discourse*, pointing out with much penetration the faults Judaism had to find with Christian teaching and then the faults the Platonic philosophy had to find with it. It was altogether the ablest attack of the kind made upon Christianity in ancient times. It is generally referred to about A.D. 178, and it has long since disappeared, so that what we know of it is derived from the quotations Origen makes from it in his reply. No less than three-fourths of Celsus' work are preserved in this way. Origen wrote this, as he did so much of his best work, at the request of Ambrose, who felt that, although almost sixty years had passed since Celsus wrote, his book had never been adequately answered. As a matter of fact, a good many of Celsus' objections to the Christian views and claims of his day were sound and could not be answered, as Origen's effort showed. Origen sometimes resorted to what now seem artificial devices to get around them, and it took all his deep religious conviction and sound religious feeling to outweigh his pagan opponent. It has been well characterized as the peak of early Christian apologetic. *Against Celsus* was written in A.D. 246–48 and is fortunately preserved in full in Greek.

Origen's other apologetic or polemic works were no more than the taking-down of his disputations with various persons: Bassus, Beryllus of Bostra, a Valentinian named Candidus, and some Jews. These are mentioned by Africanus, Eusebius, Jerome, or Rufinus but are no longer extant except for the *Dialogue with Heraclides* (see p. 142).

Letters

Origen's letters were also numerous and important. A hundred of them were gathered into a collection by Eusebius himself, perhaps in the days when he catalogued the Origen Library at Caesarea for his teacher and patron Pamphilus (*Church History* vi. 36. 3). Jerome's list of Origen's works, probably taken from that of Eusebius, now lost, mentions others. One of the letters, written to Fabianus, bishop of Rome, in defense of his works, grew to the proportions of a treatise, in two books. But, of all these letters, only two have been preserved: the one to Africanus, in defense of Susanna as part of Daniel, and the one to Gregory Thaumaturgus, who had been converted by him and had been one of his pupils. In it Origen urges his pupils to make full use, in advancing the Christian cause, of all that Greek thought had achieved.

The enormous quantity of Origen's writing makes it necessary to group it thus according to the various fields with which it dealt. But there is also a value in viewing his principal works in their chronological order. Although Origen's activity as a writer was not notable in the early part of his work at Alexandria, down to 215–16, even in those years he was learning Hebrew and producing his Hexapla. But after his return from Caesarea to the headship of the catechetical school, in 217–18, when he was about thirty-three, his literary activity began to develop fast. It was in 218 that he began his lifelong work upon his commentaries, at the suggestion of Ambrose, who provided the publishing facilities already described. In this second Alexandrian period, 217–30, he produced his four books *On First Principles* and the ten books of *Miscellanies*. After his removal to Caesarea in 232 he wrote his exhortation *On Martyrdom* (235) and his eight books *Against Celsus* (246–48), the masterpiece of early Christian apologetic.

New Testament

Especial interest attaches to Origen's New Testament. He was fully aware of the differences that existed among Christians about what books should be included in the New Testament; and, in view of these, he was careful to divide the books which he thought belonged to the New Testament into two classes, the accepted or acknowledged books, which all Christians accepted as scripture, and the disputed books, which some did not accept. As acknowledged books Origen listed the Four Gospels, fourteen letters of Paul (including Hebrews and the letters to Timothy and Titus), the Acts of the Apostles, I Peter, I John, and the Revelation of John—twenty-two in all. The disputed books, which he himself accepted as belonging to the New Testament, were James, II and III John, Jude, II Peter, Barnabas, and the *Shepherd* of Hermas. This gave him eight general epistles and two revelations, John and Hermas. This New Testament of twenty-nine books is precisely that of the Sinaitic manuscript of the fourth century, discovered by Tischendorf in 1859.

Although Origen paid little attention to literary finish in his writings, he had great literary as well as doctrinal influence. His bold liberal views were much criticized subsequently (Anastasius, bishop of Rome, condemned him in A.D. 400), but no man had more loyal and distinguished followers. His books in Caesarea passed into the hands of his great admirer Pamphilus, who formed about them the most famous Christian library of antiquity, so diligently studied and faithfully catalogued by Eusebius (*Church History* vi. 32. 3). A few years later Pamphilus wrote a *Defense of Origen*, in five books, to which Eusebius added a sixth, probably after Pamphilus' martyrdom in A.D. 309 (*Church History* vi. 23. 4; Photius *Bibliotheca* 118). "What we know of and about Origen," said Harnack, "we owe almost exclusively to Pamphilus and Eusebius." Half a century later, in A.D. 360, Gregory of Nazianzus and Basil the Great made an anthology of what they thought the best passages in Origen, which was called the *Philocalia*, and preserves much that would otherwise have been lost.

It will be seen that two-thirds of Origen's homilies are lost, and of his commentaries nineteen-twentieths of the Greek original have disappeared. The work *On the Resurrection* is gone, as is the great one *On First Principles*, except for what is almost a rewriting of it in Latin by Rufinus. The *Miscellanies*, too, in ten books, are gone, as well as the overwhelming bulk of the letters. To this neglect of his works, what seemed the dangerous liberality of his views no doubt contributed. Yet Origen certainly deserved to be called the father of Christian theology and the founder of biblical science.

In 1941 the British were using caves near Toura in Egypt for ammunition dumps, and in one of them was discovered an assortment of works by Origen and Didymus of Alexandria (late fourth century). The most interesting of the Origen papyri is the *Discussion of Origen with Heraclides and the Bishops with him, concerning the Father, the Son, and the Soul.* This work, previously unknown, is contained in a sixth-century codex which "presumably derives from Origen's text as preserved at Caesarea."[4] As a theological expert, Origen had been called upon by several bishops otherwise unknown, and he proceeded, with copious quotations from the Bible, to set them straight on such matters as the relation of the Father to the Son (Heraclides did not understand this correctly), the nature of the resurrection body, how the soul can be called "blood" in Leviticus 17:11, and the sense in which the soul is immortal. The discussion was taken down in a kind of shorthand and later corrected, presumably by the participants. The document is a unique representative of this kind of reporting in early Christianity.[5]

Other works by or derived from Origen include a treatise *On the Pascha* and a homily on I Samuel,[6] extracts from Books I and II of the treatise *Against Celsus,*[7] and extensive fragments from Books V and VI of the *Commentary on Romans.*[8] The Romans fragments show that Rufinus' Latin translation was not as bad as has sometimes been supposed.[9]

---

[4] A. D. Nock in *American Journal of Archaeology,* LV (1951), 283.

[5] J. Scherer, *Entretien d'Origène avec Héraclide et les évêques ses collègues sur le Père, le Fils, et l'âme* (Cairo, 1949). Fragments derived from another contemporary bishop are discussed by L.-M. Froidevaux in *Recherches de science religieuse,* L (1962), 32–73.

[6] O. Guéraud in *Revue de l'histoire des religions,* CXXXI (1946), 85–108.

[7] J. Scherer, *Extraits des Livres I et II du Contre Celse d'Origène* (Cairo, 1956).

[8] J. Scherer, *Le commentaire d'Origène sur Rom. III. 5–V. 7* (Cairo, 1957).

[9] H. Chadwick in *Journal of Theological Studies,* X (1959), 10–42.

13

HIPPOLYTUS AND OTHER GREEK
WRITERS OF THE THIRD
CENTURY

Life

Among the young men whom Irenaeus taught, probably
in the years he spent at Lyons, was one named Hippolytus, who
came to be his great successor as the foremost figure of Greek
Christianity in the West. He was born about A.D. 170 (165–75)
and spent his mature life in Rome, where he became a presbyter.
When Origen visited Rome, about 215, he heard Hippolytus
preach. Hippolytus was active in the campaign against the sects
and was a prolific writer. He strongly opposed the laxity of
Zephyrinus, bishop from 198 to 217, and his assistant Calixtus, regarding them both as mercenary and self-seeking, and upon the
election of Calixtus as bishop made such a protest that the Roman
church divided into two factions, one of which actually chose
Hippolytus as bishop. He continued to hold this office in opposition to Calixtus and his successors, Urbanus (222–23 to 230) and
Pontianus. In fact, in 235, in Maximin's persecution, Hippolytus
and Pontianus were sent into exile together to the mines of Sar-
dinia, where Pontianus seems to have died. Whether Hippolytus,
too, died there or survived his exile and died in Rome the following year is uncertain. But he was buried on the road to Tivoli
(Via Tiburtina) on August 13, probably A.D. 236.

The Statue

On this road, and probably near his grave, a statue of Hippolytus,
or what was left of it, was found in 1551, and while the head and
upper part of the body were gone, the marble chair proved of
great importance, because a list of the works of Hippolytus was
carved on the back of it. Upon it were also carved the tables for

calculating the date of Easter, but as these proved erroneous by as much as three days, as early as 237, the statue can hardly be of later date than that year and was probably made and set up in 236 or 237. The schism in the church as evidently healed before the death of Hippolytus.

A hundred years ago the works of Hippolytus had almost entirely disappeared, but a series of discoveries has gone far to remedy this. One of his most notable works was his *Refutation of All Heresies,* which seemed to have perished. But in 1701 a Greek work surveying the views of the Greek philosophers, the Brahmins and the Druids, was printed by Gronovius as the *Philosophumena* of Origen. In 1842 a Greek named Minas Minoides found on Mount Athos a fourteenth-century manuscript of Books iv–x of the same work, of which the part previously published was evidently Book i. These eight books E. Miller published in 1851 as Origen's *Philosophumena or Refutation of All Heresies.* But it was soon perceived that they were not the work of Origen at all but of Hippolytus, being his long-lost *Refutation of All Heresies,* mentioned by Eusebius (as *Against All Heresies* [*Church History* vi. 22. 2]) and by Jerome (*On Illustrious Men* 61), and they were republished under the name of Hippolytus by Duncker and Schneidewin in 1859. One scholar, d'Alès, has endeavored to show that Book iv really contains Books ii and iii and part at least of Book iv, but this cannot be said to have been proved. As it is, however, these discoveries and reesarches have given us one of the major works of Hippolytus almost complete.

A long series of other discoveries has brought various lost works of Hippolytus to light in Latin, Syriac, Coptic, Arabic, Ethiopic, Armenian, Georgian, and Slavic translations. The remarkable thing is that so few of them have been preserved in Greek, but Hippolytus had been out of harmony with the dominant element in the Roman church most of his later life, and Greek very soon ceased to be the language of Roman Christianity; in fact, Hippolytus is really our last Greek writer in the Western church.

The literary work of Hippolytus was done principally between A.D. 200 and 235. The inscription on the back of the chair lists at least ten of his works, but two lines are probably lost at the top, with the upper part of the chair back.[1] Eusebius lists eight works

---

[1] The list on the chair may have purposely omitted works which would have been offensive to the rival faction in the Roman church.

but says that many others were current in his day. Jerome names nineteen, and Photius, who seems to have confused Hippolytus with Gaius, mentions a number of his works (*Bibliotheca* 48, 121, and 202) but does not attempt a unified list. Upon the basis of these and the manuscript discoveries of recent years, a list of no less than forty works of Hippolytus can be reconstructed, covering the fields of scripture interpretation, polemic and doctrinal writing, church law, and chronology. Harnack listed forty-three, of which eight are preserved, complete or nearly so, in Greek or in ancient versions; twelve are lost; and twenty-three are represented only by fragments, few or many.

Scripture Interpretation

Fully half of the books of Hippolytus that we know were devoted to the interpretation of the scriptures. His interest extended all the way from Genesis to the Revelation, but he covered very few individual books completely—Ruth, Proverbs, Song of Songs, Daniel, Revelation—usually contenting himself with discussing particular narratives or prophecies here and there.

Of some twenty-six such commentaries and homilies, we have six, either in the original Greek or in early versions, the most extended being the commentary *On Daniel* in four books, written in A.D. 203-4, which is complete in Old Slavic but is preserved in large part in Greek also. We have also the commentary *On the Song of Songs* (in Georgian); *On the Blessing of Jacob* (Genesis, chap. 49) (in Greek, Armenian, and Georgian); *On the Blessing of Moses* (Deuteronomy, chap. 33) and the *Story of David and Goliath* (I Samuel, chap. 17) (these two in Armenian and Georgian); and *On the Raising of Lazarus* (John, chap. 11), preserved in Greek among the sermons of Chrysostom but in Armenian as a work of Hippolytus. These Eastern versions show how highly the Eastern churches regarded the work of Hippolytus, although he was generally forgotten in the West. Hippolytus' method of interpretation was, of course, highly allegorical; Susanna, in Daniel, symbolized the Christian church, threatened by Jews, pagans, and heretics but saved by Christ. Yet he was less atomistic and more historical in his interpretation than his Alexandrian contemporary Origen.

The sermon that Origen on his visit to Rome heard Hippolytus preach has disappeared, but Jerome says it was *On the Praise of the Lord Our Saviour (On Illustrious Men* 61). The work *On the Passover* was found in 1936 by C. Martin among the sermons of Chrysostom.

We can name at least eighteen other exegetical writings of Hippolytus, which are either entirely lost or represented only by fragments, and it is worthwhile to mention them, if for no other reason than to facilitate their discovery, in case they still exist. For we shall find them sooner if we know what we are looking for, and some of them can probably be found.

From our various sources, already mentioned, we know that in this field he wrote on:

The Six Days of Creation. There are some Greek fragments of this and the four works following

What Followed the Six Days

The Blessing of Isaac (Genesis, chap. 27)

The Blessing of Balaam (Numbers, chaps. 23 and 24)

Moses' Song (Deuteronomy, chap. 32)

The Book of Ruth. A Greek fragment

Elkanah and Hannah (I Samuel, chap. 1). Four short Greek fragments

The Witch of Endor. A Greek fragment

The Psalms (some of them). Four Greek fragments

Proverbs. Twenty-nine fragments

Ecclesiastes. One fragment

Part of Isaiah. One Greek fragment

Parts of Ezekiel. One Greek and one Syriac fragment

Zechariah (lost)

Parts of Matthew. Possible Greek and Syriac fragments

The Parable of the Talents. One Greek fragment

The Two Thieves. Three Greek fragments

The Revelation. Some Arabic fragments

Refutation

It is as an antiheretical writer, however, that we naturally think of Hippolytus, because, of his works that have come down to us, his *Refutation of All Heresies* is the longest and most interesting. The succession of discoveries that has restored at least eight of its ten books to us in Greek has already been described. Long before he wrote it, or soon after A.D. 200, Hippolytus had written a shorter work *Against All Heresies*, also known as the work *Against Thirty-two Heresies.* (This was afterward used by various writers on heresy—Epiphanius, Philastrius [A.D. 383], and the author of an anonymous work *Against All Heresies*, long ascribed to Tertullian.) He had also written a work against the Alogi, or opponents of the Logos doctrine of John—the work *In Defense of the Gospel and Revelation of John*, probably about A.D. 204–5. This book is sometimes identified with the *Heads against Gaius*,[2] which was more probably an independent work, written a little later to defend the Revelation against the claim of a Roman Christian, perhaps a presbyter, named Gaius who in his *Dialogue with Proclus*, the leading Montanist in Rome, had maintained that the Revelation was really written by the early heretic Cerinthus.[3]

But the *Refutation* was Hippolytus' great work in this field. It made use of the earlier *Refutation* written by Hippolytus' teacher Irenaeus and perhaps of Hippolytus' own earlier work *Against Thirty-two Heresies*, written a quarter-century before. Hippolytus seeks to show that the heresies had their source in Greek philosophy and in pagan religions; this is why he devoted his first book to a survey of Greek philosophies, his (lost) second and third, probably, to the mystery religions, and his fourth to astrology and magic, in preparation for his discussion of the heresies, which begins with the fifth book. His picture of the Gnostics has been criticized as based upon secondary and biased sources and as seriously misrepresenting their views. The *Refutation* was written in the years 225–30.

Two other polemic works of his are known, at least by name: one *Against Marcion*, now lost, and one *Against Artemon*, written about A.D. 230—certainly after the *Refutation*, which makes no mention of Artemon. It was also called the *Little Labyrinth*, perhaps because it formed a sort of supplement to the *Labyrinth* (as Hippolytus may perhaps call the *Refutation*, x. 5), bringing it up to date. This, too, is lost, except for three substantial fragments preserved in Eusebius *Church History* v. 28.[4]

---

[2] There are several Syriac fragments of this work in Bar-Salibi's commentary on the Revelation, written in the twelfth century.

[3] A Greek fragment of the *Dialogue* is found in Eusebius *Church History* ii. 25. 7.

[4] A work *Against Montanism* written in Rome in the time of Hippolytus has been conjectured from its apparent use in Epiphanius *Against Heresies* 48:2–13. It seems to have made use of Tertullian's work *On Ecstasy*, written in A.D. 202–3 to 204–5, and to have been in turn attacked by him in his work *On Monogamy*. But it can hardly have been the work of Hippolytus.

Works on Doctrine

Hippolytus did not neglect the field of Christian doctrine. Perhaps the earliest of his works was that *On Christ and Antichrist*, written about A.D. 200. It was written in reply to certain topics ("heads") or questions raised by his friend Theophilus about the signs of the end. Hippolytus did not regard Rome as the kingdom of Antichrist but as the fourth of the kingdoms described in the Book of Daniel. In it he made some use of the great work of his old master Irenaeus. It is often mentioned in his Daniel commentary, written in 202–4, and is extant in full in Greek.

A work *On the Resurrection*, addressed to the empress Julia Mamaea, was composed sometime during the reign of her son Alexander Severus, A.D. 222–35. Only a few Greek and Syriac fragments remain of it.

A work *On the Universe, against the Greeks and Plato*, is mentioned by medieval writers (Photius, Philoponus) as the work of Josephus or Gaius but was pretty certainly written by Hippolytus, for he mentions it as his in *Refutation* x. 28, so that it was evidently written before 225. It was in two books, but only a few Greek fragments remain. (See W. J. Malley in *Journal of Theological Studies*, XVI [1965], 13–25.)

We have also the titles of two other works—the *Address to Severina* and *On Good and the Source of Evil*—but both are lost, and there seem to be no identifiable fragments, so that their dates cannot be determined.

The Chronicle

Yet another phase of Hippolytus' literary work was as a chronicler. As early as A.D. 222–23 he had written his *Determination of the Date of Easter*, which is mentioned in the chair list and also by Eusebius (*Church History* vi. 22. 1); the Easter table carved on the side of the chair is taken from it. Aside from that, it is lost, but a similar work in Latin (*De Pascha computus*), written in A.D. 242–43 and wrongly ascribed to Cyprian, may be regarded as a corrected form of it. But now in A.D. 234 he wrote his *Chronicle* (*Chronicon*). In scope the book was a chronicle of world history from the Creation to A.D. 234, the date of its composition. The Greek original of it is lost, except for some fragments, principally a leaf of a sixth- or seventh-century papyrus book from Oxyrhynchus (*Oxyrhynchus Papyri* vi. 870) and a considerable portion found in a Madrid manuscript. But a good part of it is preserved, sometimes more or less modified, in three different Latin versions, and there is also an Armenian translation. It made use of the "Little Chronology" in the *Miscellanies* of Clement of Alexandria (i. 21. 109–36) and also of the *Chronography* of Julius Africanus, which had recently appeared in A.D. 221. Hippolytus shared the view of Africanus that the "Last Day" (of a thousand years) would follow the year of the world 6000 and was careful to prove that the year he wrote was the year of the world 5738. One of the book's most important features was the "Diamerismos" or "Division" of the earth among the posterity of Noah (Genesis, chap. 10), which was often reflected in later writers. The Madrid manuscript shows that the "Diamerismos" included the "Stadiasmos" or measurement in stadia of the Great Sea, a kind of navigation book for the Mediterranean.

The Apostolic Tradition

Recent research has restored to us still another lost work of Hippolytus and revealed another side of his literary activity. In the list of Hippolytus' works on the chair, one line reads: "The Apostolic Tradition About Gifts" (*charismata*), which probably covers two works, one the *Apostolic Tradition*, and the other *About Gifts*. These have long been reckoned among his lost writings. But a series of discoveries and researches has now resulted in the recovery of the *Apostolic Tradition*, which is identified with the so-called *Egyptian Church Order*. This work came to be so named because it first came to modern notice in a Coptic translation, brought from Egypt and published by Tattam in 1848. But, in 1900, Hauer discovered and published, from a palimpsest at Verona, a Latin form of it much nearer to the original Greek and strongly suggesting that the work was in substance not Egyptian at all. The investigations of Schwartz (1910), and others independently carried on by Connolly (1916),[5] showed that the book lying back of these versions or revisions was none other than the long lost *Apostolic Tradition* of Hippolytus, and in this view scholars have generally concurred.[6]

The book tells how bishops, presbyters, and deacons are to be

---

[5] *The So-called Egyptian Church Order and Derived Documents* (Cambridge, 1916).

[6] So B. S. Easton, *The Apostolic Tradition of Hippolytus* (Cambridge, 1934), and Gregory Dix, *The Treatise on the Apostolic Tradition of St. Hippolytus of Rome* (London, 1937).

ordained, giving the prayers to be uttered; tells of confessors, widows, virgins, new converts, crafts forbidden to Christians, of baptism, confirmation, church observances, fasts, prayers, and so forth—all in a most concise and practical fashion. It is clear that Hippolytus has the distinction of having been the leader in codifying church procedure. The book is a small compact manual, written probably about A.D. 215, in the last part of the episcopate of Zephyrinus, of whom Hippolytus complained that he was ignorant of the rules of the church (*Refutation* ix. 11).

The *Apostolic Tradition* was later rewritten and worked into the *Apostolical Constitutions*, viii. 4–32. From these the so-called *Constitutions through Hippolytus* were epitomized. The so-called *Canons of Hippolytus*, preserved in Arabic and Ethiopic, also reflect the *Apostolic Tradition*, much altered.

New Testament

Hippolytus is also significant for his testimony to the New Testament as understood at Rome in his day. He gives no list of New Testament books (unless, as some have thought, the Muratorian Fragment is a translation of something from his pen), but a close examination of his writings, or such parts of them as survive, gives us a fairly clear picture. His New Testament was not particularly different from that of his teacher Irenaeus. He accepted the Four Gospels as scripture and acknowledged thirteen letters of Paul, but not Hebrews. His famous Roman contemporary Gaius held the same view of the Pauline collection. Hippolytus also accepted Acts and three Catholic letters—I Peter and I and II John. The Revelation of John completed his New Testament, making a total of twenty-two books.

But Hippolytus knew numerous other Christian writings from the first and second centuries, among them Hebrews, the *Shepherd* of Hermas, the *Revelation of Peter*, and the *Acts of Paul*. He is the first Christian writer to reflect II Peter, and he must have known James and Jude at least slightly, for he once quotes the first verse of James with the words, "As the saying of Jude in his first letter to the Twelve Tribes proves."[7]

With Hippolytus the curtain falls upon Greek Christianity in Rome. He was a Puritan in morals and in discipline, sternly opposing a series of Roman bishops on both practical and doctrinal issues. He worked in a time of conflict with laxity, venality, and

---

[7] Hippolytus (Achelis ed.), p. 231, l. 10.

heresy within the church and proved himself a stalwart in the fight, struggling valiantly to hammer out Christian views of morals, practice, doctrine, and interpretation. Little that he accomplished can be considered final, of course, but he made a substantial contribution to Christian development. Further discoveries will undoubtedly increase our knowledge of him and his times and works, at least four-fifths of which, and perhaps much more, seems at present to have been lost.

Julius Africanus

When the emperor Septimius Severus campaigned against Osrhoene and the region of Edessa on the Upper Euphrates in A.D. 195, one of his officers was a young man from Aelia Capitolina, as the Romans called the city that replaced Jerusalem after the Bar-Cochba War, in A.D. 135. His name was Julius Africanus. He penetrated to Mount Ararat and spent some years at Edessa, where he enjoyed the friendship of King Abgar II and went hunting with the Edessene princes. Later in life we find him settled at Emmaus in Palestine and engaged in literary work. From Emmaus he led a delegation that was sent to the emperor Alexander Severus to ask that the town be restored, and in consequence it was rebuilt as Nicopolis. At Rome he designed a beautiful library for the emperor in the Pantheon. He removed to Alexandria for a time to hear the lectures of Heraclas, who later became the successor of Origen as head of the catechetical school. Africanus knew Origen and, as late as A.D. 240, exchanged letters with him. He was a devout believer in the scriptures, but he was not a presbyter or a bishop but a soldier, at home in both camps and courts, and a man of letters.

In A.D. 221 he published his *Chronography*, or *Chronicle*, in five books. It traced the course of history from the Creation, making use of the Old Testament and other chronological sources, Greek and Jewish, among them the account of the Jewish kings written by Justus of Tiberias.

The aim of Africanus was to show that human history fell into six days of a thousand years each,[8] that the coming of Christ

---

[8] It was Psalm 90 that said a thousand years were in God's sight like yesterday when it was past; the *Letter of Barnabas* said a day was a thousand years. II Peter says both (3:8). The two statements, while mathematically the same, are rhetorically opposites. On the whole, *Barnabas* seems to have influenced Africanus.

occurred in the year of the world 5500; that five hundred years later, the final thousand years, the millennium, would begin. Although controlled by this mistaken idea, the main features of this chronology (the so-called Alexandrian era) were widely adopted in the East. The *Chronography* was full of valuable excerpts from earlier chroniclers, but its scattered fragments have not yet been fully assembled. Yet it has been called the root of Christian chronography and has proved an important source for Hippolytus, for the *Chronicle* of Eusebius, and later for the *Paschal Chronicle* early in the seventh century, and Georgius Syncellus, late in the eighth.

The other chief work of Africanus was his *Cestoi*, or *Paradoxa*— a sort of notebook of strange pieces of curious information on all sorts of subjects, medical, military, magical, scientific, and literary —the miscellanies accumulated by a traveled and inquiring mind. The book was dedicated to the emperor Alexander Severus, the author's friend and patron.

The length of the *Cestoi* was variously given by later writers; Syncellus said it contained nine books, Photius said fourteen, whereas Suidas gave the number as twenty-four. But a papyrus of two columns of it, written in the middle of the third century (almost in the lifetime of Africanus) and found at Oxyrhynchus, solved the problem.[9] It preserves the end of one book and concludes: "Of Julius Africanus Cestus 18." It is evident that Suidas was right in giving the number at twenty-four. Africanus is discussing a long magical incantation supposed to have been uttered by Odysseus in summoning the shades of the dead, in *Odyssey* 11. He tells just where the manuscripts are in which he has found it— one in Aelia Capitolina, one in Nysa in Caria, and one in the Pantheon library already mentioned. Africanus wondered whether it was Homer himself or the Peisistratidae, the early editors of Homer, who had left the passage out. He recorded the lines as at any rate "a most valuable product of Epic art."

Africanus also wrote some very significant letters. One, addressed to a certain Aristides, about the genealogies of Christ, appealing to the Jewish practice of levirate marriage to reconcile their differences in Matthew and Luke, was used by Origen in his earliest homilies, on Luke. But his most famous letter is that writ-

---

[9] *Oxyrhynchus Papyri* iii. 412.

ten about A.D. 240 to Origen to show that the story of Susanna cannot have been an original part of the Book of Daniel. Africanus argued that, for one thing, Daniel's play upon words when he asked each of the wicked elders under what kind of a tree he had seen Susanna meet her lover was a Greek play and could not possibly be a translation from the Hebrew. This was certainly a point well taken, and Origen in his answer, written from Nicomedia where he was staying, although he said a good deal by way of reproof, was not able to meet it.

Here, as so often happened, the works of our author have almost entirely perished. But enough remains to show that here was a man, in the Christian church, on friendly terms with kings and emperors, keenly interested in Christian history and prophecy, and bringing a fresh and open mind to literary questions in pagan and Christian literature alike.

Dionysius of Alexandria

Three men named Dionysius were active and influential in the early church: Dionysius, bishop of Corinth (who was contemporary with Soter, bishop of Rome from A.D. 166 to 174); Dionysius, bishop of Rome, A.D. 259–68; and Dionysius the Great, bishop of Alexandria from A.D. 247 to 264, who has been called the most significant of the personal pupils of Origen.

He came of heathen parentage and was at first a pagan, then a Gnostic; a man of position and means, who stood high with the authorities. When Demetrius, bishop of Alexandria, forced Origen to break off his work there and leave the city (A.D. 230), his assistant Heraclas took his place at the head of the catechetical school, but a year later, A.D. 231, Heraclas became bishop of Alexandria and turned over the direction of the school to Dionysius. When Heraclas died, sixteen years later, Dionysius became bishop in his place but seems to have retained the headship of the school, not unworthily carrying forward the great tradition established for it by Pantaenus, Clement, and Origen.

Dionysius ably united the practical and intellectual sides of the Christian faith. He was a vigorous churchman of worldwide interests; the problems of Eastern and Western Christianity found him alert and energetic in dealing with them. He corresponded with Rome, Antioch, Laodicea in Phoenicia, Caesarea in Palestine, even Armenia, and concerned himself with questions that arose anywhere in the church, practical, doctrinal, and even critical, and with remarkable sense and skill.

Dionysius had hardly become bishop of Alexandria when a local persecution broke out there, and the following year the Decian persecution began. Like Cyprian in the same situation at Carthage, Dionysius fled before the storm, or rather he permitted himself to be rescued from the soldiers who had arrested him. It seems that a certain Timothy, a member of his household, perhaps his son, came to Dionysius' house on the way to a wedding, and, seeing what was going on, proceeded to the wedding and told the assembled company what was happening. As one man, they arose from the table, rushed to the bishop's house, put the soldiers to flight, and seizing the astounded Dionysius carried him off by force. Indeed, he thought at first that he was being mobbed or kidnaped. He was hustled upon the back of a saddleless animal and hurried off to a place of safety, where he remained with only two attendants until the death of Decius in 251. It reminds one of the seizure of Luther and his removal to the Wartburg by the emissaries of the Great Elector, for his protection.

We owe this story to the attack made afterward upon Dionysius for flight by a certain Germanus, which Dionysius answered with a full account of what actually happened (Eusebius *Church History* vi. 40 and vii. 11), in his *Letter to Germanus*, written in A.D. 259, in defense of his course in the persecutions of both Decius and Valerian.

Soon after the death of Decius and the return of Dionysius to Alexandria, the persecution of Valerian broke out and occasioned Dionysius' banishment to obscure places, first in Libya and then in the Mareotis in Egypt. The toleration edict of Gallienus, A.D. 260, made it possible for him to return to Alexandria in 261, but a new series of calamities soon set in. The prefect of Egypt revolted against Gallienus and set himself up as emperor and had to be put down. Famine and pestilence added to the misery of the Alexandrians, and amid such scenes Dionysius died, A.D. 264–65. The new bishop of Antioch, Paul of Samosata, had antagonized the churches by his views on the person of Christ—that he was mere man, though filled with divine power from his birth—and a synod was held in Antioch to settle the matter. Dionysius had been unable to attend but had sent his written opinion to the gathering. Paul was not only bishop of Antioch but also viceroy of Zenobia, the famous queen of Palmyra, who for a time wrested Egypt from the Romans.

Works

Of between fifty and sixty writings of Dionysius, including letters, only one or two letters have come down to us in full; but, thanks to Eusebius, we know something of the scope of his work and possess some important fragments of it (*Church History* vi. 40–vii. 28). He wrote an exposition of the beginning of Ecclesiastes (*Church History* vii 26. 3), fragments of which are preserved in Procopius of Gaza, and a work *On Nature*, cast in the form of a letter to his "son" Timothy, refuting the atomistic views of the Epicureans, with which he seems to have been well acquainted. Eusebius preserves portions of it in his *Preparation for the Gospel* (xiv. 23–27). There was also a work *On Temptations*, addressed to one Euphranor (*Church History* vii. 26. 2, but this has entirely disappeared.

A work *On Promises*, in two books, was called forth as a reply to a *Refutation of the Allegorists*, which had been written by Nepos, bishop of Arsinoë, before his death. Nepos seems to have been a successful hymn writer; Dionysius says that the brethren still enjoy his hymns (*Church History* vii. 24. 4). But Nepos held that the scriptures should be understood "in a more Jewish manner and that there would be a certain millennium of bodily luxury upon this earth," and appealed to the Revelation of John in support of it.

This led Dionysius in his *On Promises* to examine the claims of apostolic authorship made for the Revelation. He compared its style and ideas with those of the Gospel of John and came to the conclusion that they can hardly be from the same hand and that the Revelation must be figuratively understood. This judgment of Dionysius shows a thoroughly sound critical sense on his part and was in part responsible for the doubt with which the Revelation was ever after regarded in the Eastern church. It is characteristic of Dionysius that, while he disagreed with the millennial views of Nepos, he spoke of him in cordial and generous terms:

I confess that in many other respects I approve and love Nepos, for his faith and industry and diligence in the scriptures, and for his extensive psalmody, with which many of the brethren are still delighted, and I hold him in the more reverence because he has gone to rest before us. But the truth should be loved and honored most of all [*Church History* vii. 24. 4].

In 260–61 Dionysius wrote his *Refutation and Apology against Sabellius*, addressing it to Dionysius, bishop of Rome. It was in four books and is lost except for some fragments preserved by Athanasius in his work *On the Opinions of Dionysius* and by Basil in his work *On the Holy Spirit*, both works of the following century, and it is quoted at considerable length in Eusebius (*Preparation for the Gospel* vii 19). Athanasius came to the defense of Dionysius, who was being, as he thought, wrongfully quoted by the Arians in defense of their views on the relation of the Son to the Father. Dionysius had previously addressed four letters on Sabellianism to correspondents of his and had sent extracts from these to Xystus, bishop of Rome, in the single year of the latter's office, August, 257, to August, 258. On the basis of these, apparently, Dionysius was charged with doctrinal irregularity before Dionysius of Rome, to whom he replied with this *Refutation*. It will be seen that he was in frequent correspondence with the bishops of Rome, writing to Stephen, Xystus, and Dionysius.

The schisms of Nepos and of Sabellius were not the only ones with which Dionysius dealt. In his numerous letters sent in all directions, he discussed the rebaptism of heretics, the treatment of the lapsed, the schism of Novatian (whom he advised to give up his episcopal pretentions in the interests of the peace of the church), and finally the case of Paul of Samosata, the bishop of Antioch, whose views of the person of Christ were disturbing the Eastern church in Dionysius' last days.

Eusebius tells of at least fifty such letters, some of them virtually treatises in the form of letters, which were written by Dionysius between 249 and 264. The works *On the Sabbath*, *On Exercise*, and *On Marriage* were of this kind. It had been the custom of the bishops of Alexandria to determine each year the date at which Easter was to be celebrated and to announce this in a letter sent to all the churches concerned. Dionysius took occasion in these letters to instruct the churches on other questions of immediate importance to them, and a whole series of these letters is mentioned by Eusebius (*Church History* vii. 20–23).

If we could recover the writings of Dionyius, we should have the portrait of a wise, sincere, and able Christian leader in the trying times of Origen, Cyprian, and Novatian, the fateful middle years of the third century. But, of them all, we have less than ten pages, probably not one-twentieth of what he wrote, and we must list among the lost works of early Christian literature not only the bulk of his letters but, except for a few fragments, his major writings, *On Nature*, *On Trials*, *On Promises*, the *Refutation and Apology*, and his partial *Exposition of Ecclesiastes*.

Theognostus

After Dionysius became bishop of Alexandria, in 247, a certain Theognostus succeeded him as head of the catechetical school. He is known only for his *Outlines*, a treatise in seven books which was known to Photius in the ninth century but survives today only in brief fragments, partly because Eusebius made no mention of him in the *Church History*. These fragments reveal that Theognostus was a rather speculative theologian who perpetuated the teaching of Origen.

Pierius

There are even fewer fragments from the works of his successor Pierius, who taught at Alexandria during the last decades of the third century and wrote not only theological treatises (including one on "the God-bearer" or "Mother of God") but also exegetical works on books of the Old and New Testaments. According to Philip of Side (fifth century) both Pierius and his brother Isidore were martyrs and a large church was built at Alexandria in their memory. The martyrdom must have occurred after 309, when Pamphilus was put to death, for Philip says that Pierius wrote a treatise on his life. Jerome says that "after the persecution" Pierius lived in Rome, and it may be that the martyrdom involved confession but not death.

Peter

The last of the ante-Nicene teachers at Alexandria was Peter, who became bishop in the year 300. It was he who brought Origen's direct influence at Alexandria to an end, although he was almost constantly engaged in controversy during his brief episcopate, which ended with his martyrdom in 311. Administrative conflicts led to the Melitian schism; theological difficulties may have brought Peter to excommunicate Arius. Apart from small fragments, we possess from Peter a letter warning the Alexandrians against Melitius, self-appointed primate of Egypt, and fourteen "canons" on penance, chiefly concerned with those who had abandoned Christianity before the year 306.

Methodius

From the latter half of the third century and perhaps the beginning of the fourth we possess several writings from a certain Methodius, perhaps (but by no means certainly) bishop of Olympus in Lycia and a martyr in 311. He is significant as one of the first Christian opponents of Porphyry (whose fifteen books against the Christians appeared about 270) and as an early critic of some of Origen's doctrines. He defended the resurrection of the body and denied that the world was eternal. In spite of his criticisms, he owed much to Origen, especially regarding allegorical exegesis of the Bible. His *Banquet, or Treatise on Chastity* consists of discourses on virginity by ten Christian virgins; it is partly modeled after the *Banquet*, or *Symposium*, of Plato and contains many Platonic quotations and allusions. Methodius' other works, often in dialogue form, have been preserved primarily in Slavonic versions, along with fragments in Greek and sometimes also in Syriac and Armenian. These include *On Free Will, On Life and Rational Activity, Aglaophon or Treatise on the Resurrection of the Body, On Jewish Foods and the Red Heifer, To Sistellius on Leprosy, On the Leech and the Verse "The Heavens Declare the Glory of God"* (exegesis of Proverbs xxx. 15 and Psalm xviii. 1), *On Creatures, Against Porphyry*, and *On Martyrs*. Most of Methodius' literary output seems to be lost. He was obviously very prolific and his writings, especially the *Banquet*, show us that Christian literary culture was not confined to Alexandria.

Oddly enough, Eusebius did not mention Methodius in his extant works (although according to Jerome he did so in the sixth book which he added to Pamphilus' *Apology for Origen*);[10] in the *Praeparatio Evangelica* he ascribes a long quotation from *On Free Will* to "Maximus."[11]

---

[10] *Against Rufinus* i. 11.

[11] *Praeparatio Evangelica* vii. 22. On both passages see H. Musurillo, *St. Methodius: the Symposium* (London, 1958), 3–4, 169–70.

14

LATIN CHRISTIAN WRITERS

Christian Latin

In the latter part of the first century the writing of Latin literature was already passing into the hands of provincials, men from North Africa and Spain, like Seneca, Martial, and Quintilian. The district about Carthage was particularly active in literary lines, and it is not strange that it was there that the Bible began to be translated into Latin. It was there, and not in Rome, that Latin Christianity had its beginning and that it soon began to express itself vigorously in Latin books.

Tertullian

The first great figure in Latin Christianity was Tertullian, or Quintus Septimius Florens Tertullianus, to give him his full name. He was born in Carthage, about A.D. 155–60, of good family, and seems, from what he says in his writings, to have visited Athens and Rome in early life, studying to be a lawyer and entering fully into the excesses of heathen life in those centers. At Rome he seems to have practiced law and taught rhetoric, with marked success. There, it appears, he was converted, and he returned to Carthage a Christian. Jerome says he became a presbyter in the church there. At any rate, he threw himself into the Christian cause with tremendous vigor, especially in the crises which persecution now and then brought on for the church. These attacks called forth the notable apologetic pieces which were among his earliest writings, but a wealth of other books, practical, doctrinal, and polemic, soon followed.

The heroic behavior of Christian martyrs deeply impressed Tertullian. He may have had glimpses of it in the first year of Commodus, A.D. 180, when twelve Christians—seven men and five women—from the neighboring town of Scilli suffered martyrdom in Carthage. The simple story of their trial and fate is the earliest of Latin martyrdoms.

Apologetic Writings

In A.D. 197–98 there was another outbreak against the African Christians. Their habit of holding aloof from public shows, which were both pagan and brutal in character, kept them away from the public celebration of the victory of the emperor, Septimius Severus, over his rivals, and precipitated a fresh persecution. Tertullian came to the defense of his harassed brethren with the fiery vehemence and fervor that always characterized him. In a work addressed *To the Heathen* (*Ad Nationes*, two books) he vigorously protested against the laws condemning Christians simply as such and without first examining their behavior and manner of life. He protests also against the calumnies heaped upon them and the charges of incest, child murder, and disloyalty to the empire that were made against them. He refers to the ancient pagan practice of exposing undesired children and throws back the charges upon those who made them.

A second book of this same year, A.D. 197, was his great *Apology* (*Apologeticus*). It was addressed to the Roman governors of provinces and presents a similar argument, although in a more restrained and legal tone. He repels again the stock charges of child-slaying, incest, and cannibalism and admits that Christians do not worship the old gods but holds that they are not disloyal to the empire; although they cannot call the emperor God, they respect and rever him and are good Romans. Here Tertullian points out that persecution simply advances Christianity: "We multiply every time we are mowed down by you; the blood of Christians is seed"—the most famous of all his famous observations.

These writings were preceded in the same year, 197, by a short address *To the Martyrs* already in prison, encouraging them and cheering them on. But the *Address to the Heathen* and the *Apology* form Tertullian's main contribution to Christian defense literature, and they are powerful reinforcements of it.

Upon the death of Severus, fourteen years later, A.D. 211, and the accession of Caracalla, persecution began again. Once more, in 212–13, Tertullian wrote a short but vigorous apology addressed *To Scapula*, the proconsul of Africa, warning him, in view of well-known Roman precedents favorable to Christians, not to proceed against them.

Trenchant and timely as were his writings in the apologetic field, his practical, doctrinal, and polemic works were no less so. No ancient list of his writings has come down to us, but in the oldest manuscript we have of Tertullian, the Codex Agobardinus, given by Agobard, bishop of Lyons, who died in A.D. 840, to a church there, there is a list of twenty-one of his works, which that manuscript originally contained. From other sources, however, this list can be increased to forty-three, and possibly even to forty-five.

Practical Works

The majority of these were practical in character, dealing with Christian morality and true Christian behavior in situations of certain kinds or in relation to special groups and matters. Tertullian defends the Christian soldier who refuses to wear the chaplet or wreath on his head, regarding it as a heathenish practice (*On the Chaplet*). He condemns public games, shows, and theatrical and gladiatorial exhibitions as brutal, immoral, and interwoven with pagan rites (*On Idolatry*). He also wrote *On Veiling Virgins*, *On the Adornment of Women*, *On Baptism*, *On Patience*, *On Prayer*, *On Modesty*, and *On Repentance*.

Doctrinal Works

In the doctrinal field Tertullian was not markedly creative, for he owed much to Irenaeus and Melito. He was also much influenced by Stoic philosophy and by what he had been taught by the church at Rome, where he was converted. Yet his work *Against Praxeas* is a notable defense of the doctrine of the Trinity, particularly against the followers of the Roman Sabellius, who flourished late in the second and early in the third century and held Monarchian and modalistic views. Praxeas in his solicitude for the divine unity identified Father, Son, and Holy Spirit, so that it was the Father himself who was born of a virgin and suffered on the cross. Tertullian wrote also *On the Flesh of Christ*, *On the Resurrection of the Flesh*, and *On the Soul*—a work which Harnack calls the first book on Christian psychology.

Polemic Writings

Closely related to these were his polemic writings, attacking the positions of heretics and schismatics. In his book *On Prescription of Heretics*, which Hort called a most plausible and most mischievous book,[1] he argues that, after reasoning is exhausted with

---

[1] F. J. A. Hort, *Six Lectures on the Ante-Nicene Fathers* (London, 1895), p. 103.

such people, one must simply say, "What we hold is the belief of the church, handed down from the apostles, from bishop to bishop, in all the historic centers of Christianity, so it must be true, and there is no more to be said." This shows that when he wrote this book, at least, Tertullian was a strong adherent of the Catholic movement, which Irenaeus reflected. He was, in fact, much influenced in his polemic writings by Irenaeus, and Tertullian and Irenaeus are the first Catholic Fathers.

This appeal to the great apostolic churches, as faithful depositories of Christian tradition, naturally directed North African Christians to Rome, the only church in the West of apostolic foundation:

Since you are close upon Italy, you have Rome, from which there comes even into your hands the very authority [of the apostles]. How happy is its church, upon which apostles poured forth all their doctrine, along with their blood! Where Peter endures a passion like his Lord's! Where Paul wins his crown in a death like John's! Where the apostle John was first plunged unhurt into boiling oil, and then returned to his island exile! . . . The Law and the prophets she unites with the writings of evangelists and apostles, from which she drinks in her faith [chap. 36].

This is very much what Irenaeus says in his work *Against Heresies* (iii. 3. 2, 3) about the position of the Roman church, which he in Lyons looked up to from Gaul, just as Tertullian looked up to it from Africa.

But Tertullian's greatest polemic work was that *Against Marcion*, in five books, written over and over again, until his work on it spread over ten or twelve years of his life, from about 200 to 212. This elaborate work gives us our principal information about Marcion, and especially about his effort to put a Christian scripture consisting of the Gospel of Luke and ten letters of Paul in place of the Jewish scriptures which then made up most of the Bible of Christian churches. Other polemic writings were *Against the Jews*, *Against Hermogenes*, and *Against the Valentinians*.

We have grouped Tertullian's writings as apologetic, practical, doctrinal, and polemic. But there is also a value in surveying them in the order in which they were written, for they reveal the gradual shift in his religious views, which carried him in the course of ten years from the bosom of the Catholic church into that of the Montanist sect. He was a strong Puritan in feeling and, whatever direction he took, was fairly certain to go to extremes. His devotion to the Catholic movement and his aversion to heretics are very marked in the *Prescription of Heretics*, which he wrote in his first period when he was a thoroughgoing Catholic. It covers the years 197 to 202. He had become a Christian probably by A.D. 195, perhaps a little earlier. In 197, as we have seen, he wrote his principal apologetic books, *To the Martyrs*, *To the Heathen*, the *Apologeticus*, and also the *Testimony of the Soul*, which he thought essentially Christian by nature and itself a witness to Christianity. In the course of the next five years, 198–202, he wrote twelve other books and treatises: *On Shows* (two editions), *On the Dress of Women*, *On Baptism*, *On Repentance*, *On Patience*, *On Prayer*, *To His Wife* (against remarriage of women), *On Idolatry*, *On Prescription of Heretics*, *Against Marcion* (two editions), *Against Hermogenes*, and *Against the Jews*.

The edict of Severus in 202, forbidding anyone to become a Christian, marks a shift in Tertullian's attitude. He now begins to see truth and value in the Montanists' position—their Puritan morality, in contrast with the growing laxity of the Roman church; their spiritual emphasis, in contrast with the political cast that was coming over Roman Christianity. For five years Tertullian works to build these Montanist values into his Catholic Christianity. He is still a Catholic, but he sees the worth of Montanism, too, and strives to realize them both and to unite them.

In this period of tension he probably wrote three works now lost: *On Ecstasy*, in seven books, dealing with Montanism; *On the Hope of the Faithful* including the millennial expectations, which he shared; and *On Paradise*—these probably in 202–3 to 204–5. The *Exhortation to Chastity* and the book *On Veiling Virgins* also belong to this time, 204–5 to 206–7.

But by 207–8 the tension had become unbearable, and Tertullian with other Montanists left the church. He now produced a third edition of the first four books *Against Marcion*, his longest work, 207–8. He also wrote now *Against the Valentinians* and *Against the Followers of Apelles*, the Marcionite leader, a work now lost. These belong to 207–8. In 210 he wrote *On the Cloak* (which he wore instead of the toga), in 211 *On the Chaplet*, and in 211–12, *On Flight in Persecution*, holding it inadmissible.

In the following five years, 208–13, he wrote also the books *On the Flesh of Christ*, *On the Testimony of the Soul*, *On the*

Soul, On the Resurrection, and the fifth and final book *Against Marcion,* completing his discussion of Marcion's proposed scripture, Luke and Paul. In Books i and ii, Tertullian had dealt with Marcion's doctrine that the Creator and the Father of Jesus were different beings; in Book iii he argued that the Christian movement does not contradict the prophets but fulfills them; in Books iv and v he uses Marcion's own scripture, Luke and Paul, to establish this.

About 212 he wrote his short apology to the proconsul, *To Scapula,* and in 212 or 213 his *Scorpiace,* warning against the scorpion sting of heresy and encouraging martyrdom, which some Gnostics taught was unnecessary. In the course of the next five years he wrote *Against Praxeas* his defense of the Trinity, and soon after 217-18 his book *On Monogamy,* protesting against second marriages, and his work *On Fasting.* And finally, not long before 222-23, he wrote the work *On Modesty,* bitterly assailing the action of Calixtus, bishop of Rome, in declaring that the sins of adultery and fornication, although committed after baptism, could be forgiven by the church; it had previously been held that whereas God could forgive them, along with murder and idolatry, the church could not. Tertullian's invective against this action stands in sharp contrast to his rhapsody upon the Roman church, in his *Prescription of Heretics,* chapter 36, written twenty years before, in 198-202:

The Pontifex Maximus, that is the bishop of bishops, issues an edict: I remit, to such as have discharged the requirements of repentance (or penitence), the sins both of adultery and of fornication. O edict which cannot be inscribed "Good deed!" [chap. 1].

All three of these last works of Tertullian, in fact (*Monogamy, Fasting,* and *Modesty*), are bitter in their denunciation of the laxity that was pervading the Roman church under Zephyrinus and Calixtus. He felt strongly that it had forfeited the spiritual heritage of Christianity. "You have quenched the spirit," he cried, "You have driven away the Comforter (Paraclete)."

Augustine, almost two hundred years later, found a group of Tertullianists still meeting independently in Carthage and brought them back into the church. For it may be that by the time of Tertullian's death, soon after A.D. 222-23, he had left the Montanists and organized a little sect of his own.

Some of Tertullian's writings, like the one *On Veiling Virgins,* he wrote first in Greek. Whether he was the author of the *Martyr-dom of Perpetua and Felicitas*, women of Carthage who suffered in the persecution of A.D. 202–3, is not certain; it is extant in both Greek and Latin and is a work of moving simplicity. Perpetua was a woman of position, while Felicitas was a slave. The account is written from a Montanist point of view. Jerome also mentions a book *On the Difficulties of Marriage* addressed "to a philosophic friend," which may have been written early in life and possibly even in a lighter vein, for Jerome speaks of him as "playing" (*lusit*) with the subject.

Of the works of Tertullian, thirty-one have been preserved, and the names of more than a dozen others can be gathered from references to them in Tertullian himself, in Jerome, or in the table of contents of the Codex Agobardinus. The Greek form of the book *On Baptism* dealt also with the question of heretical baptism and was evidently a different book from the Latin work of that name. Other lost writings are the *Hope of the Faithful*, *Paradise*, *Against the Followers of Apelles*, the *Origin of the Soul*, *Fate*, *Ecstasy*, the *Garments of Aaron*, *To a Philosophic Friend*, *Flesh and Soul*, *Submission of Soul*, and the *Superstition of the World*. The Greek forms of the works *On Shows* and *On the Veiling of Virgins* have also been lost. He may also have written *On Clean and Unclean Animals* and *On Circumcision*, as Jerome intimates (*Epist.* 36:1).

Tertullian is always the advocate; there is nothing judicial about his attitude; he sees only one side. His style is impetuous, dramatic, direct, varied, often richly illustrated, sometimes full of apos-trophe and exclamation, gifted, but uncontrolled, except by over-whelming conviction. It reveals unmistakably one of the most powerful personalities of the early church, whose works have for the most part survived even though he had withdrawn from the Catholic church years before his death.

The Latin Bible

The Latin version of the Bible was just coming into being in North Africa in Tertullian's day, and he was well versed in scrip-ture, probably both Greek and Latin. Like Irenaeus, he had a New Testament, and these two are the first Christian Fathers of whom this can be said. Tertullian's included the Four Gospels, the Acts, and thirteen letters of Paul, besides I Peter, I John and

Jude, the Revelation of John, and at first the *Shepherd* of Hermas, though later in life he repudiated that book with great scorn, for what he considered its moral laxity.[2]

Tertullian also knew early Christian literature very well, especially Justin, Tatian, Melito, Theophilus, Irenaeus, and Clement. His own influence was very marked upon Minucius Felix and upon Cyprian, his great literary successor in North Africa, the bishop of Carthage from A.D. 250 to 258. Jerome reports that he once met an aged man who in his youth had known one of Cyprian's assistants, who said that Cyprian made it a rule to read something of Tertullian's every day and would often say when he wanted to consult Tertullian, "Give me the Master."

Minucius Felix

In connection with Tertullian we may discuss also the admirable work of another gifted Latin, the *Octavius* of Minucius Felix. For in the *Octavius* Minucius Felix wrote the finest of all the Latin apologies for Christianity—Renan called it the pearl of apologetic literature—and he wrote it in reply to an attack on Christianity made by one of the leading pagan Latin writers of the second century, M. Cornelius Fronto. For what Celsus did so ably in Greek in A.D. 178, in his critique of Christianity, had already been done, though less effectively, in Latin by Fronto.

We know much more about Fronto than we do about Minucius. M. Cornelius Fronto (*ca.* 100–175) was a native of Cirta in Africa who had come to Rome in the time of Hadrian and found fame and fortune there as a lawyer, orator, and writer. He became a senator and was consul in A.D. 143 but declined the proconsulship of Asia. He undertook to reform Roman literary style, advocating a return to the earliest Latin models; he exalted oratory as the greatest of arts and was himself considered second only to Cicero. He was invited by Antoninus to become the tutor of the princes Marcus and Verus. His writings had completely disappeared, however, when in 1815 Angelo Mai found in a sixth-century palimpsest at Milan part of a collection of Fronto's letters, written to the emperors Antoninus and Aurelius, among others, from A.D. 143 on. The rest of the manuscript Mai afterward found at Rome. It also contained some of Fronto's smaller literary pieces,

---

[2] *On Modesty* x. 20.

but his attack on Christianity has never been found. It may possibly have been part of an address to the senate, uttered when Christianity was beginning to show strength, about A.D. 150–60.

The Octavius

Sixty or seventy years later Minucius Felix, probably a lawyer in Rome, replied to Fronto with the dialogue, the *Octavius*. It twice mentions Fronto as an assailant of Christianity (chaps. 9 and 31), and it is not unlikely that it reproduces some of his attack in the first third of it, in which the pagan case against Christianity is presented. Fronto's was the only literary attack on Christianity made in Latin.

The scene of the *Octavius* is laid in Rome. Minucius, or Marcus, as his friends call him, tells how his friend Octavius has come from Africa to visit him, and, as the weather is fine, they and a pagan friend Caecilius go on a pleasure trip to Ostia for the sea baths. As they go, they pass a statue of Serapis, and Caecilius throws it a kiss. Octavius rebukes his superstition, and Caecilius declares he is ready to defend his attitude, if they will hear him. They agree and sit down, Minucius, as a sort of umpire, sitting between Caecilius and Octavius.

Caecilius then presents the popular case against the Christians: Christians are too ignorant to know the things they profess to know. As a matter of fact, there is no reason or providence in the universe. Rome flourished as long as it piously worshiped the gods; it is wrong for the Christians to revile them. They themselves worship a crucified man and indulge in hideous, evil, and wanton orgies. They conceal their practices and are really a wretched lot of secretive, ignorant, miserable people, unequal to the demands of this life and utterly unfitted to forecast the life to come (chaps. 5–13).

Challenged by Caecilius and encouraged by Minucius to reply, Octavius does so. Wisdom and intelligence, he declares, depend upon natural endowment, and the Christians' possession of them is not determined by the measure of wealth or advantages they may enjoy. Reasonable men have always seen reason and order in the universe and perceived that these imply a divine ruler controlling it all. Such a ruler is too great to be understood or even named; any name would fall short of him. Poets and philosophers have agreed that he is man's father and that he is one. Against such

views, old fables and the worship of dead heroes as gods ought
not to weigh at all. The heathen gods were really deified men,
images of whom the people worship. The very birds and animals
know that these images are not gods. Their rites are grotesque
and absurd, even inhuman and immoral. Roman success has been
won not by piety but by violence. Demons, not gods, are behind
the auguries and oracles, and they inspire the hideous slanders
against the Christians—that they worship monsters, devour infants,
and indulge in incest at their feasts. It is really the heathen themselves who practice murder and incest. God cannot be contained
in a temple. The Jews themselves admit in their writings that they
forsook him before he abandoned them. The philosophers have
long maintained that the universe will eventually perish, and God,
who created man, can bring him back to life, and reward or pun-
ish him, as he deserves. What Christians now suffer is not a pun-
ishment but a discipline, heroically endured. They avoid pagan
shows and practices as impious, cruel, and absurd (chaps. 16–38).
Caecilius acknowledges himself defeated by the arguments of
Octavius and forthwith accepts Christianity (chaps. 39–41).

It is generally agreed that in elegance of style Minucius' defense of Christianity decidedly excels Fronto's attack upon it,
if we may judge the latter from the clumsy and affected pieces
of Fronto discovered in the past century. The absence of scripture or of mention of Christ by name in the *Octavius* is natural
enough in a work addressed to pagan readers, as, of course, the
Octavius was.

We owe the preservation of the *Octavius* to the fact that it was
mistaken in the Middle Ages for the eighth (*octavus*) book of
Arnobius *Against the Heathen* (*Adversus nationes*) and preserved
as such, appended to the seven books of that work with no title
of its own, in the Paris manuscript of the ninth century, which is
our sole independent witness to the text of Arnobius. It was first
published, as a part of Arnobius, in 1543, but was soon recognized
(1560) by Balduinus as the long-lost *Octavius* mentioned by
Lactantius (in his *Divine Institutes* i. 11 and v. i, begun about
A.D. 303) and by Jerome (*On Illustrious Men* 58 and *Epist.* 70:5).
Jerome mentions a work *On Fate* as ascribed to Minucius but says
the style is very unlike that of the *Octavius*. No trace of it has
been found.

No problem in the field of early Christian literature has been
more hotly debated than the relative dates of the *Octavius* and of

the *Apology* (*Apologeticus*) of Tertullian; more than two hundred articles and monographs have been devoted to it. The *Apologeticus* was written in A.D. 197 and so much resembles the *Octavius* in so many points that it is clear that one was strongly influenced by the other. Jerome repeatedly speaks as though Tertullian preceded Minucius, and it would be strange if the Roman writer could think so disparagingly of the state of the empire in the course of the splendid era from Trajan to Aurelius; his attitude accords much better with the days of its palpable decline, in the middle of the third century. In the third century, moreover, the empire was getting into the lawyers' hands, and that might suggest making them the participants in the debate.

The *Octavius* was later made use of by Novatian in his work *On the Trinity*, for example, written toward A.D. 250, and also by Xystus II, bishop of Rome, if he wrote the discourse *To Novatian*, written between A.D. 253 and 258 and preserved under the name of Cyprian.[3] So the *Octavius* was probably written sometime between A.D. 238 and 249, when the empire was at a low ebb. If Novatian's work *On the Trinity* was written about A.D. 245, the *Octavius* may be dated about 240. Its mention by Lactantius, about A.D. 303, and by Jerome has been noted.

The *Octavius* is very different from the Greek apologies; it swings away from the earlier biblical apologetic toward the more sophisticated philosophical Christianity of Lactantius; it is much more like a hearing before a magistrate or, particularly, a philosophical debate before an umpire. It was modeled on Cicero's disputations—the *Orator*, the *Nature of the Gods*, and *Divination*. The pagan side is first presented with brutal frankness, and then the Christian side is just as unsparingly given.

It seems idle to look for historical characters in the persons who take part. Octavius is introduced as an old friend and teacher from Africa, and he and Caecilius are dead when the book is written, but in a work so full of art all this is probably simply part of the literary guise of the book. The appearance of the latter name, Caecilius Natalis, in a number of Cirta inscriptions of A.D. 211–17, as belonging to a leading citizen there at that time is probably little more than a coincidence.

---

[3] Another work preserved under Cyprian's name, the treatise *That Idols Are Not Gods*, also shows the influence of the *Octavius*, and it, too, may be a work of Novatian.

Cyprian of Carthage

When Tertullian was at the height of his powers, a boy was growing up in Carthage who was to do a great service to Latin Christianity in North Africa. His name was Cyprian.

Caecilius (earlier called Thascius) Cyprianus was born, probably at Carthage, about A.D. 210, or soon after. His parents were people of position and means, and he received a good education. He was engaged in the teaching of rhetoric and oratory in Carthage when he came in contact with the Christian forces there. His discussion with representatives of the new faith, especially with presbyter Caecilianus, led to his conversion, about A.D. 246. He entered into the work of the church with ardor and soon became a presbyter. In 248–49, little more than two years after his conversion, he was made bishop of Carthage in response to a popular demand on the part of the church.

The ten years that followed were years of great stress and peril for the Christians of Carthage and of great literary activity for Cyprian. Decius became emperor in A.D. 249 and soon after issued an edict which seems to have aimed at the complete extinction of the Christian movement. It ushered in the first really general persecution of the church. Cyprian saved himself by leaving Carthage, probably warned by news from Rome of what was in the wind. He was severely criticized for doing so, but afterward defended his course as taken in the interest of the church as a whole.

Throughout the Roman empire men and women were called upon to offer heathen sacrifice, before witnesses. Many complied and were given little papyrus slips recording that they had offered sacrifice to the gods, made libations, and tasted the offerings. Many such *libelli*, as they were called, have been found in Egypt.

The reign of Decius was short; he was killed in battle with the Goths in the Dobrudja in A.D. 251. There was a temporary lull in the persecution, and Cyprian, who from his place of concealment had succeeded in keeping in touch with the church at Carthage by letters and messengers, was able to return.

Important matters soon called for his attention. Through the months of Cyprian's concealment the bishop's chair in Rome had been vacant, and now it was claimed by two rival bishops, Cornelius and Novatian, the latter a man of especial culture and literary ability. They differed sharply on the treatment of the lapsed—those persons who had been driven by persecution to leave the church but now wished to return to it. Cornelius held that, upon establishing the sincerity of their repentance, they might be readmitted, but Novatian held they should not be readmitted at all. Cyprian seems at first to have favored the stricter policy, but he soon changed and, with characteristic vigor, took the side of Cornelius, who succeeded in establishing himself as bishop.

Popular animosity against the Christians was roused again by the spread of the pestilence which had first appeared in the reign of Decius, and persecution revived. Cornelius, the new bishop of Rome, was banished and died, and Cyprian himself was threatened. He made himself useful in organizing aid for those stricken with the disease. The party of Novatian had separated from the Roman church to follow his stricter principles, but now some of them were returning, and the question arose: Should they again be baptized? Cyprian maintained that they should, but the new Roman bishop Stephen (254–57) declared it unnecessary and claimed the right as the successor of St. Peter to overrule his brother bishops.

In the time of Cornelius, Cyprian had strongly maintained the unity of the church, which he found in the unity of the bishops, and although he fully recognized the historical importance of the Roman church, he boldly denied the inferences of superior authority which Stephen sought to draw from it. Stephen retorted by excommunicating the African bishops. This controversy was interrupted by the renewal of the persecution under the new emperor Valerian (A.D. 253–60), whose first edict, of A.D. 257, banished the higher clergy from their sees. Stephen died in August of that year, and in the same month Cyprian was banished to the African town of Curubis, some forty miles from Carthage.

But the edict proved ineffective. The banished bishops simply organized new churches, in the places of their banishment, and a year later Valerian issued a new and much sterner edict. The substance of it is preserved in one of Cyprian's letters (*Epist.* 80): the various classes of Christians were threatened with varying degree of confiscation, degradation, slavery, and even death, but the penalty for the clergy was death. Cyprian learned that he was to be summoned to Utica for trial, or probably condemnation, and made his escape, for, as he wrote his congregation, he wished to suffer in Carthage. When the proconsul next visited Carthage, Cyprian returned and was arrested. The following day, September 14, A.D. 258, he was tried, convicted, and beheaded.

His Letters

Into these twelve momentous years Cyprian crowded a great deal of writing in the Christian cause. The collection of his letters contains eighty-one pieces, sixty-five of which are from Cyprian's hand. The others are letters to him or to persons near him. There are also twelve more formal literary works of his, the treatises— all, of course, more or less closely related to practical church problems of the day.

The letters written or received by Cyprian during the years of his episcopate mirror the march of events in Rome and Carthage in that decade in a most illuminating way. We find ourselves right in the midst of the problems and controversies that beset those two great centers of Western Christianity, and we hear the words of their great leaders, Cyprian, Cornelius, Novatian, and a number of others, as well as Firmilian of Caesarea. A wealth of scholarly labor has established in general the years from which these letters come, and the chronological arrangement of them is perhaps the most readily comprehensible.[4]

Letters 5–43 belong to the time of Cyprian's concealment, or flight, covering about fifteen months, from December of A.D. 249 to March of 251. Even the exact order in which these thirty-nine letters were written has been pretty generally agreed upon by scholars. Cyprian was able from his place of concealment to com-municate not only with his own diocese but, through it, with the Roman church, to which he sent a number of letters in the course of these fifteen months, and no less than thirteen of his letters to his own people he collected and instructed them to for-ward to the Roman church (Nos. 5–7 and 10–19). This little group may therefore be regarded as the nucleus of the whole collection.

Two important matters appear now and again in these thirty-nine letters. One was the behavior of Cyprian in going into hiding in the time of persecution. The Roman clergy wrote to the clergy at Carthage on this matter, pointing out that a good shepherd gave

---

[4] The numbers are those of Hartel's edition in the Vienna series of Latin fathers, *Corpus Scriptorum Ecclesiasticorum* (1868–71). The English trans-lation in the *Ante-Nicene Fathers* (American ed.), Vol. V, follows a different numeration. Only one manuscript (Codex Taurinensis) contains all 81 letters.

his life for his sheep, but on this point Cyprian was able to satisfy them. They were the more easily satisfied since Cyprian agreed with them about the other matter—their attitude toward those who had lapsed in the persecution.

This was a point that divided the churches of both Carthage and Rome. There was a group in each church that believed that those who had fallen away from the faith in persecution should not be readmitted to the church at all. Such people were led in Rome by Novatian, and in Carthage by Felicissimus. Cyprian held that such persons should upon proper conditions be readmitted to the church, and this was the view of the majority of the Roman clergy. Felicissimus, however, found so many supporters for his position in the church at Carthage that a schism arose there on the subject, which caused Cyprian, hampered by his absence from the scene, the greatest difficulty.

A second group of twenty letters (Nos. 44–61, 64, 66) can be referred with confidence to the period from the spring of 251 to the summer of 253. They comprise the letters exchanged between Cyprian and two bishops of Rome, Cornelius and his successor Lucius. About the time the persecution relaxed and Cyprian returned to Carthage, Cornelius was chosen bishop of Rome (March, 251) in the face of the strong opposition of Novatian and his followers, who immediately countered by electing Novatian bishop. The situation was made more acute by the Carthaginian presbyter Novatus, who took the side of Novatian. But Cyprian sided with Cornelius, who came to be the recognized bishop. It was the natural for Cyprian to do this, as Cornelius and he were in agreement about the way the lapsed should be treated.

A third group of letters, Nos. 67–75, come from the time of Stephen, who succeeded Lucius as bishop of Rome in A.D. 254 and continued in that office until 257. Whether schismatics, like the former followers of Novatian, should be admitted to the church without rebaptism was now questioned and on this matter Cyprian and Stephen differed sharply, Cyprian holding they should be rebaptized, but Stephen maintaining that, as they had been baptized once, the impartation of the Holy Spirit through the laying-on of hands was enough. In the spring of A.D. 255 a council of African bishops was held in Carthage, and another a year later was attended by seventy-one bishops from Africa and Numidia.

On September 1, 256, a third council of bishops of Africa, Numidia, and Mauretania was held; and it voted that returning schismatics should be rebaptized but favored tolerance if an individual bishop thought differently. Firmilian of Caesarea wrote Cyprian to express his agreement with him, but Stephen, as we have seen, went so far as to excommunicate the African bishops who had refused to accept his ruling on the matter.

A fourth group of letters, Nos. 76–81, belongs to the year of Cyprian's banishment, August, 257, to September, 258. No. 81 was written not long before his execution.

There remain only seven letters, 1–4, 62, 63, and 65, that cannot be exactly enough dated to be fitted into this reconstruction of his correspondence. The whole series gives us an amazingly clear picture of Christian thought and action in Cyprian's day and of the rapid movement of events, seen for the most part through the eyes of an able, energetic, educated, devoted, and, on the whole, considerate Christian man. For the history of the church in the middle years of the third century they are of the utmost value.

His Treatises

Although some of Cyprian's letters run to considerable length, his more massive works were his treatises. They, too, like his letters, sprang from the practical conditions of church life. Twelve of them which may be regarded as genuine have been preserved, but two of these may be dismissed as little more than compilations. One is addressed to Fortunatus, who had asked Cyprian to collect the scripture passages that were calculated to fortify Christian believers in the midst of persecution. Cyprian grouped them under a series of statements, on the emptiness of idolatry, the supremacy of Christ, etc. It was entitled *To Fortunatus: On Exhortation to Martyrdom*.

The other was addressed to a certain Quirinus, who seems to have asked Cyprian to summarize the scriptures for him book by book. Cyprian laid down a series of statements of Christian truth, following each with a group of the scripture passages teaching it. The first book relates to the relation of the Jews to their scriptures and to the church, the function of the Law, and so forth. The second deals with the nature and work of Christ, presenting the passages of scripture that throw light upon it. The third book was written in response to a later request of Quirinus and presents the practical teachings of Christianity, supported with the appropriate passages of scripture. The work was called *To Quirinus: Three Books of Testimonies*, to which title was later sometimes added "against the Jews."[5]

Of the ten principal treatises, the earliest was that addressed *To Donatus*, a friend of other days, to whom Cyprian explains what drove him to be a Christian and describes the conditions of life in the pagan world in which he had grown up, its violence, brutality, and depravity, in contrast with the peace and satisfaction he had found in the Christian faith. It was evidently written soon after his conversion, probably in A.D. 246.

His second treatise, *On the Dress of Virgins*, was designed to instruct unmarried women in the church who have dedicated themselves to Christ, to dress plainly, avoid jewelry, cosmetics, mixed bathing, boisterous wedding parties, and dyeing their hair, and to tell them how to behave themselves generally. Cyprian was by this time bishop of Carthage, so that the work was probably written in A.D. 249.

In the third treatise, *On the Lapsed*, Cyprian praises the martyrs and calls upon those who had failed to acknowledge Christ in the persecution but had offered sacrifice to idols and saved themselves by accepting a *libellus* or ticket from the authorities, to repent in dust and ashes and give unmistakable evidence of the sincerity of their contrition in the hope that God will forgive them. This treatise, and the next, *On the Unity of the Church*, were probably written before he returned to Carthage from his withdrawal or flight, and when Felicissimus was making trouble at Carthage, that is, early in A.D. 251. The one *On the Lapsed* was sent, probably in the summer of that year along with that *On the Unity of the Church*, to the church at Rome, where a movement was on foot, led by Novatian, to refuse the lapsed readmission to the church on any terms.

The fourth treatise, *On the Unity of the Church*, which Cyprian seems to have brought with him when he returned to Carthage in A.D. 251, was probably later revised, when Novatian broke away from the Roman church, as a rival bishop to Cornelius,

---

[5] Collections of scripture passages bearing on particular points of Christian belief arose very early and were anticipated among the Qumran sectarians.

whose views on the lapsed he considered too lax. It was Cyprian's contention in this treatise that the guaranty of the unity of the church was the agreement of the bishops. The greatest danger to the church lay not in persecution but in heretical sects. Although the work was primarily conditioned by the spirit in the Carthaginian church precipitated by Felicissimus, it was valid also with some revision for the kindred situation in Rome brought on by Novatian, and so Cyprian sent it in its revised form with the treatise *On the Lapsed* to Rome, probably in the summer of 251.

The fifth treatise, *On the Lord's Prayer*, presents a practical interpretation of the prayer, illustrating it richly from scripture. Cyprian teaches that prayer should be accompanied by acts of charity and discusses the times at which prayer should be offered.

The sixth treatise, *To Demetrianus*, an individual otherwise unknown, who had ascribed the disasters and calamities of the times to the Christians' failure to worship the old gods, puts the blame for these things on the pagans instead, who not only refused to worship the true God but persecuted his people. It was probably written after the death of Decius (who, as we have seen, was killed in battle with the Goths), probably late in A.D. 251 or early in 252.

The seventh, *On the Mortality*, deals with the pestilence ravaging the country, and indeed the empire in 252, showing that such things were foretold by Christ and that, although death seems to overtake Christians and pagans alike, it means very different things to them. The eighth, *On Works and Charity*, urges the practice of liberal giving, especially because of the plague of 252.

The ninth, *On the Advantage of Patience*, was written in the midst of the controversy with Stephen over rebaptizing heretics and seeks to soften its acerbities. It was written early in A.D. 256.

The tenth, *On Jealousy and Envy*, explains the dangers and divisions to which those vices lead and was probably written, like that *On the Advantage of Patience*, in 256, when the struggle with Rome over the rebaptism of heretics was at its height. It shows what a powerful and searching preacher Cyprian must have been.

The "Life" of Cyprian

Much light is thrown upon the work and martyrdom of Cyprian by a short eulogistic *Life* of him written soon after his death, probably as early as 259, by his deacon Pontius. There is also an account of his trial and death written very little later, on the basis of the official report of them. Eusebius gives us some information about him in his *Church History* (vi. 43. 3; vii. 3), and Jerome deals with him in *On Illustrious Men* 67.

The *Life* by Pontius runs through the questions dealt with in the treatises so accurately that a collection of them, and probably of the letters, must have lain before the deacon when he wrote. The famous Cheltenham list of the books of scripture, found by Mommsen in a tenth-century manuscript in the library of Sir Thomas Phillipps in Cheltenham, England, in 1885 (though composed as early as A.D. 359), includes also a list of the works of Cyprian—fourteen treatises and thirty-four or thirty-five letters, concluding with the *Life of Cyprian*. The length of each work is given in stichoi, or lines of sixteen syllables. Only one of the treatises is missing—the compilation addressed *To Quirinus*—and only two of the many spurious pieces that were eventually ascribed to Cyprian have crept into the list—*Against the Jews* and *In Praise of Martyrdom*.

These pseudo-Cyprianic treatises are quite as numerous as the genuine ones, and, for their own sake as well as for their connection with Cyprian's name, they call for mention here. The most famous is the one entitled *That Idols Are Not Gods* (*Quod idola dii non sint*), a blast against idolatry, beginning with the sweeping statement that the heathen gods are simply ancient kings who have been deified, a doctrine reminiscent of Wisd. 14:15–20. This work is of interest for its manifest use of the *Octavius* of Minucius Felix, in Parts I and II, chapters 1–9, and Tertullian's *Apologeticus* in Part III, chapters 10–15. An effort has been made to show it to be the work of Novatian, but there is little basis for this, although it is a work of the latter part of the third century.

Another famous old Latin treatise that has been ascribed to Cyprian is that *Against Dice-Throwers* (*Ad Aleatores*). Harnack gave reasons for assigning it to Victor, bishop of Rome A.D. 189–99, of whom Jerome said that he was the earliest Latin Christian writer, but Koch has placed it in North Africa about 300.

A third is the chronological work composed early in A.D. 243 to correct Hippolytus' faulty formula for determining the date of Easter (*De Pascha computus*). A fourth, *To Novatian*, Harnack would assign to the Roman bishop Xystus II, A.D. 257–58, but most scholars despair of identifying its author. A fifth, *In*

Praise of Martyrdom, is in the form of a sermon, and may possibly have been written by Novatian, about the end of 249 or the beginning of 250, before he became a schismatic.

Ten other works have at various times been assigned, though on insufficient grounds, to Cyprian:

On the Trinity (really a work of Novatian)

On Shows (probably also Novatian's)

On the Advantage of Modesty (probably by Novatian)

Against the Jews (probably by Novatian)

On Rebaptism, which Harnack assigns to a Roman Ursinus, in the conflict between Cyprian and Stephen

On Mounts Sinai and Zion

On Repentance

On the Singleness of the Clergy (*De singularitate clericorum*)

To Vigilius the Bishop: On the Unbelief of the Jews

Cyprian's Feast (probably written about A.D. 400 in southern Gaul by another Cyprian, who also composed a poem covering the Hexateuch)

His New Testament

Cyprian's New Testament is clearly reflected in his treatises addressed *To Fortunatus* and *To Quirinus*, which consist so largely of quotations from scripture. It was precisely that of his Roman contemporary Hippolytus (who died ten years before Cyprian's conversion), except that Cyprian makes no use of II John. It contained the Four Gospels, the Acts, thirteen letters of Paul (that is, it did not include Hebrews), I Peter, I John, and the Revelation of John. As compared with the New Testament of Tertullian's later years, Cyprian's differs only in omitting Jude. Western Christianity still clung to the short New Testament, without Hebrews and with only two or three Catholic letters.

Cyprian's great interest in scripture is evidenced by the story about him that after his conversion he read nothing else. Of course, this is not to be taken literally; for one thing, it would conflict with that other story already told in connection with Tertullian, of Jerome's aged acquaintance who in his youth had been told by one of Cyprian's secretaries that Cyprian did not let a day pass without reading something of Tertullian and that he would call for Tertullian's works by saying, "Bring me the Master." This story is obviously related to the fact that several of Cyprian's titles and many of his ideas are derived from Tertullian.

Novatian of Rome

The ablest Christian leader at Rome in Cyprian's day was clearly Novatian. He had received baptism on a sickbed, the so-called clinical baptism, but he became a presbyter of the Roman church and evidently its leading presbyter, for when the see was vacant, after the martyrdom of Fabianus, in A.D. 250, he had charge of the affairs of the church and wrote two letters in its name to Cyprian, probably in August–September of that year (*Epistles* 30, 36). When Cornelius was elected bishop in 251, however, Novatian refused to acknowledge him as bishop and allowed himself to be chosen rival bishop, by a minority in the church, on the issue of refusing readmission to the church to those who had left the church during the persecution and now wanted to return to it. Cornelius favored readmitting them, but Novatian held they could never return to Christian fellowship. From this doctrine of a "pure" church, which was very much that held by Hippolytus twenty years earlier, Novatian and his followers came to be called Cathari, or Puritans. It must be noted that the schism had nothing to do with the doctrine of the church but only with its discipline. But Novatian and his supporters were excommunicated at a Roman synod, held in October of 251, although the Cathari succeeded in maintaining their separate existence for two and perhaps three centuries thereafter.

Novatian must have left Rome for a time in the persecution under Gallus (A.D. 251–53) or Valerian (253–60), for he seems to have written pastoral letters to his flock from some place of refuge; such as his works *On Shows, On Jewish Foods,* and *On the Advantage of Modesty*. The historian Socrates (*d.* after 439) says that he suffered martyrdom in Valerian's persecution, A.D. 257 (*Church History* iv. 28), but in 257–58 the treatise *To Novatian* was addressed to him, as Harnack thinks by Xystus II, bishop of Rome, so that we really do not know when or how he died.

Eusebius gives an account of the Novatian affair in *Church History* vi. 43, with some quotations from a letter of Cornelius to Fabius of Antioch about it, and from Dionysius of Alexandria to Novatian, urging him to relinquish his claims and return to the church. Eusebius always calls him Novatus, confusing him with the Carthaginian presbyter of that name. He accepts Cornelius' judgment of him—that he was a designing and self-seeking adventurer.

Novatian was the first considerable Latin writer of the Roman church. Jerome, in his account of him (*On Illustrious Men* 70), gives a list of nine works of his: *On the Passover, On the Sabbath, On Circumcision, On the Priesthood, On Prayer, On Jewish Foods, On Zeal, On Attalus*, and *On the Trinity* and adds that he wrote many others. The work *On the Trinity* Jerome describes as a great volume, "a sort of epitome of the work of Tertullian, which many mistakenly ascribe to Cyprian," but it is among the works of Tertullian that Novatian's book *On the Trinity* has been preserved.

His Works

No work of Novatian has come down to us under his own name, and yet some of his writings have survived as part of the writings of Tertullian or Cyprian. It would seem that the ancients found so much value in them that they could not resist copying them but could not bring themselves to credit them to the notorious Roman schismatic. In the long list of fourteen pseudo-Cyprianic writings, Harnack is satisfied that no less than five were written by Novatian: *On the Trinity, On Shows, On the Advantage of Modesty, Against the Jews*, and *In Praise of Martyrdom*. There is most doubt about the work *Against the Jews*; most scholars now recognize *On the Trinity* as certainly, and *On Shows, In Praise of Martyrdom*, and *On the Advantage of Modesty*, as probably, his.

Of the works listed by Jerome, only two, *On Jewish Foods* and *On the Trinity*, have survived. These are unquestioned writings of Novatian. *On the Trinity* was far from being "the sort of epitome of the work of Tertullian" that Jerome called it. It was the basis for Novatian's reputation as a theologian and went far to justify it. In the presence of the numerous heresies that had invaded the church, Novatian felt, as Tertullian had felt before him, that Christians should be shown what the true Christian positions were, as established by the Christian scriptures and the tradition of the church. From these had emerged the baptismal confession—the brief, compact statement of what it meant in terms of belief to be a Christian: to believe in God the Father, in Jesus Christ his Son, and in the Holy Spirit. Novatian makes this confession the framework of his discussion, which owes much to Tertullian and something also to Theophilus and Irenaeus.

His book is the work of a man trained in Stoic philosophy, skilled in dialectic, possessed of a poetical prose style, and equipped with all the resources of ancient rhetoric.

The work *On Jewish Foods* was written as a sort of pastoral when Novatian was absent from his flock, probably because of persecution, and in response to a request for such a discussion. It deals with the clean and unclean creatures named in Leviticus and arrives at an allegorical explanation of the unclean ones as symbolizing human sins and failings—indulgence, lust, and greed, essentially like that of the *Letter of Barnabas*. In this book Novatian expressly refers to previous works of his on the true *Priesthood* and on the true *Circumcision*.

If we undertake to arrange the works of Novatian in the order in which they were written, they fall into the following sequence. *On the Trinity* was written before he became a schismatic in 251, so probably before 250, perhaps as early as 245. *In Praise of Martyrdom* was also written before he became a schismatic and probably at the end of 249 or the beginning of 250. *Letters* 30 and 36 (among the *Letters of Cyprian*) Novatian wrote probably in August–September, 250. *On the Priesthood* and *On Circumcision* were written after Novatian became rival bishop in 251 and before *On Jewish Foods*, which mentions them both. *On Shows*, *On Jewish Foods*, and *On the Advantage of Modesty* are pastoral letters written to his people while he was compelled to be away from Rome to avoid arrest in the persecutions under Gallus, 251–53, or Valerian, 253–60. The works *Against the Jews* and *In Praise of Martyrdom* were already ascribed to Cyprian when what we know as the Cheltenham list of Cyprian's works was first composed, about A.D. 359.

As early as the time of Rufinus (d. 410) the work *On the Trinity* was credited to Tertullian, as Jerome reports. Both it and the work *On Jewish Foods* passed in medieval manuscripts (now lost) as writings of Tertullian and were published among his works in the first printed editions of them in 1545 and 1550. By 1579, however, both works were recognized as Novatian's and republished under his name.

Out of twelve or possibly thirteen works of Novatian of which we know, aside from the two letters to Cyprian, we now possess five, or possibly six: *On the Trinity*, *On Jewish Foods*, *On Shows*, *On the Advantage of Modesty*, *In Praise of Martyrdom*, and, if it is genuine, *Against the Jews*. Seven are lost: *On the Passover, On the Sabbath, On Circumcision, On the Priesthood, On Prayer, On Zeal,* and *On Attalus*. The twenty treatises bearing the name of Origen found some years ago by Batiffol (1900) and later ascribed to Novatian are now believed to be the work of Gregory of Iliberris (Elvira) in Spain (*d.* after 392).

Arnobius

At Sicca, in North Africa, there lived at the close of the third century a teacher of rhetoric and oratory named Arnobius. He was for a long time a pagan and a vigorous opponent of Christianity but was at length converted. Jerome says that when he asked to be admitted to the church the local bishop demanded proof of his sincerity, and he responded by writing a work *Against the Heathen,* in seven books, and was accepted forthwith. Whatever may be thought of this quaint story, from Jerome's *Chronicle* for the year 2343, or A.D. 327, *Against the Heathen* does seem to have been rather hastily written and shows very little acquaintance with the Bible, except the Gospels. Arnobius had read Plato and Cicero, however, and he also knew Clement's *Address to the Greeks* (the *Protrepticus*). It is not unlikely that he was an elderly man when he was converted, and that was why the bishop was doubtful and why later hearers of his story were so impressed.

Arnobius' book was evidently written when Diocletian's persecution was still in progress, probably in A.D. 304–10. In fact, it is a defense of Christianity, an apology. In Books i and ii he presents Christianity, and in the rest he attacks paganism. Book i takes up the argument that Christianity had brought disaster upon the world; but there had always been wars and famines before Christianity came. In fact, Christianity gives some hope of remedying such things, for war, at least, would be done away with, if Christianity prevailed. The gods should not be displeased with the Christians, for Christianity teaches the fear of God. He discusses the points brought against Christianity—that Christ was a man and that he died on a cross, both of which Arnobius seeks to reconcile with Christ's divine nature. Book ii maintains that Christ introduced the true religion and develops Arnobius' curious doctrine of the soul as not necessarily of divine origin or immortal unless it knows God and throws itself on his mercy.

Book iii meets the charge that Christians do not worship the national gods by saying that their worship of God the Creator and Father of all covers the whole ground. Book iv deals with the absurdities, trivialities, and indecencies of pagan mythology. Book v declares that these myths cannot be dismissed as mere poetic fancies, for the historians, too, have dealt with them. The mysteries are described and bitingly analyzed. Book vi deals with the temples and their idols, and Book vii with the futility of material sacrifice. The work seems to break off rather than to reach a finished end. The whole forms a bewildering series of glimpses of ancient mythologies and religious practices from the pagan world of the third and fourth centuries.

Arnobius' book seems to have been little read; Lactantius, who is said by Jerome to have been his pupil, doubtless while Arnobius was still a pagan (*On Illustrious Men* 80), shows no particular acquaintance with it in his works, sime of them written a few years later, and its subsequent influence is slight; Jerome is about the only writer who read it and speaks of it, but he does so several times. Only one manuscript of it has ever been found, written early in the ninth century, but many a better work of Christian literature has fared even worse, as we have seen. And it was as the eighth (*octavus*) book of Arnobius' *Against the Heathen*, it will be remembered, that the *Octavius* of Minucius Felix was preserved and has come down to us. In the "Gelasian Decree" on books to be received and those not to be received, really a work of the sixth century, Arnobius' work is designated as apocryphal.

Lactantius

Among those who studied rhetoric under Arnobius at Sicca, in Africa, was Lucius Caecilius Firmianus Lactantius. He came of heathen parents and was born not later than A.D. 250. Probably his first work, written before he became a Christian, was his *Symposium*, or *Banquet*, now lost. He was teaching rhetoric at his home in Africa when Diocletian, who was developing Nicomedia in Bithynia as the capital of the eastern section of the empire, summoned him to that city to teach there (*Institutes* v. 2.2). Lactantius recorded this journey in hexameter verse in his *Journey to Nicomedia*, which is also lost. A third work of his, probably from this early period, and now lost, was his *Grammar*.

Whether he became a Christian before or after he left Africa is not certain, but it was probably after. But the outbreak of Diocletian's persecution in A.D. 303 interrupted any public work he was doing at Nicomedia and limited him to writing; he was already at work upon his principal book, the *Divine Institutes*. But the intensification of the persecution in 305 forced him soon after to leave Bithynia. Galerius' edict of toleration in 311 made it possible for him to return, however, and there he seems to have remained until 317, when the emperor Constantine summoned him to Trèves, in Gaul, to become the tutor of Constantine's eldest son Crispus, then about ten years of age. Jerome says Lactantius was by that time "extremely old" and that is why his birth must be dated before or about A.D. 250. There is no record of the date of his death, but it probably occurred not far from A.D. 325.

Jerome, in *On Illustrious Men* 80, gives a list of twelve works written by Lactantius: the *Banquet*, the *Journey*, the *Grammar*, *On the Wrath of God*, the *Divine Institutes* (in seven books), an *Epitome* of it, *To Asclepiades*, *On Persecution*, *Letters to Probus* (four books), *Letters to Severus* (two books), *Letters to Demetrianus* (two books), and *On God's Workmanship*. Four of these, which were probably early gathered into a collection, are still extant: *On God's Workmanship*, the *Institutes*, the *Epitome*, and *On the Wrath of God*.

Three other works or fragments apparently of Lactantius have come down to us; one is the poem *On the Phoenix Bird*, another is the remarkable book *On the Deaths of the Persecutors*, and a third is a short fragment *On the Emotions*. The last is probably part of a letter. The book *On the Deaths of the Persecutors* is probably to be identified with the work that Jerome calls *On Persecution*. Of thirteen works of Lactantius, therefore (aside from the little fragment *On the Emotions*), we possess six—*On God's Workmanship*, the *Institutes*, the *Epitome*, the *Wrath of God*, the *Deaths of the Persecutors*, and the *Phoenix Bird*.

If we seek to relate these books chronologically to the life of Lactantius and the history of the times, the *Banquet*, the *Journey*, and probably the *Grammar* come first and, it is very likely, belong to the time before his conversion. The book *On God's Workmanship* was probably written in Nicomedia in A.D. 304, after the persecution began but before its intensification in 305. It deals in much detail with the constitution of the human frame which some said was inferior to that of the beasts, especially in its liability to disease; Lactantius points out the enormous advantage man has in the possession of mental and spiritual faculties.

The Divine Institutes

In 304 he was already at work upon the *Divine Institutes;* he refers to that undertaking in his book *On God's Workmanship* (15:6; 20:2). Two recent philosophical attacks upon Christianity, one by Hierocles, who is said to have instigated Diocletian's persecution, stirred Lactantius to offer a positive presentation of Christianity. This turned out to be his great work. He was busy with it for a number of years, beginning with 304. It was certainly substantially finished by 311, and probably well before that time, although the dedication to Constantine in 1:1 and 7:26, and implied in 2:1, 4:1, and 6:3, presupposes the new edict of toleration issued by Constantine at Milan in A.D. 313, and these touches were probably introduced into a revised edition of the book after that emperor summoned Lactantius to Trèves in 317, although some would say they were added by another hand.[6] Lactantius was therefore writing the *Institutes* at the very time that his old professor Arnobius back in North Africa was writing his work *Against the Heathen,* A.D. 304–10.

The *Institutes* form a book a good deal (almost a third) longer than the New Testament. Some idea of its contents can be gained from the titles of the seven books: (1) "On False Religion," polytheism is false; the best thought of prophets, poets, and philosophers shows that God is one; (2) "On the Origin of Error," polytheism and its causes; (3) "On False Wisdom," the errors of the philosophers; (4) "On True Wisdom and Religion," they are inseparable. The prophets foretold the life and work of Christ; (5) "On Justice," which the Christians seek to bring back to the world; (6) "On True Worship," which consists in serving God and showing justice and mercy to our fellowmen; (7) "On the Happy Life," the right use of this world, the immortality of the

---

[6] The dualistic additions to the *Institutes* also seem most naturally explained as introduced by Lactantius himself into a revised edition of the work, produced after his removal to Trèves, though why he should then fall a victim to Manichean tendencies is a difficult question; 2:20 and the extended passage at the end of 7:5 are leading examples. These dualistic additions and the occasional apostrophes of Constantine seem clearly by the same hand, which is probably that of Lactantius himself.

soul, and the life to come. Lactantius followed the millennial calculations of Julius Africanus, that Christ was born in the year of
the world 5500 and that, when the sixth "day" of a thousand years
was ended, which would be in about two hundred years (7:25),
the millennium would be ushered in, to be followed by the release
of the devil, further outbreaks against the church, and the final
resurrection and judgment.

Other Writings

In the years 313 and 314 Lactantius wrote three books: *On the
Wrath of God, On the Deaths of the Persecutors*, and the *Epitome of the Institutes*—probably in that order. The work *On the
Wrath of God* was dedicated to a certain Donatus, who had
been in prison for six years, A.D. 305–11, and was probably written
shortly after the revision of the *Institutes*, in A.D. 313. The book
On the Deaths of the Persecutors, probably to be identified with
what Jerome called *On Persecution*, must have followed almost
at once. This extraordinary work, which seems both in general
and in detail to show the influence of II Maccabees, tells the fates
of the persecuting emperors: Nero, Domitian, Decius, Valerian,
and Aurelian are briefly sketched, chapters 1–6, and the bulk of
the book, chapters 7–52, devoted to contemporary persecutors
and what became of them—Diocletian, Maximian, Galerius, and
Maximin. The cruelties perpetrated by these emperors against
the Christians and others Lactantius recites unsparingly and relates with quite understandable if not altogether Christian relish
the dreadful ends which overtook them. Of course, he sees in
the fates of these persecuting emperors the judgment of God for
their brutality and violence, not only against the church but
against many others of their subjects, high and low. And while
there may well be exaggeration here, there is no doubt that much
of what Lactantius says is true.

To this time, probably to 314, belongs also the *Epitome of the
Institutes*, written in response to a request from a brother Penta-
dius. It is a free and bold rehandling of the material of the seven
books in a much shorter form but with the inclusion of some
new material as well.

Harnack suggests that it was the striking work *On the Deaths
of the Persecutors* that led Constantine in 317 to invite Lactantius
to Trèves in Gaul to become the tutor of Crispus, the emperor's

eldest son. Although the authenticity of the book *On the Deaths of the Persecutors* and the poem *On the Phoenix* has been seriously doubted, they are probably both the work of Lactantius, and most modern scholars are disposed to accept them as his. The story of the phoenix, the bird which lives five hundred years and then makes a kind of cocoon and enters it and dies, only to have another phoenix generated by its decay, is as old as Herodotus (ii. 73), and is told also by Pliny the Elder (*Natural History* x. 2) and by Clement of Rome (*To the Corinthians* 25). Just when Lactantius wrote it cannot be determined, but it clearly belongs to his Christian period. It was later imitated by the heathen poet Claudian, about A.D. 400, in a poem of the same name.

Among the lost works of Lactantius are the eight books of his letters: *To Probus* (four books), *To Severus* (two books), and *To Demetrianus* (two books). These were sometimes more like treatises than personal communications; Damasus wrote Jerome that they sometimes ran in length to a thousand lines and complained that they had little to say about doctrine but were about metrical, geographical, and philosophical matters, in which he took little interest. Jerome once speaks (in his commentary on Galatians) of a remark in the eighth book of Lactantius' letters *To Demetrianus*, so that the three groups of letters—of four, two, and two books—probably circulated as a single collection in eight books. Except for a few fragments, they have disappeared.

Lactantius expressed an intention of writing a book *Against All Heresies* (*Institutes* iv. 30. 14) and another *Against the Jews* (*ibid*. vii 1. 26), but he seems never to have carried out these plans. Although he was not a great theologian or much interested in speculative thought, he had read very widely himself, was much used by Jerome, and was read by Augustine. The charm of his style and the wealth of his imagination went far to make up for his doctrinal weakness, and he was called the Christian Cicero.

Victorinus

Toward the close of the third century there lived in Poetovio, in Pannonia (the modern Pettau in Styria), a Christian bishop named Victorinus, who suffered martyrdom in 304 in the persecution of Diocletian. He wrote somewhat copiously, Jerome informs us (*On Illustrious Men* 18, 74) producing commentaries on Genesis, Exodus, Leviticus, Isaiah, Ezekiel, Habakkuk, Ecclesiastes, the Song of Songs, Matthew, and the Revelation, but of these only the commentary on the Revelation has come down to us. Jerome reshaped this work, omitting the highly millennial conclusion, with which he strongly disagreed, and adding sections from his contemporary Tyconius. The Spanish presbyter Beatus, late in the eighth century, made use of Jerome's work in his great commentary on the Revelation.[7]

The commentaries of Victorinus himself owned much to Origen. Indeed, Jerome thought he was more expert in Greek than in Latin and spoke slightingly of his Latinity, and Victorinus' modern editor, Haussleiter, finds his style decidedly awkward.

Victorinus also wrote a work *Against All Heresies,* which is mentioned by Jerome but has disappeared, although an effort has been made, notably by Harnack, to identify it with a work of that name that has come down to us appended to Tertullian's *Prescription of Heretics.* About the only objection that can be brought against this attractive idea is that the style seems rather better than Victorinus exhibits in the *Commentary on the Revelation.*

Another small piece from the pen of Victorinus is the fragment *De fabrica mundi* preserved in a single manuscript at Lambeth and published in 1688 by W. Cave. Although it is not mentioned in antiquity, it seems to be a genuine work of Victorinus; the style is like his, and Jerome said he wrote many other things besides the ten he listed.

---

[7] Henry A. Sanders, *Beati in Apocalipsin libri duodecim* (Rome: American Academy, 1930). Primasius in the sixth century also used it.

15

EUSEBIUS AND EARLY CHRISTIAN LITERATURE

The literature we have been discussing did not just happen to be preserved. The various books were obviously collected and used by authors themselves and by their students, and they passed into libraries both private and semi-public. The existence of such collections is explicitly attested by Eusebius and can be inferred from his own writings and from those of his predecessors. Like the New Testament and the Old, early Christian literature consists of a little library of various books assembled on and for various occasions.

Collections

One of the papyri found at Oxyrhynchus and dating from the second century (*Oxyrhynchus Papyrus* xviii. 2192) clearly shows how such collections would come into existence.

"Make copies," its unknown author writes, "of Books VI and VII of Hypsicrates' *Characters in Comedy* and send them to me. For Harpocration says that they are among Polion's books. But it is likely that others also have acquired them. He also has prose epitomes of Thersagoras' work *On Tragic Myths*.[1] According to Harpocration, Demetrius the bookseller has them. I have instructed Apollonides to send me certain books of my own which you will hear of, in good time, from Seleucus himself. If you find any, apart from those I have acquired, make copies and send them to me. Diodorus and his friends also have some which I have not acquired."

As the editors point out, this letter reflects the activities of a group of friends at Oxyrhynchus, all interested in building their libraries by hiring copyists and, occasionally, buying books. Such libraries were often cataloged, and among the papyri quite a few

---

[1] I.e., on the myths used by Greek tragic poets.

booklists have been found. Indeed, an Oxford papyrus of the
early fourth century gives a partly legible list of Christian books
in the library of some individual or community.[2] The manuscripts
in the collection include the "Shepherd" (of Hermas), "Origen"
(title lost), "Leviticus," "Job and . . ." (the rest is lost), "Acts
of the Apostles," "Apa Bal" (?), "Song of Songs," "Origen on
John," "Exodus–Numbers," and the "Great Book" (probably the
Four Gospels).

Libraries

Eusebius himself speaks of a public library at Rome where one
could find Philo's book *On Virtues* (*Church History* ii. 18. 8) as
well as the writings of Josephus (iii. 9. 2). He wrote his own
works, however, in reliance on the church libraries at Jerusalem
and Caesarea. The first of these libraries had been founded by
Alexander, bishop of Jerusalem (212–250), pupil of Pantaenus
and Clement of Alexandria and friend of Origen. Eusebius used
this library himself and listed some of the Christian writings he
found there—works by Beryllus of Bostra, Hippolytus, and Gaius
of Rome (vi. 20). To judge from a fragment of the *Cesti* of
Julius Africanus (*Oxyrhynchus Papyrus* iii. 412), the library also
contained at least the *Odyssey* of Homer. Unfortunately we know
little about what else was there. Isidore of Seville may have exaggerated when he said there were 30,000 volumes, but we have no
real basis for guessing.[3]

The second library Eusebius used was in his own see city of
Caesarea.[4] Indeed, he acquired most of his materials there, partly
by employing scribes to copy extracts for him. This library had
been established by Origen and his admirer Pamphilus and contained as large a collection of early Christian literature as could
be obtained. Eusebius himself added a good deal to the library.
He assembled more than a hundred letters by Origen (vi. 36. 3)
and was responsible for a collection of acts of the early martyrs
(iv. 15). In addition, he made use of other "collected works" or

---

[2] C. H. Roberts in *Zeitschrift für die neutestamentliche Wissenschaft*,
XXXVII (1938), 186–87.

[3] See A. Ehrhardt, "Die griechische Patriarchal-Bibliothek von Jerusalem,"
Römische Quartalschrift, V (1891), 217–65; VI (1892), 339–65.

[4] *Church History* vi. 32. 3; vii. 28. 1.

volumes of tracts, as H. J. Lawlor demonstrated.[5] A later notice about this library tells us that Euzoius, bishop of Caesarea about 367, "renewed" some of the works of Philo on skins; we thus see that Eusebius' knowledge of Philo was presumably derived from this library. It was destroyed by the Arabs in 637.

The Church History

Eusebius had already begun using the Caesarea library when, about 303, he prepared the first edition of his *Chronicle*. In it he made use of writings by Philo, Josephus, Justin, Tatian, Theophilus, Irenaeus, Tertullian, Julius Africanus, Clement, and Origen. All these authors are mentioned again in the first edition of his *Church History* (Books i–vii), completed soon afterwards. The *Chronicle* provided a skeleton for the *Church History*, which is more a history of early Christian literature than a real history either of deeds or of thought. In it there are references to the writings of about thirty-five Christian authors, in addition to lists of the writings of Philo (ii. 18) and Josephus (iii. 9).

For the early church Eusebius could use the supposedly genuine correspondence of Abgar, king of Edessa, with Jesus (i. 13) as well as some writings by the Apostolic Fathers—I Clement, seven letters by Ignatius and one by Polycarp, the *Shepherd* of Hermas, and the *Interpretations of the Dominical Oracles* by Papias (whom, on theological grounds, he preferred to date a little later). It is not at all clear that he knew either the *Didache* or the *Letter of Barnabas*. From the period a little later he could quote an excerpt from the apology by Quadratus and mention that by Aristides (iv. 3); he knew a "letter of Pilate" (ii. 2) and the letters of Pliny and Trajan, but only from the *Apology* of Tertullian (iii. 33). In the library there was a bound volume containing the acts of various martyrs—Polycarp, Pionius, Carpus with Papylus and Agathonice (iv. 15. 46–48)—and to it Eusebius himself added the account of the Gallican martyrs (v. praef. 2; v. 4. 3).

Much of his information about the later second century was derived from extensive collections already made. These included the writings of Justin (iv. 18), Dionysius of Corinth (iv. 23), Theophilus of Antioch (iv. 24), Melito of Sardis (iv. 26), Apol-

---

[5] *Eusebiana* (Oxford, 1912), 136–78.

linaris of Hierapolis (iv. 27), Tatian (iv. 29), and Bardesanes (iv. 30). He lists the works of all of these and insists that he has listed Justin's to "urge scholars to a diligent regard for his books" (iv. 8. 10). Rhetoricians were aware that such bibliographies, if simply derived from library catalogues, could give an incorrect impression of erudition,[6] and some of Eusebius' comments suggest that he knew little or nothing about the contents of the books he lists. From the end of the second century and the beginning of the third he seems to have a few dossiers of controversial writings— against Montanists (v. 16–19), works by Irenaeus (v. 20 and 26), on the paschal controversy (v. 23), miscellaneous documents (v. 27–28), and works by Serapion of Antioch (vi. 12).

When he reaches the Christian teachers of Alexandria he is much better informed—as one would expect in view of the origins of the libraries. He lists the works of Clement (vi. 13) and Origen (vi. 24–25, 32, 36),[7] and knows so many writings by Dionysius of Alexandria that he has to scatter quotations throughout the sixth and seventh books. With the earlier Alexandrians he associates three letters by Alexander of Jerusalem (vi. 11 and 14) and some works by Hippolytus (vi. 22) and Julius Africanus (vi. 31), since these men were associated with Origen. The sources he quotes in the seventh book include works by Dionysius, a rescript of the emperor Gallienus, a dossier of the proceedings against Paul of Samosata,[8] and an excerpt from the paschal canons by Anatolius of Laodicea.

The *Church History* is thus useful chiefly because of the excerpts it provides and because of the lost works it lists. It is little more than a literary chronicle. There is no attempt to explain either literary movements or historical events. Indeed, Eusebius' prefatory discussion of his plan shows how limited his range was. He intended to discuss (1) lists of apostolic successions among the bishops, (2) important events and the leaders in them, (3) famous teachers and writers, (4) heretics, (5) the disasters that came upon the Jewish nation after the crucifixion, (6) the war of the

---

[6] See Quintilian, *Inst. orat.* x. 1. 57.

[7] His "life of Origen" is not exactly a biography; see M. Hornschuh in *Zeitschrift für Kirchengeschichte*, LXXI (1960), 1–25, 193–214.

[8] Cf. H. de Riedmatten, *Les actes du procès de Paul de Samosate* (*Paradosis*, Freiburg, 1952), 15–23.

heathen against the divine word, along with the noble martyrs, and (7)—a later addition—martyrdoms in his own time. In addition, he says, he planned to pluck passages from the meadows of Christian literature (thus producing a "florilegium" or anthology) and to "indicate what church writers in each period have made use of which of the disputed books" of the New Testament "and what they have said about the canonical and acknowledged books, and anything they have said about those that are not such" (iii. 3. 3).

The result of such a chaotic plan is about what one would expect, especially since Eusebius quotes from none of the heretical writers whose heresies he discusses. Sometimes he is completely inconsistent, as when he places Hegesippus—one of his chief authorities for the early period—in "the first succession from the apostles" (ii. 23. 3), in the reign of Hadrian, 117–138 (iv. 8. 2), and in the last third of the second century (iv. 21). Longevity cannot account for this confusion. W. Telfer has shown that only the last date is right.[9] In addition, because of his lack of information or interest there are surprising gaps in his account. He knows nothing of the apologist Athenagoras and little about the apologies of Tatian and Theophilus. He has no idea where Hippolytus lived. From Tertullian he has only the *Apology* and he does not seem to have read anything by Cyprian (vi. 43. 3). It is especially unfortunate that he was so little concerned with the history of Christian thought. When he says that Bardesanes "did not completely cleanse himself from the filth of the old heresy" of the Valentinians (iv. 30. 3), we have not been told a great deal.

Could Eusebius Have Done Better?

A significant comparison can be made between the *Church History* and the *Preparation for the Gospel*, which he wrote between 312 and 318. In the latter work his aim was different: he wanted to prove the priority and superiority of "oriental" theologies, especially that of the Hebrews, to the philosophy of the Greeks (his aim was thus essentially the same as that of Hellenistic Jewish writers and earlier Christian apologists), and along the way he returned to several of the Jewish and Christian writings he had used in the *Church History*. These include Philo, Josephus,

---

[9] *Harvard Theological Review*, LIII (1960), 143–53.

Tatian, Bardesanes, Clement of Alexandria, Origen, and Dionysius of Alexandria, not to mention the Christian writing by "Maximus" (Methodius). His acquaintance with Hellenistic Jewish thought has been expanded by his readings in Alexander Polyhistor, Aristeas, and Aristobulus. And he has also come to be acquainted with a wide selection of philosophical treatises by Plato—though not by Aristotle—and by representatives of the Aristotelian, Cynic, Epicurean, Middle Platonic, and Neoplatonic schools of the second and third centuries. The general excellence of his sources in the *Preparation* and his fairly full quotations from them present a rather sharp contrast with the mediocrity of his work in the *Church History*.

This contrast can be explained in at least two ways. First, the materials he used in the *Preparation* were more adequately arranged according to the tradition of the philosophical schools than were his Christian materials. They reflect the teaching tradition of the Neoplatonic curriculum, at least for the most part,[10] whereas Eusebius was himself a pioneer in trying to combine the writings of various Christian schools with those derived from Alexandria. Second, the needs of controversy were more sharply focused in the *Preparation* than in the *Church History*. Eusebius had to present a fairly clear picture of philosophical thought in the later work, and thus both precedent and practical occasion resulted in a more adequate use of source materials. In summary, then, we may say that although we owe a good deal of our information about early Christian literature to Eusebius we might owe still more had he written the *Preparation* first and then moved toward a more adequate *Church History*.

Fortunately we are not entirely dependent on his work, indispensable though it is. (In some measure we may compare it with the Acts of the Apostles, which, taken apart from the letters of Paul—and the gospels, would not provide a very satisfactory picture of the apostolic age.) The other materials we possess include small collections of Christian documents copied and recopied in the patristic period, the Byzantine age, and late medieval times.

---

[10] We know something of this curriculum from Porphyry as quoted by Eusebius, *Church History* vi. 19. 8, and in his own *Life of Plotinus*, 72; see also J. H. Waszink, *Timaeus a Calcidio translatus commentarioque instructus* (*Plato Latinus*, ed. R. Klibansky, IV; London, Leiden, 1962), xxxv–cvi.

Sometimes we have translations of Greek works in Latin, Syriac, Armenian, or Coptic. Beyond such collections lie the works that lucky modern discoveries by archaeologists have given us. Among these should be mentioned Melito's *Paschal Homily* and Origen's *Dialogue with Heraclides*, as well as the new Gnostic library from Nag Hammadi. These discoveries encourage the belief that in the future still more will be found.

The study of early Christian literature has a significant future, especially when it is combined with the history of ideas, both theological and non-theological. The relation of Christian literature to the non-Christian literature of the time remains to be analyzed.

16

THE LOST BOOKS OF EARLY CHRISTIAN LITERATURE

With the conversion of Constantine and the adoption of Christianity by the empire, the church entered upon a period of increasingly rigorous definition of both doctrine and discipline. It was a century of great churches, great Bibles, great councils, and great names—Basil, the Gregories, Theodore, Theodoret, Athanasius, and Chrysostom in the East; and in the West, Ambrose, Rufinus, Jerome, and Augustine. It was ushered in by the Council of Nicaea and the figure of Eusebius, and it was a time of great scholars and great theologians; but the pristine radiance of the movement and the literature, the heroic period, which we have been surveying, was gone.

Although book production in the first Christian centuries had reached a high degree of proficiency, the necessity of writing every book by hand being largely offset by the abundance of slave labor, the barbarians ended all that, and the methods of book-copying in the Middle Ages were quite unequal to preserving either pagan or Christian literature, both of which suffered great losses. The wonder is that so much of either was preserved at all after the highly efficient ancient methods of publication disappeared with the old Greco-Roman civilization.

It is, of course, a melancholy business, reporting the tragic losses early Christian literature has sustained. But let us emulate our scientific friends who sometimes conclude a subject with a list of problems awaiting solution, for it is reasonable to think that we are more likely to go on finding these lost books if we have a clear idea of what we are to look for. The lost writings found in whole or in part in the last fifty years are a goodly company: the *Revelation of Peter*, the *Apology of Aristides*, Melito's *Paschal Homily*, the *Epistle of the Apostles*, the *Acts of Paul*, Irenaeus' *Demonstration of the Apostolic Preaching*, the *Odes of Solomon,* the *Apostolic Tradition* of Hippolytus, and numbers of others. And it may help in the identification of others to assemble a list of books that are now little more than names to us but that might, and in some cases certainly would, throw much needed light upon this history.

In the list "no text" is to be understood as meaning "no extended body of text." I have not taken account of scattered fragments.

The Letter of Polycarp to the Philippians; no complete Greek text

The Epistle of the Apostles; no Greek text

The Letter of the Gallican Churches; no complete text

The Shepherd of Hermas; no complete Greek text

The Revelation of Peter; no complete Greek text

The Sibylline Books, Books ix, x, and xv; no text

The Pistis Sophia; no Greek text

The Gospel of the Egyptians; no complete text

The Gospel of the Hebrews; no complete text

The Gospel of Peter; no complete text

The British Museum Gospel; no complete text

The Gospel of Thomas; no complete Greek text

The Traditions of Matthias; no text

The Secret Sayings of Matthias; no text

The Gospel of Matthias(?); no text

The Gospel of Ebionites; no text

The Gospel of Basilides; no text

The Gospel of Judas(?); no text

The Gospel of Truth; no Greek text

The Gospel of Philip; no Greek text

The Gospel of Bartholomew(?); no text

The Gospel of Barnabas(?); no text

The Gospel of Apelles(?); no text

The Gospel of Cerinthus(?); no text

The Gospel of Eve(?); no text

The Gospel of Perfection(?); no text

The Acts of Paul; no complete text

The Acts of John; no complete text

The Acts of Peter; no complete text

The Acts of Andrew; no complete text

The Clementine Recognitions; no complete Greek text

The Preaching of Peter; no text
The Apology of Quadratus; no text
Aristo, *Dialogue of Jason and Papiscus;* no text
The Apology of Aristides; no complete Greek text
Justin, *Dialogue with Trypho;* no complete text
    Against the Greeks; no text
    Against All Heresies (the Refutation?); no text
    On the Sovereignty of God; no text
    Psaltes; no text
    On the Soul; no text
The Letter to Diognetus; no complete text
Tatian, *The Diatessaron;* no Greek or Syriac text
    Problems; no text
    On Perfection according to the Saviour; no Greek text
    On Animals; no text
Rhodo, *Solutions;* no text
    Against the Heresy of Marcion; no text
    On the Six Days' Work of Creation; no text
Marcion, *The Contradictions;* no text
The Teaching of the Apostles, short form; no Greek text
Papias, *Interpretations of Sayings of the Lord;* no text
The Odes of Solomon; no complete Greek text
Hegesippus, *Memoirs;* no text
Melito, *On the Conduct of Life and the Prophets;* no text
    On the Church; no text
    On the Lord's Day; no text
    On the Faith of Man; no text
    On His Creation; no text
    On the Obedience of Faith; no text
    On the Senses; no text
    On the Soul and Body; no text
    On Baptism; no text
    On Truth; no text
    On the Creation and Generation of Christ; no text
    On Prophecy; no text
    On Hospitality; no text
    A Key [to the Scriptures]; no text
    On the Devil and the Revelation of John; no text
    The Apology; no text
    Selections from the Old Testament; no text

Theophilus of Antioch, *Against the Heresy of Hermogenes;* no
  text
     Against Marcion; no text
     A Gospel Harmony(?); no text
Irenaeus, *Refutation of Gnosticism;* no Greek text
     Demonstration of the Apostolic Preaching; no Greek text
     On Knowledge; no text
     On Schism; no text
     On the Ogdoad; no text
     On Sovereignty; no text
Clement of Alexandria, *The Outlines* [of Scripture]; no text
     On the Passover; no text
     On Fasting; no text
     On Evil-speaking; no text
     On Patience; no text
     On Providence; no text
     On the Prophet Amos(?); no text
Tertullian, *On Baptism;* no Greek text
     On the Hope of the Faithful; no text
     On Paradise; no text
     Against the Followers of Apelles; no text
     On the Origin of the Soul; no text
     On Fate; no text
     On Ecstasy; no text
     The Garments of Aaron; no text
     To a Philosophic Friend; no text
     On Flesh and Soul; no text
     On Submission of Soul; no text
     The Superstition of the World; no text
     On Shows; no Greek text
     On the Veiling of Virgins; no Greek text
     On Clean and Unclean Animals(?); no text
     On Circumcision(?); no text
Hippolytus, *Refutation of All Heresies;* no complete Greek text
     On Daniel; no complete Greek text
     On the Song of Songs; no Greek text
     On the Blessing of Moses; no Greek text
     On the Story of David and Goliath; no Greek text
     The Six Days of Creation; no text
     What Followed the Six Days; no text
     The Blessing of Jacob; no text

    The Blessing of Balaam; no text
    Moses' Song; no text
    Elkanah and Hannah; no text
    The Witch of Endor; no text
    On the Psalms; no text
    On Proverbs; no text
    On Ecclesiastes; no text
    On Isaiah (part); no text
    On Ezekiel (part); no text
    On Zechariah; no text
    On Matthew (part); no text
    The Parable of the Talents; no text
    The Two Thieves; no text
    On the Revelation; no text
    Against Marcion; no text
    Against Artemon, the Little Labyrinth; no text
    Against Thirty-two Heresies; no text
    Heads against Gaius (?); no text
    In Defense of the Gospel and Revelation of John; no text
    On the Resurrection; no text
    On the Universe—against the Greeks and Plato; no text
    On Good and the Source of Evil; no text
    Address to Severina; no text
    Determination of the Date of Easter; no text
    The Chronicle; no Greek text
    The Apostolic Tradition; no Greek text
Gaius, *Dialogue with Proclus;* no text
Origen, *The Hexapla;* no text (a Syriac version of the Septuagint
    column)
    Homilies; 554 out of 574 lost in Greek; 388 not even in the
        Latin version
    Commentaries; 275 out of 291 lost in Greek; very little pre-
        served in Latin
    On First Principles; no complete Greek text
    Letters; Eusebius' collection of 100 lost, except for 2
    Miscellanies, 10 books; no text
Julius Africanus, *Chronography;* no text
    Cestoi, or *Paradoxa;* no text
    Letter to Aristides; no text
Dionysius of Alexandria, *On Nature;* no complete text

On Trials; no text
On Promises; no complete text
The Refutation and Apology; no text
Exposition of Ecclesiastes (partial); no text
On Temptations; no text
Fifty Letters, most of them; no text

Nepos of Arsinoë, *Refutation of the Allegorists;* no text
Novatian, *On the Passover;* no text
On the Sabbath; no text
On Circumcision; no text
On the Priesthood; no text
On Prayer; no text
On Zeal; no text
On Attalus; no text

Pamphilus, *Defense of Origen;* no Greek text; only Book i in Latin
Lactantius, *The Banquet* (*Symposium*); no text
Journey to Nicomedia; no text
Grammar; no text
Letters to Probus, four books; no text
Letters to Severus, two books; no text
Letters to Demetrianus, two books; no text

Victorinus, *Against All Heresies;* no certain text
Commentaries on Genesis, Exodus, Leviticus, Isaiah, Ezekiel, Habakkuk, Ecclesiastes, Song of Songs, Matthew; no text

There were, of course, a host of minor writers whom I have not enumerated, some of whose writings might prove of unexpected significance, and the above list is not complete even for all the authors named. But the progress of excavation and research may well bring us in the next half-century not a few of the books listed above as lost.

SELECT BIBLIOGRAPHY

Abbreviations

ACW   Ancient Christian Writers, Westminster, Md.
CSEL   Corpus Scriptorum Ecclesiasticorum Latinorum, Vienna
GCS   Die griechischen christlichen Schriftsteller, Berlin-Leipzig
LCL   Loeb Classical Library, London, Cambridge, Mass.
SC   Sources chrétiennes, Paris
TU   Texte und Untersuchungen, Berlin-Leipzig

CHAPTER I. EARLY CHRISTIAN LITERATURE

ALTANER, B. *Patrology.* London, 1960.

BARDENHEWER, O. *Geschichte der altkirchlichen Literatur.* 5 vols (Vols. I–II, to Eusebius). 2d ed. Freiburg, 1913–32.

CROSS, F. L. *The Early Christian Fathers.* London, 1960.

CRUTTWELL, C. T. *A Literary History of Early Christianity.* 2 vols. London, 1893.

DIBELIUS, M. *A Fresh Approach to the New Testament and Early Christian Literature.* New York, 1936.

HARNACK, A. *Geschichte der altchristlichen Literatur.* 3 vols. Leipzig, 1893–1904.

HENNECKE, E. and SCHNEEMELCHER, W. *Neutestamentliche Apokryphen. I. Evangelien.* Tübingen, 1959. (English translation by R. McL. WILSON, Philadelphia, 1962; Volume II in preparation.)

JAMES, M. R. *The Apocryphal New Testament.* Oxford, 1924.

PUECH, A. *Histoire de la littérature grecque chrétienne depuis les origines jusqu'à la fin du iv⁰ siècle.* 3 vols. Paris, 1928–30.

QUASTEN, J. *Patrology.* 3 vols. Westminster, Md., 1950–60.

Gnostic Literature

GRANT, R. M. *Gnosticism: An Anthology.* London, New York, 1961.

HARNACK, A. VON. *Marcion: das Evangelium vom fremden Gott.* 2d ed. TU, XLV, 1924.

VÖLKER, W. *Quellen zur Geschichte der christlichen Gnosis.* Tübingen, 1932.

See also bibliographies to chapters 2–5.

CHAPTER 2. LETTERS

AUDET, J. P. *La Didachè: instructions des apôtres.* Paris, 1958.

BAUER, W. *Die Briefe des Ignatius von Antiochia und der Polykarpbrief.* Tübingen, 1920.

BIHLMEYER, K. and SCHNEEMELCHER, W. *Die apostolischen Väter,* Vol. I. Tübingen, 1956.

CORWIN, V. *St. Ignatius and Christianity at Antioch.* New Haven, 1960.

DELEHAYE, H. *Les passions des martyrs et les genres littéraires.* Brussels, 1921.

DIEKAMP, F. *Patres Apostolici.* (*Patres Apostolici,* ed. F. X. FUNK, Vol. II.) Tübingen, 1913 (best text of Pseudo-Ignatius, etc.)

GOODSPEED, E. J. *The Apostolic Fathers.* New York, 1950.

———. *Index Patristicus.* Naperville, Ill., 1960.

GRANT, R. M. (ed.). *The Apostolic Fathers.* 6 vols. New York, 1964 ff.

HARRISON, P. N. *Polycarp's Two Epistles to the Philippians.* Cambridge, 1936.

KNOPF, R. *Lehre der Zwölf Apostel; Zwei Clemensbriefe.* Tübingen, 1920.

LAKE, K. *The Apostolic Fathers.* 2 vols. LCL, 1913.

LIGHTFOOT, J. B. *The Apostolic Fathers.* 5 vols. 2d ed. London, New York, 1889–90.

MALININE, M. *et al. De Resurrectione* (*Epistula ad Rheginum*). Zurich, 1963.

MUILENBURG, J. *The Literary Relations of the Epistle of Barnabas and the Teaching of the Twelve Apostles.* Marburg, 1929.

QUISPEL, G. *Ptolémée: Epître à Flora.* SC, 1949.

RICHARDSON, C. C. *Early Christian Fathers* (*The Library of Christian Classics*). Philadelphia, 1953.

TESTUZ, M. *Papyrus Bodmer X-XII: X: Correspondance apocryphe des Corinthiens et de l'apôtre Paul.* Geneva, 1959.

CHAPTER 3. REVELATIONS

BÖHLIG, A. and LABIB, P. *Koptisch-gnostische Apokalypsen aus Codex V von Nag Hammadi.* Halle-Wittenberg, 1963.

———. *Die koptisch-gnostische Schrift ohne Titel aus Codex II von Nag Hammadi.* Berlin, 1962.

BONNER, C. *A Papyrus Codex of the Shepherd of Hermas.* Ann Arbor, Mich., 1934.

DIBELIUS, M. *Der Hirt des Hermas.* Tübingen, 1923.

GEFFCKEN, J. *Die Oracula Sibyllina.* GCS, 1902.

GIET, S. *Hermas et les Pasteurs.* Paris, 1963.

GIVERSEN, S. *Apocryphon Johannis.* Copenhagen, 1963.

JOLY, R. *Hermas: Le Pasteur*. SC, 1958.

KRAUSE, M. and LARIB, P. *Die drei Versionen des Apokryphon des Johannes im Koptischen Museum zu Alt-Kairo*. Wiesbaden, 1962.

KURFESS, A. *Sibyllinische Weissagungen*. Munich, 1951.

ROBINSON, J. A. and JAMES, M. R. *The Gospel According to Peter and the Revelation of Peter*. London, 1892.

SCHMIDT, C. and TILL, W. C. *Die Pistis Sophia*. GCS, 1954.

TERRY, M. S. *The Sibylline Oracles*. 2d ed., New York, 1899.

TILL, W. C. *Die gnostischen Schriften des koptischen Papyrus Berolinensis 8502*. TU, LX, 1955.

WHITTAKER, M. *Der Hirt des Hermas*. GCS, 1956.

CHAPTER 4. GOSPELS

BELL, H. I. and SKEAT, T. C. *Fragments of an Unknown Gospel and Other Early Christian Papyri*. London, 1935.

GRANT, R. M., FREEDMAN, D. N., and SCHOEDEL, W. R. *The Secret Sayings of Jesus*. New York, London, 1960.

GROBEL, K. *The Gospel of Truth*. Nashville, Tenn., 1960.

GUILLAUMONT, A. *et al. The Gospel According to Thomas. Coptic Text and English Translation*. Leiden, New York, 1959.

HENNECKE, E. See bibliography to chapter 1.

MALININE, M. *et al. Evangelium Veritatis*. Zurich, 1956.

STRYCKER, E. DE. *La forme la plus ancienne du Protévangile de Jacques*. Brussels, 1961.

TESTUZ, M. *Papyrus Bodmer V: Nativité de Marie*. Geneva, 1958.

TILL, W. C. *Das Evangelium nach Philippos*. Berlin, 1963.

VAGANAY, L. *L'Evangile de Pierre*. Paris, 1930.

WILSON, R. McL. *The Gospel of Philip*. London, New York, 1962.

———. *Studies in the Gospel of Thomas*. London, 1960.

CHAPTER 5. ACTS

HENNECKE, E. See Bibliography to chapter 1.

KLIJN, A. F. J. *The Acts of Thomas*. 1962.

LIPSIUS, R. A. and BONNET, M. *Acta Apostolorum Apocrypha*. 3 vols. Leipzig, 1891–1903.

MUSIRILLO, H. A. *Acts of the Pagan Martyrs*. Oxford, 1954.

SCHMIDT, C. and SCHUBART, W. *Praxeis Paulou*. Hamburg, 1936.

CHAPTER 6. HYMNS, HOMILIES, AND EXEGESIS

BONNER, C. *The Homily on the Passion by Melito Bishop of Sardis*. London, 1940.

HARRIS, J. R. *The Odes and Psalms of Solomon*. 2d ed. Cambridge, 1911.

HARRIS, J. R. and MINGANA, A. *The Odes and Psalms of Solomon.*
2 vols. Manchester, 1916, 1920.

LOHSE, B. *Die Passa-Homilie des Bischofs Meliton von Sardes.* Leiden,
1958.

PERLER, O. *Ein Hymnus zur Ostervigil von Meliton? (Papyrus Bodmer XII).* Freiburg, 1960.

TESTUZ, M. *Papyrus Bodmer XIII. Méliton de Sardes: Homélie sur
la Pâque.* Geneva, 1960.

CHAPTER 7. THE FIRST APOLOGIES

A. *Texts and word-index of the Apologies*

GOODSPEED, E. J. *Die ältesten Apologeten.* Göttingen, 1914.
———. *Index Apologeticus.* Göttingen, 1912.
OTTO, J. C. T. *Corpus apologetarum christianorum saeculi secundi.*
9 vols. Jena, 1851–81 (various editions).

B. *General studies of the Apologists*

CASSAMASSA, M. *Gli apologisti greci.* Rome, 1944.
GEFFCKEN, J. *Zwei griechischen Apologeten.* Berlin-Leipzig, 1907.
PELLEGRINO, M. *Gli apologeti greci del II secolo.* Rome, 1947.
PUECH, A. *Les apologistes grecs du deuxième siècle de notre ère.*
Paris, 1912.
See also bibliographies to chapters 8 and 9.

C. *Aristides*

GEFFCKEN, J. (as above).
VONA, C. *L'apologia di Aristide.* Rome, 1950.

CHAPTER 8. THE AGE OF JUSTIN

ANDRESEN, C. *Logos und Nomos.* Berlin, 1955.
ARCHAMBAULT, G. *Justin: Dialogue avec Tryphon.* 2 vols. Paris, 1909.
GOODENOUGH, E. R. *The Theology of Justin Martyr.* Jena, 1923.
OTTO, J. C. T. See bibliography to chapter 7.
PRIGENT, P. *Justin et l'Ancien Testament.* Paris, 1964.
SCHMID, W. In *Zeitschrift für die neutestamentliche Wissenschaft,*
XL (1941), 87–138 (on text).
WILLIAMS, A. L. *Justin Martyr: The Dialogue with Trypho.* London,
1930.

The Letter to Diognetus

BILLET, B. In *Recherches de science religieuse,* XLV (1957), 409–18
(on lacunae).
MARROU, H. I. *A Diognète.* SC, 1951.
MEECHAM, H. G. *The Epistle to Diognetus.* Manchester, 1949.

CHAPTER 9. THE SUCCESSORS OF JUSTIN

A. *Tatian*

ELZE, M. *Tatian und seine Theologie*. Göttingen, 1960.

KRAELING, C. H. *A Greek Fragment of Tatian's Diatesseron from Dura*. London, 1935.

PUECH, A. *Recherches sur le Discours aux grecs de Tatien*. Paris, 1903.

SCHWARTZ, E. *Tatiani Oratio ad Graecos*. TU, IV, 1, 188.

B. *Athenagoras*

CRECHAN, J. *Athenagoras*. ACW, 1956.

GEFFCKEN, J. See bibliography to chapter 7.

UBALDI, P. and PELLEGRINO, M. *Atenagora: La supplica per i cristiani, Della risurrezione dei morti*. Torino, 1947.

C. *Theophilus*

GRANT, R. M., in *Harvard Theological Review*, XL (1947), 227–56; XLIII (1950), 189–96; in *Vigiliae Christianae*, VI (1952), 146–59; XII (1958), 136–44; XIII (1959), 33–45; text in preparation.

NAUTIN, P., in *Vigiliae Christianae*, XI (1957), 212–25 (on text of Book II).

CHAPTER 10. ANTIHERETICAL WRITERS OF THE LATE SECOND CENTURY: IRENAEUS AND HEGESIPPUS

A. *Texts, translations, and word-indexes of Irenaeus*

HARVEY, W. W. *Sancti Irenaei Episcopi Lugdunensis Libri quinque Adversus Haereses*. 2 vols. Cambridge, 1857.

REYNDERS, B. *Lexique comparé du texte grec et des versions . . . de l' "Adversus Haereses."* Louvain, 1954.

——. *Vocabulaire de la "Démonstration" et des fragments de saint Irénée*. Chevetogne, 1958.

SAGNARD, F. M. *La gnose valentinienne et le témoignage de saint Irénée*. Paris, 1947 (text of part of Book I).

——. *Irénée: Contre les hérésies, Livre III*. SC, 1952.

SMITH, J. P. *St. Irenaeus: Proof of the Apostolic Preaching*. ACW, 1952.

UEBEL, F. *Eirene*, Vol. III. Prague, 1964 (text of Jena papyrus).

B. *Studies of Irenaeus*

BENOIT, A. *St. Irénée: Introduction à l'étude de sa théologie*. Paris, 1960.

LOOFS, F. *Theophilus von Antiochien und die anderen theologischen Quellen bei Irenaeus*. TU, XLVI, 2, 1930.

CHAPTER 11. THE ALEXANDRIANS: CLEMENT

BUTTERWORTH, G. W. *Clement of Alexandria*. LCL, 1919.
CASEY, R. P. *The Excerpta ex Theodoto of Clement of Alexandria.* London, 1935.
CHADWICK, H. and OULTON, J. E. L. *Alexandrian Christianity (The Library of Christian Classics)*. Philadelphia, 1954.
HORT, F. J. A. and MAYOR, J. B. *Clement of Alexandria: Miscellanies Book VII*. London, 1902.
SAGNARD, F. M. *Clément d'Alexandrie: Extraits de Théodote*. SC, 1948.
SMITH, M. In *New York Times*, December 30, 1960 (new fragment; edition in preparation).
STÄHLIN, O. *Clemens Alexandrinus*. 4 vols. GCS, 1905–36.

CHAPTER 12. THE ALEXANDRIANS: ORIGEN

BUTTERWORTH, G. W. *Origen On First Principles*. London, 1936.
CADIOU, R. *La jeunesse d'Origène*. Paris, 1936.
CHADWICK, H. *Origen Contra Celsum*. Cambridge, 1953.
DANIÉLOU, J. *Origène*. Paris, 1949.
KOETSCHAU, P., *et al. Origines Werke*. 12 vols. to date. GCS, 1899——.
ROBINSON, J. A. *The Philocalia of Origen*. Cambridge, 1893.
SCHERER, J. *Entretien d'Origène avec Héraclide et les évêques ses collègues sur le Père, le Fils, et l'âme*. Cairo, 1949.
——. *Extraits des livres I et II du Contre Celse d'Origène*. Cairo, 1956.

CHAPTER 13. HIPPOLYTUS AND OTHER GREEK WRITERS OF THE THIRD CENTURY

A. Hippolytus

BONWETSCH, G. N. *et al. Hippolytus*. 5 vols. GCS, 1897–1929.
BOTTE, B. *Hippolyte de Rome: La tradition apostolique*. SC, 1946.
D'ALÈS, A. *La théologie de saint Hippolyte*. Paris, 1906.
DIX, G. *The Treatise on the Apostolic Tradition of St. Hippolytus of Rome*. London, 1937.
EASTON, B. S. *The Apostolic Tradition of Hippolytus*. Cambridge, 1934.
LEFEVRE, M. and BARDY, G. *Hippolyte: Commentaire sur Daniel*. SC, 1947.
NAUTIN, P. *Le dossier d'Hippolyte et de Méliton*. Paris, 1953.

B. Other writers

BONWETSCH, G. N. *Methodius*. GCS, 1917.

BOUMA, S. J. *Dionysius van Alexandrie.* Purmerend, Holland, 1943.

CONNOLLY, R. H. *Didascalia Apostolorum.* Oxford, 1929.

FELTOE, C. L. *The Letters and Other Remains of Dionysius of Alexandria.* Cambridge, 1904.

FUNK, F. X. *Didascalia et Constitutiones Apostolorum.* Paderborn, 1905.

GELZER, H. *Sextus Julius Africanus und die byzantinische Chronographie.* 2 vols. Leipzig, 1880, 1898.

GRENFELL, B. P. and HUNT, A. S. *The Oxyrhynchus Papyri,* Vol. III (no. 412). London, 1903 (Julius Africanus).

KOETSCHAU, P. *Des Gregorios Thaumatourgos Dankrede an Origenes.* Freiburg, 1894.

RADFORD, L. B. *Three Teachers of Alexandria: Theognostus, Pierius and Peter.* Cambridge, 1908.

REICHARDT, W. *Die Briefe des Sextus Julius Africanus an Aristides und Origenes.* TU, XXXIV, 3, 1909.

VIELLEFOND, J. R. *Fragments des Cestes provenant de la collection des tacticiens grecs.* Paris, 1932.

CHAPTER 14. LATIN CHRISTIAN WRITERS

A. *Tertullian*

BECKER, C. *Tertullians Apologeticum: Werden und Leistung.* Munich, 1954.

DEKKERS, E. *et al. Tertulliani opera.* 2 vols. *Corpus Christianorum, Series Latina,* Vols. I–II. The Hague, 1954.

EVANS, E. *Tertullian's Treatise Against Praxeas.* London, 1948.

——. *Tertullian's Treatise on the Incarnation.* London, 1956.

——. *Tertullian's Treatise on the Resurrection.* London, 1960.

GREENSLADE, S. L. *Early Latin Theology (The Library of Christian Classics).* Philadelphia, 1956.

WASZINK, J. H. *Tertullian De Anima.* Amsterdam, 1947.

——. *Tertullian: The Treatise Against Hermogenes.* ACW, 1957.

B. *Minucius Felix*

QUISPEL, G. *M. Minucii Felicis Octavius.* Leiden, 1949.

C. *Cyprian*

BÉVENOT, M. *The Tradition of Manuscripts: A Study in the Transmission of St. Cyprian's Treatises.* Oxford, 1961.

HARTEL, G. S. *Thasci Caecilii Cypriani opera.* 3 vols. CSEL, 1868–71.

D. *Novatian*

FAUSSET, W. Y. *Novatian's Treatise on the Trinity.* Cambridge, 1909.

E. Arnobius

REIFFERSCHEID, A. *Arnobii Adversus nationes Libri VII.* CSEL, 1875.

F. Lactantius

BRANDT, S. and LAUBMANN, G. L. *Caeli Firmiani Lactanti opera.* 3 vols. CSEL, 1890–97.

G. Victorinus

HAUSSLEITER, J. *Victorini episcopi Petavionensis opera.* CSEL, 1916.

CHAPTER 15. EUSEBIUS AND EARLY CHRISTIAN LITERATURE

LAKE, K. and OULTON, J. E. L. *Eusebius: The Ecclesiastical History.* 2 vols. LCL, 1926, 1932.

LAWLOR, H. J. *Eusebiana: Essays on the Ecclesiastical History of Eusebius Bishop of Caesarea.* Oxford, 1912.

LAWLOR, H. J. and OULTON, J. E. L. *Eusebius: The Ecclesiastical History and the Martyrs of Palestine.* 2 vols. London, 1927–28.

McGIFFERT, A. C. *Eusebius (Select Library of Nicene and Post-Nicene Fathers of the Christian Church, Second Series).* New York, 1890.

MRAS, K. *Eusebius: Die Praeparatio Evangelica.* 2 vols. GCS, 1956.

SCHWARTZ, E. *Eusebius: Die Kirchengeschichte.* 3 vols. GCS, 1903–1909.

WALLACE-HADRILL, D. S. *Eusebius of Caesarea.* London, 1960.

INDEX

1. Ancient Authors and Writings

2. Modern Scholars

DATE DUE
